THE DISINTERESTED WITNESS

Northwestern University

Studies in Phenomenology

and

Existential Philosophy

THE DISINTERESTED WITNESS

A Fragment of Advaita Vedānta Phenomenology

Bina Gupta

Northwestern University Press
Evanston, Illinois

Northwestern University Press
625 Colfax Street
Evanston, Illinois 60208-4210

Printed in the United States of America

ISBN cloth 0-8101-1564-6
paper 0-8101-1565-4

Library of Congress Cataloging-in-Publication Data

Gupta, Bina, 1947–
The disinterested witness : a fragment of Advaita Vedānta phenomenolgy / Bina Gupta.
p. cm. — (Northwestern University studies in phenomenology and existential philosophy)
Includes bibliographical references and index.
ISBN 0-8101-1564-6 (alk. paper). — ISBN 0-8101-1565-4 (pbk. : alk. paper)
1. Advaita. 2. Apperception. 3. Philosophy, Comparative. I. Title. II. Series: Northwestern University studies in phenomenology & existential philosophy.
B132.A3G867 1998
181'.482—dc21 98-5545
CIP

The paper used in this publication meets the minimum requirements of the American National Standard for Information Sciences—Permanence of Paper for Printed Library Materials, ANSI Z39.48-1984.

To

J. N. Mohanty,

a consummate philosopher,

who personifies

prajñā, kṣānti, and *karuṇā*

Contents

Author's Note

This book began as a study of the Advaita Vedānta notion of the witness-consciousness. However, it ended up as a comparison between that notion and some similar notions in Western phenomenology. Accordingly, it may also be construed as a contribution to what is generally called "comparative philosophy"—that is, a comparison of the philosophies of the East and the West. A word about this aspect of the project is in order.

Philosophy East and West is a favorite project of some intellectuals today. Such a project clearly has an extra-philosophical use and motivation, viz., that of bringing different and seemingly unconnected parts of different cultures together. My interest in this project, however, has been strictly philosophical. I would like to make this clear at the outset.

There are many approaches to such comparative philosophical endeavor. One approach, which is perhaps widely followed, is to highlight or bring out fundamental differences between different cultural groups, in this case between India and the West. When carried to an extreme, such an approach translates into a radical relativism that results in denying any common rational norms or ideas between the two philosophical traditions. My goal in this work is not to refute such relativism. However, an unprejudiced study of the Vedānta texts will demonstrate, I believe, that while there are important differences, there are also shared concerns, questions and answers to these questions, between Vedānta and Western philosophical thinking.

Some readers might still wonder whether the demonstration of shared common norms and ideas results from a modern contemporary reader's interpretation of these texts. I believe that one's reading or interpretation of the texts is strengthened by an appeal to the data of one's phenomenological investigation of one's own conscious experience. In this sense phenomenology seems to provide us with a point outside of cultural relativisms. Some philosophers might believe that phenomenology is a Western mode of thinking, and historically this might be so. But the beauty of phenomenology is that it permits us to look at experience rather than language, and so leads us to a point where linguistic and interpretive differences, though recognized, are transcended in the horizon of pure experiential consciousness and its structures. This claim, again, I cannot justify directly in this project; I can only do so indirectly by means of the readings of the Vedānta texts and by recalling the findings of Western phenomenology.

It seems to me that an escape from language to consciousness is possible. At the first level, our consciousness and experience are imprisoned in the local, linguistic and cultural norms. However, unless we can escape from these norms into some common structures and norms of consciousness such as the witness-consciousness presented here, we cannot even assert relativism as a thesis. The point that I wish to make is as follows: The very exercise of comparing / contrasting implies assuming a position as witness-consciousness. Any claim, irrespective of whether it is about the perceived commonalities or differences between the East and the West, presupposes a reflective stance in which one is a witness to these differences and/or commonalities. If my present thesis is correct, then the idea of the witness-consciousness found in the Advaita Vedānta commentaries does in fact provide a glaring example and a vantage point for cross-cultural comparison.

Finally, I would like to warn my readers that if in securing a copy of this book they were hoping to find an esoteric philosophy that is practiced and preached by esoteric holy persons in India, they will be disappointed. "Vedānta," as used in this study, refers to philosophy in the strictly philosophical sense. As a philosophy, it has its own logic, epistemology and metaphysics. It adheres to the highest standards of conceptual rigor, though its logic and its mode of expression may be different from the predominantly Western mode of thinking. It has been challenged and defended by thousands of years of philosophical works; it entered into a highly logical dialogue with other schools of Indian philosophy and in the process developed a large volume of philosophical literature. This is not because as a Western-trained philosopher I am trying to make Advaita Vedānta appear to be something that it is not, but this is how Vedānta was taken to be by thousands of years of Indian philosophers. In saying so, I am not trying to deny Vedānta's religious, mystical and spiritual side. The goal here is simply to draw attention to the philosophical side of Vedānta and focus on one of its important epistemological notions, viz., the notion of the witness-consciousness. It is Vedānta in this sense that is taken to be India's greatest intellectual and spiritual achievement.

Preface

This study on the concept of the witness-consciousness (*sākṣin*) represents the second phase of my research on Advaita Vedānta. I became interested in the notion of the witness-consciousness while working on my book *Perceiving in Advaita Vedānta: Epistemological Analysis and Interpretation* (Bucknell University Press, 1991). Two sections of that work deal with the notion of *sākṣin* and some of the issues related to it.

For a long time, it has seemed regrettable to me that in spite of the central position the concept of *sākṣin* occupies in Advaita Vedānta epistemology, there does not exist a comprehensive and in-depth study on this concept. That is why, soon after completing my book on the Advaita theory of perception, I devoted myself to a study of the Advaita literature on *sākṣin.* The present book is the result of that research. I hope that this will, among other things, fill in a major gap in the writings on Advaita Vedānta.

Advaita Vedānta, one of the most widely known and influential schools of Indian philosophy, postulates *brahman* or undifferentiated pure consciousness (*cit*) as the only reality; it is one without a second. This pure consciousness, on account of nescience, appears as the empirical world where the plurality of names and forms is manifested. Thus, we find at least two levels in Advaita: the level of reality and the level of appearance. The Advaitins beautifully explicate how these two levels of consciousness yield a unifying perspective. These two levels, argues the Advaitin, are incommensurable: When *brahman* is known, nothing remains to be known. However, until *brahman* realization, all knowing that takes place in the empirical world holds good. Thus the obvious questions are: How and why do the real and the apparent become confused? The Advaitins explain both the involvement of the real with the apparent and the subsequent retracing of the real from the apparent in an epistemological context by postulating the concept of the *sākṣin* or the witness-consciousness. It is the most enigmatic epistemological concept of this school. In the absence of this notion, no knowledge at all would be possible.

While the Advaitins establish the witness-consciousness (*sākṣin*) on epistemological grounds, this concept is conspicuously absent in many other schools of Indian philosophy. The Advaitins argue that when an object is cognized the object is indeed manifested; however, the object is not the only thing that is manifested—cognition of an object is accompanied by an immediate self-awareness of the cognition. To be specific, in an external perception, when an object—say a pitcher—is known through a mental mode with the help of a sense organ, the mental mode is also known without the mediation of another mental mode. In short, particular cognitions presuppose a continuous principle of self-awareness; this principle is none other than the witness-consciousness.

This work is entirely devoted to Advaita Vedānta—and I should add that its focus is chiefly, but not exclusively, on the Vivaraṇa school of Advaita Vedānta. I begin my investigation by looking at the Upaniṣads in order to determine the extent to which the idea of *sākṣin* is to be found in them. Next I try to ascertain to what extent, and in what form—as well as for what use—this idea (rather than just the word "*sākṣin*") is to be found in Śaṃkara's own writings. As is well known, the ideas of Śaṃkara were first fully developed and systematized by his followers. The concept of *sākṣin* is no exception. They developed the ramifications of this notion from an epistemological perspective and brought them to the forefront for the first time. Accordingly, a major part of the book is devoted to an analysis of the post-Śaṃkara commentarial literature and of monographs within the Vivaraṇa school. I am aware that there are different formulations of the concept of the witness-consciousness in other schools of Vedānta and also in the Sāṃkhya and Yoga systems of Indian philosophy. I hope to be able to study them in a future work.

In general, this book is an attempt to understand the important and interesting Advaitin concept of *sākṣin*. I have attempted to demonstrate that the notion of witness-consciousness is essential for any sound theory of knowledge. The goal of this study is twofold. The first goal is to explore the role and importance of the notion of *sākṣin* in Advaita epistemology and to formulate a critique dealing with the wide range of epistemological issues and dilemmas inherent in this notion. I hope this will result in a scholarly interpretation of the notion of *sākṣin* and of its ramifications for the Advaita two-tiered theory of knowledge. The second goal is to bring out the phenomenological relevance of this concept for Advaita Vedānta. It seems to me that there has been very little done to bring out the phenomenological content in Advaita. Although the renowned phenomenologist J. N. Mohanty provides various pointers at the phenomenological content in Advaita Vedānta (*The Concept of Intentionality*

[St. Louis: Warren H. Green, Inc., 1972], 136–37; "Phenomenology in Indian Philosophy," in *Essays on Indian Philosophy: Traditional and Modern*, ed. Puroshottama Bilimoria [Delhi: Oxford University Press, 1993], 252–54), he has not done an in-depth investigation of this content in his numerous works. Debabrata Sinha has tried to make sense of the concept of *cit*, or what he calls "transcendental subjectivity," from a phenomenological perspective (*The Idealist Standpoint: A Study in the Vedāntic Metaphysic of Experience* [Santiniketan: Visva-Bharati, Centre of Advanced Study in Philosophy, 1965]). Sinha, however, primarily focuses his attention on the phenomenological content of *cit* as a metaphysic of experience, not on the process of knowing. Also, Sinha's book does not provide an exegetical analysis; it is a freelance analysis of the *cit*, so to speak.

Keeping in mind the importance of the notion of *sākṣin*, it is surprising that no systematic study on this notion has previously been done. It seems to me that the concept of *sākṣin* is so fundamental to Advaita epistemology that it has more or less been taken for granted as requiring no further elucidation or investigation. A few articles on the notion of *sākṣin*, however, do exist. I have surveyed this literature. The critical interpretation contained herein relies primarily on the interpretation of *sākṣin* worked out in the post-Śaṃkara Sanskrit commentaries. In translating passages from these Sanskrit commentaries, I have tried to remain faithful to the original texts while at the same time making their content accessible to my readers. Important original Sanskrit passages have been transliterated in the endnotes.

I would like my readers to be aware of some of the stylistic conventions that I have tried to follow in my use of terms in this study. On the whole, I have provided translations of all Sanskrit terms. However, I have retained commonly used terms such as "*jīva*," "*Īśvara*" and "*brahman*." My use of "*sākṣin*" at some places and "witness-consciousness" at other places might appear to be arbitrary. This, however, is not the case. When "*sākṣin*" refers to the word or concept or when I am involved in an exegetical analysis of this notion, I have used "*sākṣin*." When I am interpreting these sources, I have tried to employ the translation "witness-consciousness." Usually and for the most part, I have adhered to this principle; any deviations from this practice are in the interest of clarity. I have translated key Advaitin metaphysical and epistemological terms in order to make the work more accessible to a wider audience. However, I found some of the technical Sanskrit terms almost impossible to translate into English without jeopardizing clarity. For example, the term "*jīvasākṣin*" when translated would read "the witness-consciousness belonging to the individual self." Use of such English translations in the text would have resulted in clumsy sentences. In such cases, I have tried to give the translation in parentheses on its first usage in the text and again when several pages have elapsed since its last occurrence. I have also included a glossary of terms at the end of the book.

This book, however, is not merely an exegetical study of the Sanskrit texts. I believe that, in writing this book I have been guided by a systematic philosophical interest. I have tried to show, among other things, that the notion of a witness-consciousness has an important role to play in both Indian and Western epistemological theories. I have attempted to show how something very much like the witness-consciousness is recognized in various Western epistemological theories beginning with Kant. Notwithstanding the differences between the Advaita Vedānta account and the Western theories, I have attempted to show that something very similar to the idea of witness-consciousness is recognized in the Western philosophical tradition. Although in some respects the Vedānta theory is new, Western philosophers should take it seriously and explore its validity for their own sake.

Finally, I recognize that some of the material discussed in this book is very complex. This complexity is confounded by the problems involved in translating complex philosophical concepts from Sanskrit to English. I apologize for any difficulty the reader may encounter in following my exegesis and interpretation of the Sanskrit texts. If this work challenges the readers to further investigate the issues raised herein, I will have succeeded in my effort.

It is both a duty and a pleasure to express my sincere thanks to those friends, scholars, and students who have contributed to this work in various ways. It is not possible to list them all individually. Two individuals to whom I owe much, however, deserve special mention: late Professor Krishna Sivaraman and Professor J. N. Mohanty. I would like to thank Professor Sivaraman for introducing me to the concept of *sākṣin.* I would also like to express my thanks to Professor J. N. Mohanty for inspiring me to work on this concept. He has contributed to this volume in at least two ways: (1) During one of the research conferences of the Society for Asian and Comparative Philosophy (Honolulu, January 1995), Professor Mohanty made some enthusiastic and insightful comments about the importance of this concept. As luck would have it, at that time I was on research leave from the University of Missouri to write a book on the ramifications of the concept of *sākṣin* in the context of Advaita epistemology. My discussions with him during this conference reinforced my belief about the importance of my ongoing project and the need for a book on Advaita phenomenology. (2) His numerous works and papers on Indian philosophy and Western phenomenology have contributed immensely to my understanding of the various issues involved in this work. I owe him a special debt and, hence, my heartfelt thanks.

Additionally, I would like to thank Ms. Beverly Ayyar for her assistance in carrying out many tedious tasks that go with the preparation of a manuscript. She typed most of the manuscript and suggested editorial changes, many of which have been incorporated. I am grateful to the University of Missouri for granting me a research leave during the 1994–95 academic year. I also want to thank the Research Council of the University of Missouri–Columbia for providing me with the funds to help defray some of the costs that I incurred in connection with this project. I would also like to thank Ms. Melanie Johnson-Moxley for preparing the index. Finally, I would like to thank my husband, Madan, and daughter, Swati, for believing in me, supporting me, and being there for me when I needed them.

Abbreviations

AS	*Advaitasiddhi*, Parimal Publications, New Delhi
AV	*Ātmajñopadeshavidhi*
BSBh	*Brahma-Sūtra-Bhāṣya of Śrī Śaṅkarācārya*
BU	*Bṛhadāraṇyaka Upaniṣad*
BUBh	*Bṛhadāraṇyaka Upaniṣadbhāṣya*
BUBV	*Bṛhadāraṇyakopaniṣadbhāṣyavārtika*
BUBVS	*Bṛhadāraṇyakavārtikasāra*
CU	*Chāndogya Upaniṣad*
CUBh	*Chāndogya Upaniṣadbhāṣya*
KUBh	*Kena Upaniṣadbhāṣya*
MAU	*Māṇḍūkya Upaniṣad*
MAUBh	*Māṇḍūkya Upaniṣadbhāṣya*
MU	*Muṇḍaka Upaniṣad*
MUBh	*Muṇḍaka Upaniṣadbhāṣya*
NS	*The Naiṣkarmya Siddhi of Śrī Sureśvara*
PD	*Pañcadaśī*
PP	*Pañcapādikā*, Vizianagaram Sanskrit Series edition
PPV	*Pañcapādikāvivaraṇa*, Madras Government Manuscripts Library edition
PU	*Praśna Upaniṣad*
PUBh	*Praśna Upaniṣadbhāṣya*

SB	*Siddhāntabindu of Madhusūdana with the Commentary of Abhyankar*, Bhandarkar Oriental Research Institute edition
SBMA	*Siddhāntabindu* with *Nyāyaratnāvalī*, Mount Abu edition
SLS	*Siddhāntaleśasaṅgraha*, Madras University Series edition
SS	*Saṃkṣepaśārīraka of Sarvajñātman*, Radhakrishnan Institute, University of Madras edition
SV	*Sambandha Vārtika.*
Svetā. U	*Śvetāśvatara Upaniṣad*
Svetā. UBh	*Śvetāśvatara Upaniṣadbhāṣya*
TP	*Tattvapradīpikā*, Nirṇayasāgar edition
TU	*Taittirīya Upaniṣad*
TUBh	*Taittirīya Upaniṣadbhāṣya*
TUBV	*The Tattirīyopaniṣad Bhāṣya-Vārtika of Sureśvara*, University of Madras edition
Upadeśa	*Upadeśasāhasrī*
VC	*Viveka Cūḍāmaṇi*
VP	*Vedānta Paribhāṣā*
VPS	*Vivaraṇaprameyasaṅgraha*
VV	*Vākyavṛtti*

1

Introduction

Historical Background: The Basic Issues

Vedānta is arguably the most important school of Indian philosophical thought. Vedāntic texts have been the subject of numerous commentaries, which have given rise to several schools of Vedānta. Advaita Vedānta is the nondualistic system of Vedānta expounded primarily by Śaṃkara (ca. 788–820). It has been, and continues to be, the most widely accepted system of thought among philosophers in India, and it is one of the most challenging and provocative philosophical achievements to be found in the East or the West.

In recent times a great deal of work has been done on many facets of Advaita philosophy, but relatively little attention has been paid to its epistemology. Professor Eliot Deutsch points out that "except in the later phases of the tradition, and even here to a limited extent, . . . there is little awareness of epistemology as a distinct philosophical discipline."[1] One possible explanation for this phenomenon is the Advaitic taxonomy. Advaita does not treat epistemological issues separately; it interweaves them with metaphysical considerations.

The goal of Advaita Vedānta is to show the ultimate nonreality of all distinctions; reality is not constituted of parts. The "oneness" that Advaita upholds does not require variety and multiplicity in order to be affirmed. All claims of distinction have meaning only against the background recognition of that identity. A philosopher's job is to peel away the layers of apparent distinctions that have accrued, rather than to establish the identity. Philosophy is only a means of approaching reality directly. It is the road that takes one up to, but not into, the goal of becoming a part of that reality.

Brahman, the ultimate reality, is of the nature of pure consciousness (*cit*). It is the only reality that there is, one only without a second, nondual. It is the source of whatever could appear in consciousness, a single undifferentiated whole. It is impervious to any ascription that might be imposed on it. It is a whole that transcends any effort to describe it, inasmuch as any effort to characterize it as "this" or "that" denies its essentially infinite nature. Accordingly, any effort to talk about *brahman,* even to think about it, is to undertake the impossible. Thinking and talking presuppose description, and description is inherently limiting.

The problem is one of undertaking a journey toward a goal that is completely transcendent. How can a finite, imperfect, limited being achieve an identity with *brahman* in which all subject/object distinction is obliterated? Since *brahman*'s nonduality seems inconsistent with the plurality of empirical existence, what is the status of this plurality? The task is to elucidate reality as the essence inherent in all appearances. It not only transcends the world of appearance, but is present in all that appears. Transcendence and immanence are not incompatible; they are two facets of the same situation. If the empirically given world had a reality of its own, then one could indeed speak of *brahman*'s transcendence, as contrasted with its immanence within the empirical. Only *brahman* exists; therefore, it is transcendent. However, it remains the case that when one strips away the cloak of the empirically given, one is left only with *brahman*: the reality of the empirical world.

Thus, it is incumbent upon the nondualists (Advaitins) to explain how reality and appearance become interrelated and, therefore, confused. When both paths take us through the realm of that which is only apparent, how do we retrace the paths that, on the one hand, lead to this confusion, but, on the other hand, lead away from this confusion? From an ontological point of view, this movement, this process, this journey never did and never could occur. Nevertheless, the appearance of the movement, at least to those to whom the movement seems real, is a fact about them. This interrelationship between the real and the apparent gives rise to two different, but complementary, approaches to the absolute. For consciousness to be an object in the world is for it to be a subject presented with other objects. Both, nevertheless, have the same essential being and, accordingly, can only be understood as different aspects of one reality. There appears to be a difference, there is a phenomenal difference, but each is of the same essence—the only reality. They are brought together and have intercourse with each other through *brahman*, and *brahman* is only reached by understanding that which is essential to both the knower and to that which is known.

The initial involvement of the real in what is nonreal and the subsequent withdrawal or retracing of the real from the nonreal are addressed as problems in epistemology. From the noetic perspective, being in the world is confrontation between what is present as an object and that to which it is thus present. These are, respectively, the objective and the subjective poles of the knowledge relation. Even though appearing as two different sorts of entities, with natures apparently opposed to each other, like light and darkness, they are essentially one and the same reality. The platform on which the two meet and make one relevant to the other is reality in the ultimate sense (*brahman*). That reality is sought by an analysis of the knower and the known. The knower and the reality to be known coalesce into one, i.e., *ātman*[2] is *brahman.*

It is important to remember here that consciousness (*cit*) and existence (*sat*) are not two modes of being that exist side by side in being. They are two alternate descriptions of being that have the same denotation, but connote different things—very much like Frege's "morning star" and "evening star," which have the same referent but different meanings. Likewise, "existence" and "consciousness" have different meanings, but refer to the same being. *Brahman* is the object par excellence. It is not pure subject, because subjectivity is surrendered in the realization of being. It is so objective that the knowing act merges into it. The process of knowing culminates in the unveiling of being, the emergence of being when the veil is removed.

The epistemological inquiry thus takes the form of an investigation into the nature of the ground on which all duality, including the duality of the knower and the known, is based. Investigation of this apparent duality, and of the reality upon which it is founded, involves us in two separate activities. Initially we must understand the world of objects, the world of phenomena, and that which generates or founds their status as objects. Additionally, we need to understand what it is to be a subject, a knower. We need an analysis of what it is to be a knower, and what is involved in knowing. What is it that knows? What is it that makes this knower both "this"—i.e., the object known—and a knower? How do we distinguish the knower from both the object that it knows, and more importantly, from the object that another knower knows? The Advaitins, of course, try to answer these questions. As part of the effort to completely explicate the process of knowing, they put forth the concept of *sākṣin,* the witness-consciousness.[3]

What or Who Is "*Sākṣin*"?

A review of various Advaita commentaries reveals various descriptions of this important notion. Given below are some of these descriptions. The importance and relevance of these characterizations will become obvious to the reader as we proceed in our journey to make sense of this important notion.

1. The *sākṣin* is indubitable, unerring, eternal. It is always directly manifested and its manifestation is not due to any extrinsic reason.[4]

2. The *sākṣin* is the neutral (pure) consciousness as qualified by a modification of the inner sense.[5]

3. The *sākṣin* is that which is never concealed.[6]

4. The *sākṣin* manifests ignorance.[7]

5. That which directly manifests is the *sākṣin*.[8]

6. The *sākṣin* is that which illuminates everything.[9]

Etymologically "*sākṣin*" means direct and immediate perception, or that which directly or immediately perceives, the agent of such perception. As a consequence of this meaning, the term "*sākṣin*" also stands for a witness, both in the context of a court of law, and in the context of epistemology, the context that concerns us here. It refers to a witness in the sense of the phenomenologically pure observer, the observer who observes without bringing anything to the observation. It signifies seeing without being the agent of the act under consideration. Its interests are not involved in what occurs. It signifies the self, which though not itself involved in the cognitive process, functions as a disinterested, uninvolved onlooker or witness-consciousness. The witness-consciousness in Advaita, though indifferent or detached, is intelligent. Its indifference or detachment is really its refusal to acknowledge the illusory distinctions of names and forms which fragment reality.

The concept of the *sākṣin* in Advaita is the single most important postulate of the principle of revelation operative in experience—cognitive and noncognitive alike. A phenomenological exploration leads to the recovery of this principle as a necessary ingredient in any epistemological process. In simple terms, it represents an attempt to understand experience and its implications. The object as such is not the focus of attention. Rather, the focus of attention, vis-à-vis the object, is consciousness, which functions as the medium of manifestation of the object.

The *sākṣin* at once reveals the ground of the empirical world that is experienced and the ground of the notion of the "I." It bridges the gap between the metaphysically real and the empirical, or, better yet, provides the link between the empirical and the real. As Debabrata Sinha notes:

> on the one hand, *sākṣin* which participates in the process of empirical activity (*vyavahārāṅgatva*) cognitive or otherwise, is not taken as completely *transcendent* in character. On the other hand, *sākṣin* need not exhaust itself within the confines of the empirical individual (*jīva*). In approaching the concept of *sākṣin*, its *jīva*-transcending character comes first into consideration. The primary point of departure in the question of *sākṣin* is the empirical individual, who not only cognizes but also feels and enjoys.[10]

Sākṣin, in other words, is a form of apprehension that is direct, nonrelational, nonpropositional, and nonevaluative in both cognitive and practical affairs. It is the basis of all knowledge.

Given the Advaita account that in every cognition, of whatever sort and of whatever object, besides the cognitive process appropriate to that kind of cognition and to that object, there must necessarily be an accompanying witness-consciousness, I have translated "*sākṣin*" as "witness-consciousness" in this study. A good approximation to this view is to be found among Western writers, as in the following paragraph from Husserl's *Cartesian Meditations*:

> If the Ego, as naturally immersed in the world, experiencingly and otherwise, is called "*interested*" *in the world,* then the phenomenologically altered—and, as so altered, continually maintained—attitude consists in a *splitting of the Ego*: in that the phenomenological Ego establishes himself as "*disinterested on-looker,*" above the naively interested Ego. That this takes place is then itself accessible by means of a new reflection, which as transcendental, likewise demands the very same attitude of looking on "*disinterestedly*"—the Ego's sole remaining interest being to see and to describe adequately what he sees, purely as seen, as what is seen and seen in such and such a manner.[11]

I take it to be an "approximation" because, e.g., when Husserl talks about the "*splitting of the Ego,*" this is a concept that does not and, for that matter, cannot appear in the Advaita theory. However, what Husserl calls the "*disinterested on-looker*" very closely captures the concept of the witness-consciousness. This *on-looker,* argues Husserl, is revealed in reflection. The existence of this *on-looker,* however, is not, for Husserl, a necessary condition for the occurrence of any cognition. The Advaitins, on the other hand, maintain that without this *on-looker* no cognition at all would be possible.

Phenomenological Method

Advaita Vedānta philosophy provides us with a detailed account of the different levels of consciousness and, in that sense, has a rich description of the various levels and modalities of consciousness. Accordingly, one finds in Advaita a phenomenology of perception that is a type of identity theory, inasmuch as the Advaitins maintain that in perceptual cognitions the subject and the object become nondifferent. Since undifferentiated consciousness is the only reality, the subject in a cognitive situation is consciousness conditioned by the cognitive apparatus of the empirical percipient while the object is the same consciousness, but conditioned by the object under consideration as well. For the Advaitins, this nondifference typifies or, better yet, *is* perceptual cognition

Apart from a phenomenology of perception, one also finds in Advaita a phenomenology of the levels of consciousness. An important part of this phenomenology of consciousness is that, at a certain level, consciousness is simply a witness to its own operations and divergent modes. My attempt in this book is not to lay down the entire phenomenological theory of consciousness in Vedānta, but only a part of it; namely, the idea of a consciousness or a level of consciousness that simply witnesses, without getting involved in, the ongoing process of experience. So, I call this phenomenology a "fragment." In the absence of such a consciousness, no knowledge or experience would be possible. It is not a product of a speculative theory, nor is it a metaphysical construction; it is an experience of consciousness that can be confirmed or verified by reflection on one's own self or, better yet, by self-experience. Regardless of whether we are involved in sensation, cognitive efforts, or any other modality of experience, there is always a level of consciousness within each one of us where we stand apart at a certain distance and simply observe our experiences without getting involved in those experiences.[12]

The goal of Vedānta is to separate these levels of consciousness in order to demonstrate what role they play in cognition and in our experiences. All this amounts to arguing that consciousness in its entirety is not involved in or engaged in the world; that there is always a level of consciousness deep within each of us that stands apart and observes what the rest of our conscious life undergoes—pleasure or pain, knowledge or ignorance. The Advaitins further demonstrate that in the absence of this observation, there could be no cognition. Many modern philosophers oppose such a conception. Heidegger, for example, criticizes the view of the disinterested spectator.[13] The Advaitins, on the other hand, argue that without such a consciousness we cannot give an account of knowing, not knowing, and other cognitive mental states.

Although I am using the term "phenomenology" to describe the method employed in Advaita Vedānta, I am by no means suggesting that it is used there in the same sense as it is used by Husserl in his phenomenology. Phenomenology, as a twentieth-century movement, signifies a disavowal of any ontological commitment whatsoever. It is an attempt to lay a foundation for science in experiential terms; it is restricted in its application to empirical experience. The primary goal of Husserl's phenomenology was to demonstrate philosophy as a rigorous science:

> Philosophy . . . does not want to leave anything unsolved; it wants to reduce everything to primary "presuppositions" which do not need to be clarified because they are immediately evident and cannot even be clarified. It is only in this sense that philosophy as the "science of ultimate grounds" is a rigorous science.[14]

A phenomenologist suspends or brackets the belief in the existence of things. In Husserl's own words:

> This means suspending all beliefs characteristic of the "natural attitude," the attitude of common sense and science; in short, everything that is not "apodictic." Our perception of a chair, for instance, involves the belief that a physical chair is present "out there." This belief is neither necessarily true nor necessarily false. In the phenomenologically reduced state of the given we are to hold in abeyance every such belief.[15]

Marvin Farber explains the basic phenomenological method of bracketing as follows:

> Instead of the universal doubt of Descartes, then, Husserl proposes this universal "*epoché.*" A new scientific domain is thus determined. All the sciences which refer to the natural world are also eliminated: no use is made of their propositions and results. They may only be "assumed" in brackets, and not as propositions presuming validity. That which remains when the entire world is eliminated (including us with all "cogitare") is "pure" or "transcendental" consciousness. That is the phenomenological residuum.[16]

For Husserl, "transcendental" consciousness is an intellectual residuum, something that is disclosed through the process of phenomenological reduction. To do phenomenology, for Husserl, amounts to returning to the the pure subject (the transcendental ego), which forms the foundation and constitution of all objectivity. This enables the reflective thinker to comprehend intuitively how the pure subject at once constitutes the objects and also serves as the source of all objectivity.

Both Śaṃkara and Husserl focus their attention away from things and direct it to experience. Husserl begins with the given qua given; his goal is to provide a founding for science. This is neither the goal nor the result in Advaita Vedānta. The orientation in Śaṃkara comes from illusion and sublation, questions concerning the real, the nonreal (appearance), and the unreal arise and become meaningful only in that context. In our everyday experiences, regardless of whether we are perceiving an object or a state of mind, we generally do not raise the question of whether our experience is true or false. The question arises only when one moves from an affirmation to a negation of the data presented in our experience; when, as a matter of psychological necessity, we cannot accept both the initial experience and the new experience that negates the initial experience as true. The experience of negation, in other words, provides an occasion for using such terms as "real" and "unreal." In the terminology of Advaita, the real is that which is never canceled or sublated (*abādhita*); what is nonreal is canceled or sublated by another experience, it belongs to the realm of appearance; and the unreal, since it does not become an object of either an actual or a possible experience, does not fall under the purview of phenomenological inspection.

The Advaitins use the notion of appearance as a heuristic device to understand reality. The entire conceptualization of something as an appearance arises because of the disclosure of depth. When the depth opens itself and one becomes aware of it retrospectively, one speaks of the distinction between depth and surface. In contemplation as correction, one becomes aware of what is depth and what is surface. Prior to that, we are always at the level of the surface, but we do not even know that we are at the level of the surface. Unless we have a critical experience, like the snake-rope or the shell-silver illusion, the occasion does not arise for understanding an appearance *as* an appearance.

In the opening section of his commentary on *Brahmasūtra* (BS), Śaṃkara gives the following definition of the "false" (*mithyā*):[17] "the appearance elsewhere of what one perceived earlier, with a nature that is similar to recollection (*smṛti*)." The appearance essentially involves a confusion between the real and that which is nonreal. In the appearance of a snake, its qualities are superimposed on the rope, which is given to us as "this." The snake that is seen in the snake-appearance is different from the snake that was seen in a zoo, and yet the appearance is like, but not quite identical to, a recollection. Erroneous perceptions thus involve three stages: (1) One perceives a snake, (2) this perception is canceled, and (3) then there is an interpretation of this cancellation or, in other words, a correction takes place. The last stage is the most significant one for our purposes, because it is at this stage that we become aware of the distinction between the real and the nonreal. Cancellation in this context does not amount to a suspension of belief in the content as initially appraised, but rather amounts to the refusal to admit that the initial belief had any content at all. The Advaitins recognize that the snake and the rope cannot both be equally real. They hold that the snake is not unreal, because it is experienced—there was something there to be perceived. But it cannot be both real and unreal at the same time. So, the Advaitins conclude that the content of appearance is indeterminable. In other words, an erroneous cognition is a cognition not of the real, but of that which is not determinable as real.

The potential of the idea of superimposition (*adhyāropa*) for a phenomenological investigation must not be underestimated. Instead of simply treating it as a ploy for affirming the absolute reality of *brahman*, one can use it for analyzing experience by disclosing layers within experience. It can be used as a measuring rod for analyzing experience. The method used in erroneous cognition exemplifies a phenomenological approach in the sense of uncovering the deeper layers of experience presupposed in our ordinary, surface-level experience. The goal is to isolate an imperceptible dimension of experience through an analysis of that experience. Hence, phenomenological analysis is used to uncover reality or pure consciousness.

In any experience, at the prereflective stage, the presented data appears as an undifferentiated mass. When forms unfold progressively, one realizes that in the lower stages these forms were not discriminated. For example, initially one's body might be taken to be just one object among others. When differentiation sets in, one realizes that one's body, from a phenomenological point of view, is subjective relative to the objects in the external world. Likewise, the mind may be taken to be subjective relative to the body, insofar as it has a kind of subjectivity that is freer than that of the body. The point that the Advaitins are trying to make is as follows: In relation to our body, we are able to objectify the external object as "this," so the body is subjective relative to the object; in the case of the mind, we are able to objectify our body as "this," so the mind is subjective relative to the body. Similarly, mental functions can be objectified in relation to something that is still more inward, more subjective, more free than the mind. As Kalidas Bhattacharyya observes:

> These states are mental, but they are *objects* at the same time. Felt, in themselves, as relatively more subjective than either body or physical things, they are yet experienced as objects too, and discovered too that way by introspection (*anuvyavasāya*) or mental operation (*mānasa-pratyakṣa*), as the case may be, quite in the same way as things of the world are experienced in—and one may add, though unnecessarily, "as discovered that way by"—the primary first-order cognition. Mental states which are primary objects are said to be objects to *introspection*, and other states which are noncognitive—feelings and wills, for example—are objects for mental perception.[18]

Mental functions, in other words, are objectified as "what are experienced" (*dṛśyam*), assuming such forms as "I am happy" or "I am unhappy." The Advaitins extend this analysis further and point out that there is a dimension of consciousness that is more inward than mental states. It can be experientially isolated. And finally, when the language descriptive of content becoming an object is replaced by the language of manifestation, the procedure of isolating leads us to "*sākṣin*," the witness-consciousness, and then leads eventually to pure consciousness itself. In the process of explaining the above thesis, Bhattacharyya further notes:

> The relation between body and the world, between mind and body and between pure consciousness and mind . . . is unlike any ordinary case of distinguishing where when X is distinguished out the remainder is understood as a clear positive definite Y equivalent to the given situation minus X. Dissociation of the stages of freedom, as thus of a different sort, can be best represented by saying that what is now dissociated had earlier, by an inscrutable act of self-negation, deformed itself positively as the given that was started from. This is the Advaita principle of *ajñāna*.[19]

It is significant to note in this context that the act of isolating itself is not akin to abstracting colorlessness from a color, but amounts to attending what was previously unattended. To put it differently, what was previously undistinguished due to ignorance (*ajñāna* or *avidyā*)[20] is now distinguished with clarity. What thus arrives last in the order of knowing is first in the order of being; it has been present and functioning from the very start. Thus, the method used in Vedānta, although in many ways similar to Husserl's phenomenological method, is different.

It is indeed true that the overall intention of Husserl's phenomenology is to focus on the experience in which the true forms are revealed, rather than on natural perception. "Natural knowledge," notes Husserl:

> progressively takes possession of a reality at first existing for us as a matter of course and as something to be investigated further as regards its extent and content, its elements, its relations and laws. Thus the various sciences of the natural sort (*natürlichen Wissenschaften*) come into being and flourish, the natural sciences . . . the sciences of culture (*Geisteswissenschaften*) and, on the other side, the mathematical sciences, the sciences of numbers, classes, relations, and so on.[21]

Husserl contrasts the philosophical mode with the natural mode of reflection: "But philosophy lies in a wholly new dimension. It needs an entirely new point of departure and an entirely new method distinguishing it in principle from any 'natural science.' "[22] Husserl's transcendental subjectivity is not beyond experience; it is the essence of the purified region of experience. From a functional point of view, it is the principle on which all possible forms of knowing and experience are grounded. However, it cannot be used to describe the notion of the witness-consciousness or the self (*ātman*) of Vedānta.

The goal in Advaita Vedānta is not to lay a foundation for science but rather to discover the transcendental depth through an immanent inspection of experience. It is indeed true that, from one perspective, *brahman*-knowledge as the goal of Advaitic inquiry is the foundation of all cognitive endeavors. However, paradoxical as it may sound, the task of laying the foundation is to demonstrate that all species of knowledge are species of ignorance. One can talk about progress of knowledge in the phenomenal realm governed by ignorance. However, *brahman*-knowledge does not play any role in this process of progress, notwithstanding the fact that all knowledge in the empirical sphere is rooted in the knowledge of *brahman*.

Thus, although Advaitins recognize the reflective standpoint as distinct from the natural, it is always taken to be a part of the natural. The value of the reflective standpoint, however, must not be underestimated; it is necessary insofar as it paves the way for a transnatural or transcendental perspective. The program of transcendental phenomenology integral to the philosophic climate of European rationalism rules out anything that may be taken to transcend the intellect. Advaita Vedānta, on the other hand, does not simply stop at a mere analysis of the natural attitude and experience. Rather, it is interested in recovering a deeper layer of experience than that of surface experience. Husserl's phenomenology is simply a construct for understanding experience like any scientific construct. Husserl does not appeal to such radical existential situations as call for a new orientation of one's entire vocabulary and thought.

Advaita Vedānta is committed to the distinction between what is an appearance and what is not an appearance. It is committed to the distinction between appearance and reality, between surface and depth, between what shows forth and what remains hidden. The goal is to recover that which is not given in one's immediate inspection, but which, however, opens up through an analysis where immediate inspection is used as the take-off point.

Thus, the difference between Husserl's phenomenological method and the Advaitic analysis is as follows: Phenomenology, as a contemporary Western movement, is a study of appearances as they show themselves, a study of things as they are immediately open for reflective analysis. Western phenomenology thus involves a resolute attempt to stick to the appearances qua appearances, a refusal to go behind the appearances, but still claims to be an attempt to return to the thing-in-itself: By knowing the experience and its structure, it analyzes the structure to see whether one can lay a foundation for science, mathematics and so on, from within that framework. It does not raise the question of whether there are deeper layers of consciousness; it self-consciously remains at the surface level, refusing to accept that there is anything more than the surface, because an investigation of deeper layers of consciousness would not amount to doing philosophy, but psychology. Like commonsense theory and ordinary language analysis, Western phenomenology is an attempt to hold fast to ordinariness, because any effort to stretch the discourse strains the discourse.

In the words of Thèvenaz, I believe, phenomenology is:

> a method for changing our relation to the world, for becoming more acutely aware of it. But at the same time and by that very fact, it is already a certain attitude vis-à-vis the world, or more exactly a certain attitude vis-à-vis our relation to the world. Phenomenology combines the most radical break with our ordinary and natural attitude vis-à-vis the world (in this sense, it is an ascesis of the mind) with the deepening or the consecration of this original attitude (in this sense, it is respect for the real and engagement in the world). Consciousness takes its distance with regard to things; it gives itself complete freedom in respect to them, but one realizes at once this is in order to be more faithful to our essential insertion in the world. . . . The phenomenological method thus permits pushing on simultaneously and with one movement towards the roots of subjectivity and the foundation of the objective world.[23]

In short, the phenomenological method provides us with a better understanding of the world by an analysis of consciousness. It helps us both to elucidate and to analyze the constructs by which we come to understand reality.

The Vedāntic method is phenomenological in the sense that its focus is on experience instead of objects. Consciousness is the light that illumines the objects. The object is of interest to us because the object is made manifest by the light of consciousness. So it is a self-analysis of that light that is called phenomenological. This is what I have developed in this book. It is indeed true that in Advaita the transcendental, pure consciousness is a necessary condition of all phenomena. The Advaitins, however, postulate *sākṣin* (the witness-consciousness) as the witness of the object. Additionally, the Advaitins also make use of the idea of ignorance (*avidyā*). Thus, there is ignorance, there is a consciousness that witnesses this ignorance, there is consciousness of the ignorance, and when ignorance is removed, the consciousness and the object become nondifferent. The witness-consciousness is the presupposition of all knowing; it illuminates all that is known, thereby making knowledge possible. It is at once intrinsic to the cognizing of the empirical self and yet is more fundamental than the merely empirical. It is the basic Advaitin epistemological principle, their solution to the problems of epistemology.

The Purpose and the Plan of the Book

The purpose for writing such a book may be purely historical or exegetical or philosophical, or a combination of two of these three. This work is not historical, i.e., it does not deal with the chronological development of the concept of the witness-consciousness. Although I discuss what Advaitins (e.g., Śaṃkara, the founder of this school) and the later Advaitins (e.g., Sureśvara, Madhusūdana, Padmapāda, Prakāśātman) held and point out the differences between them, the goal in this work is not to show how and in what stages this development came about. So my focus in this work is not one of philosophical history. It can certainly be said to be exegetical in view of the fact that I have translated and interpreted some of the key passages that discuss the concept of the witness-consciousness in the Sanskrit commentaries belonging to the post-Śaṃkara period. The ultimate purpose of this work, however, is philosophical. I examine the arguments given by the Advaitins in support of this concept, the functions that they assign to it, and provide my reasons for accepting or rejecting what they have advanced. My goal is to demonstrate why such a consciousness is deemed necessary in Advaita, what advantages Advaita has over the other systems of Indian thought that deny the existence and necessity of such a consciousness, and, finally, to suggest that the witness-consciousness may indeed be a necessary component of any sound epistemological theory, regardless of whether one is talking about Western or Indian philosophical thinking. Thus, my interest in this book is philosophical and exegetical.

Apart from this introductory first chapter, the book contains an additional five chapters for a total of six chapters.

In the second chapter I trace the evolution and growth of the crystallizations of the epistemological ideas associated with the concept of the witness-consciousness in some major Upaniṣads. I begin my analysis by examining the denotation of the term. Although the term "*sākṣin*" is virtually nonexistent in the Upaniṣads, the epistemological ideas surrounding this concept do indeed occur there. Hence, I have selected certain key terms and passages from the Upaniṣads, especially the *Bṛhadāraṇyaka Upaniṣad* (BU), that foreshadow the development of this important concept. The Upaniṣads reiterate one central point: Consciousness or self is a necessary condition for all knowing, i.e., all actions, thoughts, and cognitions presuppose an immediate and direct awareness. This Upaniṣadic notion of awareness anticipates the development of the notion of the witness-consciousness in Śaṃkara and post-Śaṃkara Advaita epistemology. I close this chapter with a discussion of the various states of consciousness in the *Māṇḍūkya Upaniṣad* (MAU) and Gauḍapāda's *Kārikā* to show how the notion of the witness-consciousness is anticipated by these states.

In the third chapter I discuss the notion of *sākṣin* in the writings of Śaṃkara. This chapter contains translations of all the passages and verses, to my knowledge, in which the term "*sākṣin*" occurs in his writings. An analysis of these passages and verses reveals that Śaṃkara provides divergent, though not mutually exclusive, characterizations of this term. I show that these divergent characterizations can be grouped under two headings: *sākṣin* as pure consciousness and *sākṣin* as pure consciousness limited by the inner sense. I argue that while Śaṃkara uses the notion of the witness-consciousness to preserve his nondualistic thesis, he neither develops the epistemological ramifications of the concept of *sākṣin* systematically, nor does he provide a discussion of the metaphysical issues associated with this notion. Analyses of these epistemological and metaphysical issues surrounding the notion of *sākṣin* form the subject matter of the fourth and fifth chapters, respectively.

To be specific, in the fourth chapter I unpack and evaluate the epistemological ramifications of the Advaitin theory of the witness-consciousness and the role it plays in the Advaita epistemology. The chapter begins with a review of some of the fundamental concepts and distinctions that one finds in the Advaita literatures and is followed by my analysis of the Advaitin theory of perceiving. In this chapter, I provide a detailed analysis of the objects apprehended by the witness-consciousness alone: namely, mental states, illusory objects, and ignorance. My analysis focuses on two central Advaitin questions: (1) why these three objects are, and can only be, revealed by the witness-consciousness; and (2) what is entailed in the claim that everything is an object of the witness-consciousness, either as known or as unknown. I close the chapter with a discussion of the role and importance of the notion of the witness-consciousness in Advaita epistemology. I explore such issues as: How is the witness-consciousness known? Why must one postulate such a consciousness?

What is the necessity of ignorance? What does it mean to say that the mind goes out and assumes the form of the object? Why does pure consciousness associate itself with the inner sense? How can ignorance at once reside in consciousness and conceal it? The answers that the Advaitins provide are discussed in detail in the body of the text. Suffice it to say here that I believe I have demonstrated that the Advaitins provide ample phenomenological data for postulating the existence of the witness-consciousness and have successfully defended the necessity of such a consciousness for any viable theory of knowledge. How much of Advaitin metaphysics one can appropriate into one's own thinking I will leave for the individual reader to decide.

In the fifth chapter, I focus on the nature of *sākṣin.* I discuss issues such as what the nature of *sākṣin* is, whether it is one or many, and whether it is the same or different from the empirical cognizer. I also evaluate *sākṣin*'s relationship with other metaphysical entities—e.g., God (*Īśvara*), the self (*ātman*), and empirical individuals (*jīva*-s)—in order to demonstrate that although the Advaitins systematically develop the epistemological ramifications of the notion of *sākṣin,* they do not take the same care to explicate the metaphysical underpinning of this notion.

In the final chapter of the book, I attempt to make the concept of *sākṣin* accessible to Western readers. I compare and contrast the notion of the witness-consciousness with similar ideas in Kant, Husserl, Freud, and Sartre. I show that while these Western thinkers do not develop this concept explicitly, they implicitly assume the existence of something very similar to it in their own systems. In this chapter, I clearly bring out one fundamental difference between Indian and Western epistemology: Knowledge in the Indian context is not limited to knowing, as it is in the Western context, but also encompasses within its scope not-knowing. Not-knowing or ignorance for the Advaitins is not simply a lack of knowledge; it is rather something positive. Indeed, the very attempt to know by finite human beings points to a previous recognition of ignorance. Thus, it is not an exaggeration to say that any sound theory of knowledge must incorporate a theory of ignorance. Knowledge and ignorance mutually implicate each other; they are inseparable opposites. This fact is largely ignored by Western philosophers since Socrates. Whether or not one accepts the nondualistic Advaitin thesis has no bearing on the fact that a sound theory of knowledge presupposes a notion of ignorance. The Advaitins not only accept the theory of ignorance, they also systematically develop its ramifications for a theory of knowledge. Therein lies their unique contribution to epistemology.

2

The Advaita Notion of *Sākṣin* (Witness-Consciousness): Its Anticipations in the *Upaniṣads* and Gauḍapāda

I

In the previous chapter, I maintained that the witness-consciousness in Advaita mediates the polarity of the real and the apparent. It is eternal, nondual, and remains unchanged. While pure consciousness is eternal and is nondifferent from *brahman*, it also persists in empirical-practical experiences. Accordingly, it is more fundamental than the merely empirical. Pure consciousness, on account of the limiting adjunct, viz., ignorance, appears as the witness-consciousness.[1] The witness-consciousness in Advaita is the basic presupposition of all knowledge:

> it is wrong to speak of *sākṣin* as knowable, for it is the element of awareness in all knowing; and to assume that it is knowable would be to imply another knowing element—a process which leads to the fallacy of infinite regress. But the *sākṣin* does not therefore remain unrealized, for being self-luminous, by its very nature, it does not require to be made known at all. Its presence is necessarily equivalent to its revelation and it is therefore never missed [as] the pure element of awareness in all knowing.[2]

Thus, the witness-consciousness as the principle of revelation is not different from the self-luminous *ātman*. Standing behind all objects of knowledge, it furnishes illumination for all that is known, making that knowledge possible. Accordingly, the witness-consciousness carries with it a kind of accessibility that is not available to either *brahman* or *ātman*. It is completely independent, existing in its own right, and not in relationship to anything else; it is seamless, eternal existence, the ground of our understanding of "I," and the ultimate reality that the "I" names. It is the basic Advaita Vedānta epistemological principle, the Advaitin's solution to the basic problem of epistemology, viz.: how is knowledge possible?

The above characterization highlights the following key epistemological ideas surrounding the notion of the witness-consciousness:

1. The witness-consciousness, although the basis of all knowing, is different from the object known. It is implied in every act of knowing. It is the ultimate subject; it can never become an object of knowledge.

2. It is the pure element of awareness in all knowing. It is one, immutable, indivisible reality.

3. It shines in its own light; it is self-luminous.

4. It is different from the empirical individual (*jīva*), who cognizes and enjoys. In other words, it is different from the empirical individual who is caught up in the triple states of waking, dreaming, and dreamless sleep.

II

My goal in this chapter is to trace the evolution and growth and the early crystallizations of the above four key epistemological ideas associated with the notion of the witness-consciousness in some selected Upaniṣads.[3] It is important to bear in mind that although the term "*sākṣin*" does not occur in the Upaniṣads, the divergent characterizations of the self that this notion implies, especially when viewed in the epistemological context, undoubtedly occur in the Upaniṣads. I will demonstrate not only that these characterizations occur in the Upaniṣads, but that they are clearly presented and developed there. The Upaniṣads are replete with terms that foreshadow the important notion of the witness-consciousness. For example, some of the concepts that have been used in detail in the Upaniṣads are "seer" (*draṣṭā* or *vijñātā*),[4] "inner controller" or "the inner ruler" (*antaryāmin*),[5] "self-light" or "self-shining" (*ātmajyoti*),[6] or "self-luminous" (*svyaṃjyoti*).[7] These Upaniṣadic concepts echo the same point in different ways: that which lies beyond the plurality of names and forms—i.e., the self—is not accessible through empirical modes of knowing. *Bṛhadāraṇyaka Upaniṣad* (BU) analyzes these terms in detail; it also contains a lengthy analysis of knowing and its presuppositions. Accordingly, *Bṛhadāraṇyaka Upaniṣad* will be the primary focus of my investigation. These terms, however, are not unique to *Bṛhadāraṇyaka Upaniṣad.* They are scattered all over the various Upaniṣads. I will try to show that these terms as used in divergent Upaniṣads anticipate the four key ideas surrounding the notion of the witness-consciousness discussed above. Wherever necessary, I will bring in passages and/or terms from other Upaniṣads to substantiate my claim.

The source of *sākṣin* as a philosophical concept is obscure. It is virtually nonexistent in the Upaniṣads,[8] although compounds, such as *sarvasākṣin* (witness of all)[9] and *nityasākṣin* (eternal witness)[10] do occur. It is difficult to assign any precise referent to these concepts. They could be construed as referring to *brahman, sākṣin,* or even *Īśvara.* There is too little evidence to make an informed decision. These scattered references, however, can undoubtedly be construed as anticipating the later systematic development of this concept.

The Upaniṣads frequently characterize the self as the seer. The definition of the self is one of the central concerns of the Upaniṣads. For example, among the Upaniṣadic teachers, Yājñavalkya[11] is well known for his instructions regarding the knowledge of the self. In the course of discoursing with his wife, Maitreyī, the sage Yājñavalkya informs her that the self is the basis of all knowledge. It is different from the objects known. Therefore, it cannot be known in the manner in which the objects are known. One of the key passages in which the term "seer" (*draṣṭā*) occurs presents the best evidence for a forerunner of *sākṣin* in the *Bṛhadāraṇyaka Upaniṣad*:

> [You] cannot see the seer of seeing, [you cannot] hear the hearer of hearing, [you cannot] think the thinker of thinking, [you cannot] know the knower of knowing.[12]

When this passage is translated into epistemological terms, it states that the self is not knowable by any empirical means of knowledge. In other words, the self or the *ātman* is described as the eternal sight or the seer; it is eternally real and immutable. Likewise, *sākṣin* also etymologically signifies direct perception;[13] it is the eternal seer that cannot be comprehended by any empirical means of knowledge.

The above teaching is given by Yājñavalkya in the context of explaining to Uṣhāsta the real nature of the self. The self cannot be known like another physical object—say, a pitcher. The self forms the basis of both the subjective and the objective poles of experience. Functions of the body—seeing, hearing, knowing, etc.—occur not in the self but in the outside world. Yājñavalkya emphatically declares that one could not see the seer of the sight, the hearer of hearing, and so on. Rather, the self is the knower of all; it is the eternal witness. For him, the self is the ultimate subject that can never be made an object of knowledge. That is why it can only be described as "*neti, neti*" ("not this, not this"). No description of it is possible except denying all empirical attributes. It is not an exaggeration to say that this passage is an anticipation of the later conception that the cognitive functions are apperceived by the seer (*sākṣin*), which in itself is not an object of any more ultimate awareness.

Again, another passage reiterates the self as the basic presupposition of all knowing:

> That this self entered here into all these bodies up to the fingernail tips, just as a razor would be hidden in its case, or as fire, which sustains the universe, lies in its source. [People] do not realize it, for [as seen] it is incomplete [when viewed piecemeal]. . . . Of all these, the self alone is to be known, because one knows all through it, just as one can trace [a missing animal] through its footprints.[14]

This passage affirms that by knowing the self one acquires complete knowledge of all its names and forms. In other words, the unmanifest differentiates itself into names and forms. This very self enters into all bodies up to the nail-ends, like a razor enters into the razor case, or fire enters into the wood: while breathing it is known as the life-energy (*prāṇa*), while speaking as the speech, while seeing as the eye, while hearing as the ear, and while thinking as the mind. These are the various names of the self corresponding to its actions. Those who worship one or another of these names are ignorant. On the other hand, those who worship the self know all the names, because the self is the unitary basis of all knowing. Once again, this passage foreshadows the later notion of *sākṣin*, insofar as no cognition can result in the absence of such a consciousness in Advaita.

The *Kena Upaniṣad* makes the same point when it states that the self is other than the known and the unknown:

> [He] is known by one who does not know him; he who is certain to know him does not know him; those who rightly know, do not think they know him; those who do not have right knowledge, think that they know.[15]

In other words, to whom the self is not known, to him it is known; to whom it is known, he does not know it. It is unknown to those who think they understand it; it is known to those who know they do not understand it. In concrete terms, it amounts to saying that *brahman* or the self is not an object of knowledge: if one thinks that one knows the self and can describe it as an object perceived in the ordinary world, then he does not know it. On the other hand, those who are convinced that the self is not an object of knowledge do indeed know it. The self cannot be comprehended by the senses and logic, but only by intuitive realization.

The self, in other words, is other than the known (as an object) and the unknown (*anyad eva tad viditād atho aviditād adhi*).

The *Taittirīya Upaniṣad* (TU) echoes the same idea when it states that words return baffled from the self, not being able to attain it along with the mind (*yato vāco nivartante aprāpya manasā saha . . .*).[16] The self cannot be grasped by logic and reasoning, much less articulated in language. Words and thought are applicable to the realm of names and forms where plurality is manifested; they are simply pointers and in that sense useful.

The *Kaṭha Upaniṣad* reiterates this point, when it states:

> [The self] is not to be reached by words, nor by the mind, and not by the eyes. How can it be experienced by those who are other than those who say "the self exists"?[17]

In other words, the self is to be comprehended as "It is." The witness-consciousness, like the self, is different from objects that are known: it is the pure element of awareness in all knowing; it can never become an object.

Since the self is not an object of any empirical knowledge, it is never objectified. The "I" is a superimposition; it is not-self. When the self is called an "I," it is only from the outside. It is not an inherent characteristic of the self. The self is essentially *brahman*: this very same self is said to be the self of the world. In response to the question by Uddālaka Āruṇi about the inner controller (*antaryāmin*) of the world, Yājñavalkya in *Bṛhadāraṇyaka Upaniṣad* states that the principle which lies behind everything—which controls everything from within—is the inner controller. This inner controller is the immortal self:

> [It is] the unseen seer, the unheard hearer, the unthought thinker, the unknown knower. There is no seer other than him, no hearer other than him, no thinker other than him, no knower other than him. He is your self, the inner controller, the immortal. Other than him is the sufferer.[18]

The above passage highlights the idea that the self is one. Duality does not constitute the essence of the self; the duality is apparent, not real. The self is said to be the seer (*dṛṣṭā*) or the knower because it illuminates the cognitive as well as the other modes of the mind. It is the ground of all empirical knowledge. To put it differently, the self is said to be the seer only in its relation to the modes of the mind, the modes that owe their existence to the light of consciousness. All cognitions point to the activity of the self. The Upaniṣads nowhere explicitly deny the activity of the self: it is taken to be the thinker, not an object of thinking; the perceiver, not an object of perception. Specific activities start at a given point in time and terminate at another point; what remains constant through them all is the self—the pure consciousness that makes manifestation possible. In this context, however, we must not lose sight of the fact that the self does not illuminate these modes as their agent (*kartā*). The self is changeless and without any attributes whatsoever. The agency of seeing or knowing cannot belong to such a changeless self. The self is immutable pure consciousness; it is the witness of all events, psychical and physical. The essence of all being is the unconditionally immediate self.[19] It is the indwelling essence of the individual; it is the ultimate knower. It is always self-revealed. The Upaniṣads repeatedly affirm: "Verily, in the beginning everything was *brahman,* it knew itself alone."[20] However, on account of ignorance, it acts as a doer, an enjoyer, and so on. When ignorance is destroyed, "it knows itself" (*tad ātmānam evāvet*).

Being of the nature of pure consciousness, the self shines of itself. *Bṛhadāraṇyaka Upaniṣad* provides a detailed discussion of the self as its own light, which, once again, anticipates the notion of the *sākṣin.* In the famous discourse of Sage Yājñavalkya and King Janaka, the King asks the Sage: "Of what light is this *puruṣa*?" In other words, the King desires to know the source of illumination that makes it possible for human beings to function in this world. The Sage initially informs the King that it is the light of the Sun. This answer, however, does not satisfy the King. He further asks: "When the sun has set, what light does a person have?" The Sage informs him that it is the light of the moon. This reply does not satisfy the King either. Thus, he queries further: "With the setting of the sun and the moon, what light does a person have?" Yājñavalkya then replies: "It is the light of the fire." The King persists in questioning and asks what happens when the sun and the moon and the fire are out. The Sage informs him that it is the *vāc* or the word that guides a person. The King finally asks: "What is the source of light when the *vāc* is also at rest?" Yājñavalkya replies: "The self is indeed his light; with the self as light, he sits, runs around, does his work and returns."[21] The self as its own light, once again, foreshadows the *sākṣin* of Advaita. Like the self of the Upaniṣads, the *sākṣin* is self-effulgent: it is self-luminous.

The sought-after "light" in this context is more basic than the physical light that makes the perception of physical objects possible. It is significant to note that the above reply is given in response to the question "what light does a person here have?" In the waking state a person moves with the help of various lights that are outside his/her body. But, we must ask, what serves as a light for a person in dreams and in deep sleep? One cannot see dream objects without illumination of some sort. From deep sleep, one awakes with the remembrance that one slept happily and knew nothing. This must show that some kind of light functions in deep sleep as well as in dreams. Therefore, Janaka asks about the light that serves a person when he is asleep. Yājñavalkya answers that the self is the light that serves a person in all the states: waking, dreaming, and dreamless sleep. Light in this context does not signify simply consciousness and its conditions in an abstract sense, but also that which helps one to sit, walk about, work, and return. It is self-effulgent and eternal.

Janaka does not comprehend Yājñavalkya's response. So, he further asks, "which is the self?"[22] To put it differently, since a human being is an aggregate (of the senses, the mind, the intellect, and the ego) with divergent properties and functions, which of these components is the self? Yājñavalkya informs the king that the self is *vijñānamaya*; it is identified with the intellect. The transparent intellect, on account of its proximity to the self, assumes the characteristics of the self; like the light reflected in a glass globe assumes the shape, color, etc., of the globe. The intellect performs the function of thinking. However, the self, assuming the likeness of the intellect, creates the appearance of thinking. The self's light illumines the internal as well as the external objects.[23] Śaṃkara, in his commentary on *Bṛhadāraṇyaka Upaniṣad*, reinforces this point when he says that "the intellect, being transparent and next to the self, easily catches the reflection of the intelligence of the self."[24]

To overcome such problems, a kind of physico-psychological method is used that progressively unfolds the essence of *ātman*. In the *Chāndogya Upaniṣad* (CU), Indra and Virocana approach Prajāpati for knowledge of the immortal self.[25] They desire to know the self that is free from sin, old age, death, hunger, thirst, etc. Initially, Prajāpati informs them that the true self is nothing but the self seen in a reflection; that the self is the same as the body. This answer satisfies Virocana. Indra, however, is not satisfied with Prajāpati's explanation. So, he returns to Prajāpati for further instruction about the self. Prajāpati tells him that the dream-consciousness is his true self. Indra is still not satisfied. He returns to Prajāpati a second time for further explanation. Prajāpati tells Indra that the self is experienced in deep sleep: "When a person is asleep with senses withdrawn, [when one] is serene, and sees no dream—that is the self. This is immortal, this is *brahman*."[26] Indra is not satisfied with this answer either, because this explanation suggests that when everything is withdrawn and only unconsciousness remains, that unconsciousness is the self. Indra returns to Prajāpati for the third time and this time lives with him for five years. Finally, Prajāpati reveals to Indra the true nature of the self—the self is immortal, the body is destructible: the body is but the abode of the immortal self.[27] The real self continues in all states. This passage stresses the continuity of the real self. The self is progressively identified with the bodily self, the dreaming self, and the self of dreamless sleep, until finally it is declared to be that which is not affected by the changing modes. It is that which is present in all three states.

Again, the description of the self as self-luminous (*svayaṃjyoti*) in *Bṛhadāraṇyaka Upaniṣad*, where the ultimacy of the self is again explicated by indicating that the seer is unseen and that the knower cannot be known, anticipates the notion of *sākṣin*. The sun illuminates objects in waking life. Since the sun does not shine inside us, but yet objects are revealed to the dreaming self, there must be another source of illumination. It is said:

> When he goes to sleep, he takes with him the material of this all-embracing world, himself pulls it apart, himself builds it up; dreams by his own nature and own light; then this person becomes self-illuminating.[28]

In the waking state, a person is aware of the subject-object distinction. While dreaming, since one is only aware of dream objects, the waking individual himself becomes both the subject and the object, so to speak. The impressions of the waking state furnish the materials for the dream state. In the dream state, the body is set aside for all practical purposes. When, in dreams, the mind detaches itself from external objects, the self manifests those impressions. The power of manifestation belongs to the self, which serves as the light in all three states. The dream world, being its own creation, is lighted by the eternal vision of the self. This is what is meant by "its own radiance" (*svena bhāsā*). In other words, the self itself becomes the light, and, accordingly, must shine by its own light.

Thus, the self is continuous in all three states. It passes from the dream state to waking life and from waking life back to the dream state very much like a fish that swims from one bank of the river to another.[29] The self, though continuous, is not identical with any of the three states. In both dreaming and waking states duality is present. In deep sleep, however, there is a lack of relatedness that is bliss (*samprasanna*). As a hawk or a falcon, having flown around in the sky, becomes exhausted, folds its wings and goes to his nest to rest, similarly the self in the deep sleep state passes into a dreamless state in which it has no desire, no pleasure, and no dreams.[30]

> While one does not see anything there, one sees everything there. Seeing, one sees not; for there cannot be any absence of the sight of the seer, owing to the imperishability [of the seer]; there is not that second entity differentiated from it which it can see.[31]

The thrust of the passage is as follows: The self does not perceive any object in deep sleep, because although it is (really) seeing in that state, it does not see in the usual manner—through the eyes. Consciousness is imperishable; there is no cessation of the seeing of the seer. In the state of deep sleep, there is nothing else but pure consciousness. As fire never loses its property of burning or the sun of shining, similarly the seer, the self, never loses its power of seeing. Here a distinction is made between two kinds of sight: the phenomenal and the eternal. The former takes place with the eyes; such a seeing is an accidental attribute of the self that has a beginning as well as an end. However, the sight that the self possesses by its very nature, like the burning of fire or the shining of the sun, is eternal. Eternal seeing is an essential attribute of the self. When it is associated with phenomenal sight, its limiting adjunct, it is described as the seer and is differentiated into the seer and the sight. It is metaphorically described at times as seeing and at other times as not seeing, although it is the same forever. In reality, the seer and the sight are identical. The self exists within all; it is immutable. The eternal seer of the Upaniṣads is none other than the *sākṣin* of the later Advaita.

Thus, the seeing of the seer, being its own intrinsic nature, never ceases; even in deep sleep, where there is nothing to be seen, it sees. It cannot be distinguished from not seeing, since there is no other thing to be seen or not to be seen. Seeing can be empirically realized only when an other is posited by ignorance. There can be no seeing when everything becomes the self and there is nothing to be seen. This notion of the self—remaining the same in all three states, being the self-effulgent light in them—clearly anticipates the later notion of the witness-consciousness.

What is stated here is obvious. The self is articulated as that which continues in the three states of waking, dreaming, and deep dreamless sleep, and is therefore not identical with any of them. This is a clear description of the notion of the self as witness standing behind everything that is known (known discursively in wakeful life, known dreamingly in dreams, and known as unknown in deep sleep) shining forth in its own light, revealing eternally and continuously.[32]

The three states of the self discussed above become the focus of investigation in some major Upaniṣads. It is one of the common methods adopted in the Upaniṣads for arriving at the knowledge of the self. For example, the entire *Māṇḍūkya Upaniṣad* (MAU) is devoted to a discussion of these three states of the self. It contains one of the most succinct and systematic treatments of this method. At the outset, this Upaniṣad identifies the sound *aum* with all-that-there-is. *Aum* is what was, what is, and what will be. It signifies a correlation between the microcosms and the macrocosmos. It is also what is beyond time, that which is the unmanifest basis of the manifest universe. *Aum* stands for *brahman*; it is the most effectual sound symbol of *brahman*. The word "*aum*" consists of three letters, *a, u, m*, which correspond to the three forms in which the self appears, respectively, in the states of waking, dreaming, and dreamless deep sleep. Knowledge of *brahman* encompasses not only the three states, but also the fourth state—*turīya* (the transcendent), the undifferentiated state of pure consciousness that is beyond the changing and conditioned phenomenal modes of existence.

The three states of the self are known as: *viśva, taijasa*, and *prājña*:

> The universal self [*vaiśvānara*], with the waking state [*jāgarita sthāna*] as its manifestation, with consciousness directed outward, of seven limbs and nineteen mouths, is the enjoyer of gross things, is the first quarter.
>
> The second quarter is the *taijasa* or the luminous, with the dream state as its manifestation, with consciousness directed inward, with seven limbs and nineteen mouths, it is the enjoyer of consciousness not related to objects.
>
> Where the sleeper desires no desires, sees no dream, that is deep sleep [*suṣupta*]. The third quarter has deep sleep for its manifestation; it has become one, is of the nature of enlightenment, full of bliss, an enjoyer of bliss, with consciousness as its face.[33]

Viśva is the waking self. In this state, the self cognizes external objects. It has seven limbs[34] and nineteen mouths.[35] Since it is only in this state that the self is conscious of external objects, its experiences are sensuous. The waking self is the first state (*pāda*) of *brahman*. It is the outermost appearance of the self. *Taijasa*, the dreaming self, is the second state in which the mind enjoys impressions imprinted upon the mind during the waking experience, which are then presented as if real. In this state, the self is "internally conscious"; it experiences subtle objects created out of the mental impressions of the first state. This state is contradicted by waking experiences. Dream-objects, regardless of how real they might appear in one's dreams, disappear upon waking up. Dream-objects are not treated consistently throughout the history of Vedānta, the later tradition explaining them as simply products of nescience. The third state, *prājña*, is a state of dreamless sleep during which the mind and the senses are quiescent. Consequently, in this state there is a cessation of normal consciousness; the subject-object distinction no longer exists, nor does distinction among objects. There are no desires, no dreams. There is no experience of pleasure and pain. It is an entirely undifferentiated state. There is a sense of bliss, however, because there is a temporary union between the absolute and the embodied self.

It is a state in which the knowing self, while still capable of knowing, does not have anything to know. This self still has the capability of knowing all objects and therefore is called *prājña*: "It is not a state of consciousness in the ordinary sense; but it is not a state of blank or absolute consciousness either, for some sort of awareness is associated with it. It is not, however, 'the objectless knowing subject' that endures in it . . . ; for along with the object, the subject as such also disappears then. It is rather a state of nonreflective awareness, if we may so term it."[36]

The phenomenon of deep sleep is especially significant since in it all mental activities are suspended and the consciousness of individuality is absent. It points to the fact that knowledge of duality is only a conditional and temporary feature of finite lives. From deep sleep, one awakes and recalls that he slept happily and remembered nothing. In the deep sleep state distinctions are not overcome. The self, being hidden by a kind of undifferentiated darkness, absorbs duality and multiplicity. Deep sleep demonstrates that something permanent, unchanging, and foundational to all experiences must be present even when the consciousness of external objects is not present. This state is different from *turīya*, the state of release, which is the underlying substratum of the the triple states of waking, dreaming, and dreamless sleep.

III

This tripartite distinction, by means of which the self successively occupies, yet remains independent of, the three states, is elaborated by Gauḍapāda:

> The all-pervasive, as outward directed consciousness, is *viśva*; as inward directed it is *taijasa*; as nothing but a mass of consciousness it is *prājña*. Though one, it is thought of in three ways.[37]
>
> Of the *viśva*, the right eye is the face, it dwells there to shine forth. The *taijasa* abides in the mind within. The *prājña* lies in the space in the heart. he thus dwells in the body in three ways.[38]

What we have are three states of embodiment of the self that remain pure, unrelated, and with a oneness confirmed by the judgment "I am he." *Viśva, taijasa*, and *prājña*, all three are the self, but only as embodied. As *viśva*, the self can not only perceive objects, but it can also approach these objects mentally by remembering or imagining them. The dreaming self is the same as the waking self, but it can only approach objects of impressions mentally, fabricating dream-objects from the residual impressions of the objects of perception or the memories of objects. In this sense, *taijasa* is parasitic on *viśva*. When consciousness rests in itself, all imagery ceases, and the self is *prājña*. The self exists although all mental processes stop; only the vital airs and the potentiality of having mental processes persists. The vital airs persist actually, not potentially; we breathe and our other autonomic functions continue during deep sleep. The undifferentiated nature of the self is clearest in this state. The fact that the *prājña* self reawakens, and can say "I am he," proves that, even if only in the state of potentiality, *prājña* had been embodied. It is only when there is not even potentially the chance of embodiment that *prājña* passes into *turīya*, the real unconditional nature of the self. The "I" reemerges after deep sleep; it is not recreated. The self, though in itself *turīya*, is embodied in different forms or states.

Gauḍapāda argues that a determination of what characterizes *viśva* and *taijasa* is necessary so that we are able to ascertain the true nature of *turīya*. Keeping this in view, Gauḍapāda states: "*Viśva* and *taijasa* are taken to be bound to cause and effect. But *prājña* is bound to cause [alone]. In *turīya*, there is neither cause nor effect."[39]

The above first asserts that whereas *viśva* and *taijasa* are conditioned by cause and effect, *prājña* is conditioned by cause alone; that "these two" (*dvau tau*) do not exist in *turīya*. This verse is ambiguous, because the referents of "these two" is not clear. On one interpretation, "these two" could be taken to assert that causation is not real, considering the fact that neither cause nor effect exists in *turīya*, which is reality in the absolute sense. On another interpretation, "these two" may be taken to refer to the states of waking and dreaming, which are said to be conditioned by cause and effect, and that the state of deep sleep is conditioned by cause alone insofar as all effects must exist in this state in an undifferentiated form. Both interpretations are plausible. Śaṃkara in his commentary on this verse states that in an effect the result is actualized and in the causal state the effect remains latent. *Viśva* and *taijasa* are conditioned by cause and effect; nonapprehension and misapprehension of reality characterize these two states. *Prājña*, however, is bound by cause alone, insofar as the nonapprehension of reality is alone responsible for the arising of the state of *prājña*. This explains, argues Śaṃkara, why the causal and the resultant conditions—the nonapprehension and misapprehension of reality—do not exist in *turīya*.[40] The point that is being made in these verses is as follows: Since the effect actualizes only when certain conditions are fulfilled and at all other times only remains potentially contained in the cause, *viśva* and *taijasa* are governed by causality; they are conditioned by both nonapprehension and misapprehension. Ignorance—the state of not knowing—is the substance of causal potentiality. Its actualization is knowing otherwise; it is the state of being positively mistaken.

Gauḍapāda explains the distinction between *prājña* and *turīya* further:

> *Prājña* knows nothing, neither itself nor the other, neither truth nor falsehood, but the *turīya*, the fourth, is all-seeing, ever and always.[41]
>
> Both *prājña* and *turīya* are, in common, unaware of duality. The former is in seed sleep [i.e., the source of cognition of name and forms]; this seed sleep is absent in *turīya*. Of these two, *prājña* alone is conditioned by cause.[42]

Śaṃkara in his commentary on the above verses explains what Gauḍpāda was trying to convey to his readers. In the first verse, Śaṃkara raises two issues: First, why is it that *prājña* is conditioned by cause alone? Second, why are the two conditions of nonapprehension and misapprehension absent in *turīya*? Unlike *viśva* and *taijasa*, *prājña* does not apprehend the external world that arises as a result of ignorance: it does not comprehend either itself or others. It therefore is in a state of not-knowing, covered by undifferentiated darkness. *Turīya*, on the other hand, is not conditioned by cause or effect. Therefore, false perceptions or misperceptions of reality that result from nonapprehension are not possible in *turīya*. Nonapprehension of reality during *prājña* is the cause (seed) of the misapprehension during dreaming and waking. *Turīya* does not contain any such seed. It is, like the sun, ever luminous: it consists of light and is opposed to the darkness that characterizes *prājña*. *Turīya* is the effulgent and all-pervasive source of objects. It is beyond ignorance. It is at once *sarvadṛk*, the seer of everything that there is, as well as the witness of everything that exists. It exists in all beings during the waking and the dreaming states, and is called the seer of everything.[43] There is nothing besides *turīya*. Therefore, it is never associated with causal conditions that may result from nonapprehension of reality. Accordingly, nonapprehension as well as misapprehension of reality are not possible in *turīya*.

In his commentary on the second verse, Śaṃkara states that this verse is intended to remove the confusion as to why, since nonapprehension characterizes both *prājña* and *turīya*, it is *prājña* alone that is conditioned by the cause and not *turīya*. It is because *prājña* is the seed sleep (*bījanidrāyuta*), i.e., it is sleep that is characterized by the noncognition of reality. *Prājña* is deep sleep—the nonapprehension of reality that gives rise to the cognitions of variety and multiplicity. It is the causal state that immediately precedes the state of waking up. *Turīya,* on the other hand, is the nondual witness and is by nature pure consciousness itself. Therefore, it is said that *turīya* is not governed by the conditions of cause or effect.[44] In the case of *prājña,* the undifferentiated darkness absorbs duality while still containing it; in the case of *turīya,* there is not even the potentiality of duality, and no darkness. These are different states. The dormant darkness is present in deep sleep; however, it does not, it cannot, condition *turīya. Prājña* anticipates the later notion of *sākṣin. Prājña* consciousness is the self as unified; distinctions are not overcome in this state but rather are present in an undifferentiated state. It is an indivisible entity, which accounts for its being called *prajñānaghana,* a lump of consciousness.[45] The senses do not function in this state and therefore the "I" as explicit awareness is absent; this state thus approximates the notion of the witness-consciousness. "The self in this state is not aware of itself, or of others, and is therefore shrouded by undifferentiated darkness in which duality is absorbed. . . . But it is only the self in the third stage that is epistemologically significant as containing the potentiality for a cognitive relation characteristic of wakeful life."[46]

Several other Upaniṣads argue along the same lines. For example, *Kaṭha Upaniṣad* makes a clear distinction between the self that is associated with the body, the senses, and the mind, on the one hand, and the self that is pure and not associated with either the body or the mind or the sense, on the other hand.[47] The first is empirical; it is the changing consciousness. The pure self does not change; it is the ground of all changes. It is *brahman,* beyond the intellect (*buddhi*) and the witness of all (*sarvasākṣīn*). Although it witnesses objects, it does not enjoy them.[48] But how can *sākṣin* be equated with the supreme reality, as it is here, and still be relegated to the empirical enjoyer (*bhoktā*)? *Māṇḍūkya Kārikā* provides the following answer: *brahman* is witness of all (*sarvasākṣīn*) or sees all (*sarvadṛk*) only to the extent that its nature as seer is not affected when there is nothing to see; *sākṣin,* on the other hand, is the witness of everything that appears; it is literally a seer.[49] Even when in deep sleep there is nothing to see, *sākṣin* sees that there is nothing (no-thing) presented to perception. Thus, the self in deep sleep is not a seer in the ordinary sense of the word, because such activity is applicable due to the inner sense alone, which is operative during both the waking and the dreaming stages. In deep sleep nothing is seen because there is no object to be seen. This, however, should not be taken to mean that there is cessation of consciousness during deep sleep. Indeed, pure consciousness does not cease to exist during deep sleep; the vision of the seer constitutes its essence, which is unaffected by either the presence or the absence of objects. In fact, the Upaniṣads repeatedly reiterate that the self is the place of deep sleep: "'Now, when one is sound asleep, composed, serene, and knows no dream—that is the self (*ātman*),' said he. 'That is the immortal, the fearless. That is *brahman*.'"[50]

Again:

> [Deep sleep] is that form of his which is beyond desires, free from evil, without fear. As a man, when in the embrace of a beloved wife, knows nothing within or without, so this person, when in the embrace of the intelligent self, knows nothing within or without. Verily, that is his [true] form in which his desire is satisfied, in which the self is his desire, in which he is without desire, without sorrow.[51]

This also explains the seemingly contradictory claims that pure consciousness (*cit*) cannot be known as an object of mediate knowledge, but that it is known as involved in every act of knowing. The absolute self does not possess enjoyership; its enjoyership is created by the limiting adjuncts, e.g., intellect. Another Upaniṣad reiterates the same point when it states that "the absolute self thinks as it were, and shakes as it were, and so on."[52] Passages such as "for where there is duality, as it were, there one smells, sees, hears, speaks, thinks, and knows of another. However, when everything becomes the very self of the knower of *brahman*, then what and through what should one know?"[53] reinforce the idea that when pure consciousness individuates itself into subject and object, there results knowledge—the distinction between the knower and the known. Śaṃkara and his followers use such passages to highlight the single most important distinction that they make between the absolutely real (*pāramārthika*) and empirically real (*vyāvahārika*) perspectives. This distinction is the pivot around which revolves the entire edifice of the Advaita system: What holds good from the absolutely real perspective does not also hold good from the empirically real perspective. To put it differently, knowledge takes place in the phenomenal world and therefore is not attributable to the pure self.

The Upaniṣadic conception of self as light raises an important question: If the self is pure consciousness, what is its relation to the empirical world of names and forms? The Upaniṣads do not provide a clear answer to this question. However, this issue receives a systematic treatment in the hands of Śaṃkara and his followers. They use the conception of the self as light to underscore the freedom of the self. The self-luminous nature of the self points to the fact that each individual is aware of his/her own existence spontaneously. Such a self-awareness is not arrived at as the result of an inferential process. All thoughts, actions, and cognitions proceed from this self-awareness, which is immediate and direct. It is none other than the *sākṣin* of Śaṃkara and his followers.

The point that is being made in the various Upaniṣads is as follows: Consciousness is a necessary condition for the assertion that there are things. To say that there are things, and yet no consciousness, is to contradict oneself. The experientially variable can only be isolated against an invariable background. Without an invariable consciousness, there can be no objects. Such a consciousness can never be absent, not even in deep sleep.[54]

Thus, the Upaniṣads repeatedly emphasize that the self is different from the mind or the intellect. It is also different from the perceptual triad—the perceiver, the act of perceiving, and the perceived object. It is pure consciousness. It is of the nature of light; it is self-luminous. All these ideas indirectly point to the conception of *sākṣin* that one finds in Advaita Vedānta. The *Bṛhadāraṇyaka Upaniṣad* passage "*yat sākṣād aparokṣād brahma*"[55] articulates *brahman* as direct and immediate and thus directly anticipates the notion of *sākṣin.* This Upaniṣadic passage is cited by the later Advaitins in the context of the question "What directly and manifestly is the *brahman*?" Thus, such a *brahman* is defined (or rather left undefined). *Brahman* is the essence of all that there is. *Brahman* in this context is not *sākṣin* in the technical sense, or even for that matter in a nontechnical sense, but rather an undifferentiated and undifferentiable principle that can signify indifferently either *sākṣin* or *brahman,* as we shall see in the next chapter. The writings of Śaṃkara illustrate this point clearly.

3

Śaṃkara on *Sākṣin*

I

In keeping with his relentless commitment to nondualism, Śaṃkara undertakes his philosophical investigation into the idea of the nondual reality known as *brahman* or *ātman*. In his writings,[1] he seeks to give a systematic and rationalistic account of the theory of the self that he largely takes from the Upaniṣads. The whole notion of *ātman* remains unchanged from that of the Upaniṣads, while he endeavors to systematize and explain the diverse and at times inconsistent Upaniṣadic teachings. Reflecting on the inconsistencies of the Upaniṣads, he sometimes speaks of *ātman* as *brahman*, and at other times as the witness-consciousness, even at other times as *Īśvara*. In his discussion, one gets a clear picture of the nature and functioning of the *ātman*. However, it is not so clear when he discusses the immanent self of empirical experience. *Brahman, Īśvara, sākṣin*, and even *ātman* appear to be synonymous in many contexts, and the distinct nuances of the meanings of these terms are not clearly explicated. Following the Upaniṣads, Śaṃkara in his writings variously characterizes *ātman*. To list a few, he notes:

1. *Ātman* is self-luminous. The conscious [self-luminous] self, for Śaṃkara, is beyond the sun and the moon, etc.; everything exists and shines through the light of *ātman*; however, *ātman*, being self-effulgent, does not shine or manifest by any other light.[2]
2. *Ātman* is self-established [*svayaṃsiddha*].[3]
3. Undifferentiated self or consciousness is the only reality.[4]
4. *Ātman* is imperceptible, because it is never perceived.[5]
5. *Ātman* cannot know itself even as fire cannot burn itself.[6]
6. *Ātman* cannot be an object of perception because it cannot be split into the knower [*jñātṛ*] and the knowable [*jñeya*].[7]
7. Unlike the knowledge gained through the eye, the vision of the *ātman* does not cease to exist.[8]
8. The *ātman* is always of the nature of homogeneous consciousness.[9]

These characterizations of *ātman* raise a number of questions: What is the real nature of *ātman*? Is it knowable or unknowable? Since it is not an object of perception, is it unknowable? If it is knowable, how is it known? Are the above characterizations self-contradictory? If they are self-contradictory, are the contradictions real or only apparent?

Before proceeding any further, let us briefly discuss these characterizations to determine whether they shed any light on the questions raised above.

Ātman is said to be self-luminous because it reveals; it does not create. It reveals other objects (*ananyāvabāsyatve sati svetara sarvāvabhāsakatvaṃ svayaṃprakāśatvam*). While other objects are established via consciousness, consciousness itself is the presupposition of all knowing. Therefore, it is self-established.

It is pure distinctionless, self-shining consciousness, which is non-different from *brahman.* It is that state of being in which all subject-object distinction is obliterated. It is unconditioned; no one can either doubt or deny it. It is undifferentiated, since it is free from all external and internal differentiations. There are two varieties of external differentiation: heterogeneous (*vijātīya*) or homogeneous (*sajātīya*). A physical object—say, a table—is different from (*vijātīya*) another physical object, say, a chair. It (a table) is also different from (*sajātīya*) other tables. *Ātman* does not possess any internal (*svagata*) distinction either; the sort of differentiation that exists among different parts of the same object is foreign to it. One leg of a table, for example, is different from the other legs (*svagata*). *Ātman* does not have parts, and accordingly, it does not and cannot possess any kind of internal differentiation either. Hence, there is nothing either similar or dissimilar to consciousness.

Ātman is nonintentional, that is, it is not consciousness "of" and "for" something. It exists eternally as the reality (*brahman*); and it is a solid mass of knowledge (*vijñānaghana eva*). To be intentional means to have an object. *Ātman* is pure; it is a consciousness from which all content has been subtracted. One cannot even think of the absence of *ātman,* of it having ceased to be or not having come into existence, because the very act of thinking implies the presence of consciousness. It does not have either a beginning or an end; it is eternal and timeless. Time only arises within it. It is uncaused because nothing does or could precede it. It is unborn (*aja*). It is one or, better yet, not many.

Thus, we may say that *ātman* or self, for Śaṃkara, is one, pure, self-luminous, self-established, undifferentiated, nonintentional, eternal and timeless consciousness.

How can such a self or consciousness be known? Since it is not an object of perception, is it unknowable? Is it known or unknown? If it is known, does it know itself directly or is it known via some other object?

One might argue that the self is unknowable, given the fact that the Upaniṣads repeatedly reiterate that the self is unknowable and that it is never apprehended as "this" or "that." The unknowability of the self in this context must not be construed to mean that it is unknown. Rather, it means that the self cannot become its own object; it is the foundation of all knowledge.[10] It cannot be known as objects are known. One and the same entity cannot be both the subject and the object of knowledge at the same time. Moreover, since everything besides the self is unconscious, the conscious self cannot be known by anything unconscious. It cannot be said to be unknown either because it is immediate. That is why it is said to be different from both the known and the unknown. No contradiction is involved in saying that it is neither known nor unknown: *ātman* is other than the known; it is above the unknown.[11] Hacker notes:

> [Self-luminosity] implies that the self is known in a manner different from the way in which objects become known. The self is not an object. It is not necessary to prove . . . that the self exists. On the contrary, the self's luminosity is the presupposition for any object's being known. One may say in a paradox that the self is unknowable because it cannot become an object of knowledge, but it is at the same time better known than any object inasmuch as no object can be cognized save in the light of the self.[12]

The self is not known as a physical object, say, a pitcher, is known. It is not completely unknown either because it is known as the "I." It is unknown as an eye is unseen in the act of seeing. "[T]he self is not presented like heaven or Mount Meru . . . for it is the very self of those that present it. A presentation by someone has for its object something to be presented, and this is possible only when there is a difference."[13] Thus, the self is not completely unknown; it is accessible as the "I."

For Śaṃkara, one is aware of *ātman* within oneself. It is impossible to deny it. It is real and present in human experience. Nothing can be said about it except that it exists. It is known directly and immediately, it manifests in every human being as self-awareness or self-consciousness; it is the witness-consciousness of all events, physical as well as psychical. *Ātman* as pure consciousness is one without a second, but it also persists in empirical experience and is known as the agent and the enjoyer of activities. That is why the Upaniṣads repeatedly state that although pure consciousness cannot be "known as an object of mediate knowledge, yet it is involved in every act of knowing." The known are many, the knower is one; it is unlimited, changeless, and self-evident.

If the self is pure consciousness, however, it is at the same time said to be related to the flux and flow of empirical experiences. On the Advaita account, the self, on account of nescience (*avidyā*), appears as the *sākṣin*. Thus, the obvious questions: What or who is this *sākṣin*? What role does it play in Śaṃkara's philosophy? What is the relevance of this concept in his system?

II

I will begin my discussion by providing translations of all the passages and verses in Śaṃkara's writings in which the term "*sākṣin*," to my knowledge, occurs.

(1) By superimposing what is known by the "I" upon the inner self, which is the witness-consciousness of all its [i.e., of the "I," or the inner organ] endless modifications [*pracāra*], [it] superimposes the inner self, the witness-consciousness of everything, upon the inner organ, etc., which are mistaken for it.[14]

(2) It may be objected that since the *a͞tmā* is designated by the "I," it cannot be said that it is known from the Upaniṣads. [The reply is] "no," it is said to be the witness-consciousness of that self. That is the witness, which is not the object of the sense of "I"; the witness-consciousness is different from the agent.[15]

(3) The state of ignorance of the empirical self, blinded by the darkness of ignorance, nondiscrimination between the highest being and the cause-effect organ aggregate, is established by the god who is the highest self who, in the state of ignorance, resides in all beings and presides over all actions and is the witness-consciousness of all things. . . .[16]

(4) Just as a person who is dreaming is not touched by the illusion of the dream experience, because waking and satisfaction do not invariably go together, so the witness-consciousness of the three states, which is one and nondeviating, is not affected by any of these deviating states.[17]

(5) By the mere apprehension of cognition [*vijñāna*], there does not arise a desire to apprehend the witness-consciousness of the cognition; therefore the apprehension of an infinite regress is not justified. Of the two, the witness-consciousness and the cognition, being by nature different, the relation of the cognizer and cognized is possible. Because the witness-consciousness, which is self-established, cannot be denied.[18]

(6) Just as I am the witness of the movements of my intellect [*buddhi*], so I am also of the others. I can neither be rejected or accepted; therefore I am the highest self.[19]

(7) The self does not have changefulness, impurity and materiality. Being the witness of all intellects, it is not of limited knowledge like the intellect.[20]

(8) It is like ether in all beings, but free from the defects of material things. It is the witness, consciousness without qualities, pure, *Brahman*; so I am alone.[21]

(9) The object (that which is to be perceived) is different from the perceiver, because it is perceived, like a jar; the seer and the seen do not belong to the same class, otherwise being the witness-consciousness would be like the intellect.[22]

(10) Being the witness of all cognitions, it is changeless and all-pervading. If it were to change [i.e., an object], it would have become of limited knowledge like the intellect, etc.[23]

(11) [Self] is consciousness, self-shining, the seeing, immediate awareness and inactive. [It] is the witness-consciousness directly cognized inside everybody, constant, qualityless, and nondual.[24]

(12) Everything rooted in the intellect, including the I-notion, is [a qualifying attribute] of the witness. Pervading everything by means of its reflection but without being in contact with anything, the self is itself of the nature of knowledge.[25]

(13) Just as one knows himself to be the tenth person from the sentence "you are the tenth," so from sentences such as "thou art that," one knows one's own self, which is the constant perceiver of the inner sense.[26]

(14) The supreme self, which is different from all modifications of *prakṛti*, which is of the nature of pure awareness, which manifests all without difference, these endless [entities] existent and nonexistent—this self enjoys itself as "I," through the states such as the waking, etc., as the direct witness of *buddhi*.[27]

(15) When both reasoning and *śruti* eliminate the five sheaths, what

remains after their negation is the witness, which is of the nature of awareness.[28]

(16) The self who is a light unto itself, who is other than the five sheaths, who is the witness-consciousness of the three states, who, while being, is unchanging, who is without blemishes, who is always blissful; it should be known, [and] realized as one's own self.[29]

(17) A thing is the witness of another thing when the latter is experienced by the former. For an object which is not experienced by anyone, there is no need for positing witness-hood.[30]

(18) This is witness to itself, because it is experienced by itself. The directly experienced self is this, and nothing other than it.[31]

(19) Control [merge] the speech in the mind, the mind in the intellect, intellect in the witness-consciousness, and the witness-consciousness is the indeterminate full self—after which you will reach the highest peace.[32]

(20) Why do you not know yourself as the consciousness that is the witness-consciousness of the inner sense and its modifications, which is of the nature of bliss and truly existent?[33]

(21) Always know yourself to be existence-consciousness-bliss, the witness-consciousness of the intellect, and give up the misconception of the identity of the self and the body, etc.[34]

(22) The thou is the consciousness which is of the nature of the witness. The property of being the witness is the property of being the knower on the part of the self while the self remains unchanging.[35]

(23) The self, which is free from all change, which is of the nature of seeing, which is nondifferent and of the nature of pure consciousness, and witness of all cognitions, as soon as it comes into the proximity of the object, assumes the property of being the seer, depending on the manifestation of the object by the intelligence, etc., otherwise there is no seerhood [in it].[36]

(24) . . . the self which is of the nature of consciousness, devoid of change and of parts, all-pervading like space and time, etc., [is] the witness of both the seer and the seen. . . .[37]

(25) There exists some entity which is itself eternal and is the support of the sense of "I," which is the witness-consciousness of the three states, and which is different from the five sheaths.[38]

(26) That the self is different from and is the witness of the body, its properties, its actions, and its states, is self-established.[39]

(27) One who, again, pervades over, regulates both knowledge and ignorance, is different from these two, because of being the witness.[40]

(28) He is the witness-consciousness of all beings, seer of all—owing to the definition "one who directly sees."[41]

(29) Just as the reflection of the sun falls on the water, so does the highest self as reflected in the intellect, and as witness-consciousness of all modifications, is here called "*ātman.*"[42]

(30) That is the highest light, not manifested by an other, self-shining, those wise men who know the self, the witness-consciousness of all awareness by the intellect of all objects such as sound, they, the knowers of the self, follow the knowledge of the self.[43]

III

A careful examination of the above passages reveals that Śaṃkara provides at least five different, though not mutually exclusive, characterizations of *sākṣin*:

1. *Sākṣin* as the witness of the intellect (1, 2, 5, 6, 7, 9, 10, 12, 13, 14, 17, 20, 21 and 29);
2. *Sākṣin* as the nondual, propertyless *brahman* (8, 11, 20, 21, 22, 23 and 28);
3. *Sākṣin* as identical to *ātman* (15, 16, 18, 19, 23 and 30);
4. *Sākṣin* as the witness of all three states (4, 14, 16 and 25); and
5. *Sākṣin* as the same as *Īśvara* (3, 7 and 27).

I will analyze some of the passages to ascertain the implications and ramifications of these characterizations. For my analysis, I have chosen the first five passages, which are from Śaṃkara's commentary on *Brahmasūtra.* I have selected Śaṃkara's commentary on *Brahmasūtra* for three primary reasons: (a) *Brahmasūtra* is the foundational text of the entire Vedānta school of Indian philosophy; (b) Śaṃkara's authorship of the commentary on it is accepted as authentic by all the scholars working in the area of Indian philosophy; (c) I believe that a contextual analysis of the passages selected will not only familiarize my readers with some of the main theses of Śaṃkara's philosophy but will also to some degree help me to ascertain what role this notion plays in his philosophy; and finally, (d) one of the goals of this study is to assess what role, if any, this notion plays in the Vivaraṇa and Bhāmatī traditions, the two sub-schools of Advaita.[44] An analysis of the passages selected will, I hope, set the stage for a discussion of this notion in these two post-Śaṃkara traditions.

For Śaṃkara, *brahman* is the only reality. The multiplicity of names and forms experienced at the phenomenal level,[45] the level at which philosophical inquiry transpires, is real only from an empirical/practical standpoint. Śaṃkara's realistic epistemology contends that every cognition points to an objective referent, regardless of its veridicality or falsity. So the issue is: How real are the things that we experience in the phenomenal realm? Plurality is real as long as one remains in the empirical world. Reality is never contradicted; it is never sublated (*bādhita*). It *was, is,* and *will be* real. Thus, Śaṃkara must provide some explanation not only of the existence of the subject-object dichotomy from an epistemological perspective, but also of the problem of one and many from a metaphysical point of view.

Ātman, for Śaṃkara, is the self of all (*sarvasya ātmā*). In the order of discovery, in the order of knowing things, appearance comes first. In the order of existence, however, *brahman* comes first. The former is the epistemic order, which explains why Śaṃkara begins his investigation in his commentary on the *Brahmasūtra* with the idea of superimposition.[46] For Śaṃkara, superimposition gives rise to "I-ness" (*aham*), resulting in a confusion between *this* (*idam*) and *not-this* (*anidam*). Pure consciousness, when superimposed, becomes an "I." Accordingly, one makes a distinction among many "I's." In fact, the distinctions among the knower, the known, and the means of knowledge are the result of the mutual superimpositions of the self and the not-self. This mutual superimposition is the subject matter of the first passage cited above.

At the outset of his commentary on *Brahmasūtra,* Śaṃkara postulates the self and the not-self as two fundamental components of human experience, which are opposed to each other as light and darkness. The self can never become the not-self and vice versa. Nor can the properties of the one be superimposed on the other. However, our everyday experience revolves around a beginningless confounding between the two, in the forms "I am this," and "This is mine." In the first form, the distinction of the self and the body is forgotten. In the latter form, however, the distinction between the self and the body is not forgotten, though the attributes of the two are mixed up. The former can assume either of these two forms: (a) "I am this body," or (b) "This body is I." In (a) the body per se is superimposed on the self, whereas in (b) the self is superimposed on the body.

Śaṃkara adduces numerous examples to demonstrate the varieties of superimposition: It may be the superimposition of (a) the body on the self, e.g., "I am a man," "I am a woman"; (b) the properties of the body on the self, e.g., "I am fat," "I am thin"; (c) mental states such as desires, doubt, pleasure, pain, e.g., "I am happy," "I am virtuous"; and (d) the properties of the sense organs on the self, e.g., "I am blind," "I am deaf." Thus, the superimposition not only assumes the form of the "I" but also of the "mine." The former is the superimposition of the substance (*dharmin*), the latter of the attribute (*dharma*). The reciprocal superimposition of the self and the not-self, and of the properties of the one on the other, results in the bondage of the empirical self. The empirical self acts and enjoys because of erroneous identification of the inner self with the inner sense (*antaḥkaraṇa*).[47]

So, the self is not absolutely beyond comprehension because it is apprehended as the content of the "I." The self is known as "I" to empirical individuals; nobody doubts this fact. We know the self directly, immediately. The self is not an object of thought; it is not the conclusion of a rational argument. However, to direct the empirical mind to its experience, Śaṃkara gives us a kind of "*cogito ergo sum*," which may be expressed as follows: "It is not possible to refute the self, for he who is doing the refutation is the self."[48] No one can doubt the existence of *ātman* because it is involved even in doubting. Only an adventitious object can be repudiated; denying the self would amount to a denial of one's own nature. As fire cannot deny its own heat, similarly, the self, being self-established, can never doubt itself.[49]

At this point, the question may be raised, if the self is never an object, how can objects and their properties be superimposed upon it? Śaṃkara states that the self (pure consciousness) is apprehended as an object when one becomes aware of oneself as "I am." The "I" that is the referent of the self-consciousness of the empirical individual is bound by the limitations of the body, the mind, and the senses. The referent of "*pratyagātman*," the inmost or the innermost self, is neither the doer (*kartā*) nor the enjoyer (*bhoktā*).[50] One superimposes not only the inner sense, the possessor of egoity, on the self—the witness of everything—but also the self on the inner sense. Thus, beginningless superimposition, which is in the form of the multiplicity of names and forms, results, conjuring up the notions of agency and enjoyer that empirical individuals experience. Behind all these experiences, there is the witness-consciousness, which is at once different from and the witness of the individual ego. Such a witness is said to be "*pratyagātman*" or the inner self as opposed to the "*ahaṃpratyaya*" or the "I-consciousness," the individual referred to by the "I." Such an inmost self is said to be "*svapracāra sākṣī*" or "the witness of all its manifestations." Thus, the superimposition of the self on the senses, intellect, and so on endows the empirical individual with consciousness, while the superimposition of the intellect on the *ātman* endows the empirical individual with the notion that he/she is the doer of actions and the enjoyer of fruits.

Śaṃkara again and again returns to the notion of agency to establish that it belongs to the "owner of the body" (i.e., the self). But we have still to ask, does it belong to it naturally or due to limiting adjuncts? Śaṃkara defends the view that agency belongs to the self as connected with the inner sense, not to the pure self. The causal conditions depend on consciousness for their efficacy; this consciousness belongs to the self. The agency depends upon the "I-consciousness," which in itself is an object of experience. Therefore, agency of the self is due to the limiting adjuncts.[51]

One might wonder, how do we know that such a self exists? The second passage quoted above provides an answer to this question. Śaṃkara begins his discussion of this aphorism[52] by pointing out that according to some (Indian) philosophers (i.e., the Mīmāṃsakas), the Vedic sentences derive their meaning and significance only in connection with some injunction. Since no injunction is possible with regard to a thing that is already established, argue the Mīmāṃsakas, the Vedas dealing with ritual cannot provide us with any evidence about *brahman* as the source of the world.

Śaṃkara, on the other hand, argues that the self is known only from the Upaniṣads. In reality, the self is *brahman.* It is different from that which is subject to changes. The self cannot be denied because the very denial implies that there is somebody doing the denying. One may wonder, at this point, even assuming that the self is contained in the "I" notion, whether the self is known from the Upaniṣads alone.

In response to the question whether it is consistent with the view that the self is known from the Upaniṣads alone, Śaṃkara explains that no contradiction is involved in the characterizations of the self given above. The self is not given to us as an object in the sense of an ego. What is so given to us is our empirical self, which is subject to change. The real self, on the other hand, is different from the empirical self. The empirical self is given to us as an object; it is illumined by the real self. The ever-present, real self is the witness of everything.

Therefore, the self is not found in the ritualistic portions of the Vedas, nor can it be made part of an injunction. In this context, we must not lose sight of the fact that knowledge, for Śaṃkara, reveals an object; it does not act upon the object. Knowledge arises when the object and the requisite means of knowing it are present. For the Mīmāṃsakas and the Buddhists, on the other hand, knowledge is an activity of the self regarding an object.

For Śaṃkara, however, knowledge apprehends the object *as it is:* it unveils the object; it does not create or transform the object. The actual object (i.e., *vastu*) is different from the intentional object of thought (*viṣaya*). Śaṃkara argues: "Knowledge of the true nature of an actual object does not depend upon the intellect of a person. What does it depend on then? It depends on the actual object."[53] Again:

> Knowledge arises by a cause or means of true cognition. A means of true cognition has for its object the actual object as it is in reality. Therefore, knowledge is not something to be done, not done, or [done] in some other way, because knowledge depends only on the actual object and not upon injunctions nor upon man.[54]

The thrust of the Advaita theory of knowledge, as articulated by Śaṃkara, is that the object of knowledge should exist before our knowledge of it. Knowledge always presupposes the priority of the object—a priority that is not merely temporal but points in some cases to the eternally accomplished character of the object, a *siddha vastu.* In other words, it signifies that an object is not brought into being through knowing it. This is the distinctive characteristic of knowledge that distinguishes knowledge from noncognitive experiences, say, volition. This has important ramifications from an epistemological perspective. The actual object (*vastu*), in other words, is that which is meant; the content (*viṣaya*) is that which is actually present in it. It is important to remember here that the content in a knowledge situation is neither true nor false. It is the act of judging—in which one either affirms or denies the actuality of an object corresponding to the content—that is said to be true or false. Thus knowledge is a mode of consciousness; it is determined by its object. Śaṃkara further argues that the contents of our objective experience are different from the real self. Behind the plurality of experiences that the individual "I" undergoes, there is the *sākṣin*—the principle of manifestation.

The third passage asserts that God is the efficient cause of everything that we experience in the phenomenal world. On account of nescience, the self acts as enjoyer and doer, and this is accomplished by the will of God, the witness residing in all finite beings. The notion of God as the efficient cause of the world raises another important issue: What is the relationship between *brahman* and the world? *Brahman*, for Śaṃkara, is both the efficient and the material cause of the world. He subscribes to *vivartavāda*:[55] the theory that although the effect pre-exists in the material cause, it is simply an apparent, and not a real, modification of the cause. In other words, the effect, or the phenomenal world, is simply an appearance of the cause, *brahman*. The effect is ontologically nondifferent from the cause; a simple change in the outward form does not imply a change in the substance. As a magician is not affected by the illusion that he conjures up for others, similarly, the self is not affected by the plurality of names and forms.

The fourth passage reiterates the same point with an analysis of the states of waking, dreaming, and deep sleep. As a person in the waking state is not affected by the dreams experienced (since the latter do not persist in the waking state or, for that matter, in the deep sleep state), similarly, the self, the witness-consciousness (*sākṣin*), is not affected by these states, because these states are mutually exclusive. Śaṃkara makes the same point in *Upadeśasāhasrī* (*Upadeśa*), when he states that by distinguishing the invariable from the variable, the seer from the seen, one realizes that the unvarying consciousness is the true self; it is distinct from the three states.[56]

In the waking state, *ātman* is aware of external objects, performs actions, and is taken to be an experiencer. Both the inner sense and the five sense organs are at work. In the dreaming state, the five senses are no longer at work, but the inner sense continues to function. One is aware of objects present only to the dreamer. In the state of deep sleep, both the five senses and the inner sense cease to function, and the self in this state is a mass of undifferentiated consciousness. One does not perceive anything in the deep sleep state. It is usually believed that there is a cessation of consciousness in this state. Śaṃkara reminds his readers that the apparent lack of consciousness is not really because of the lack of consciousness itself, but because of the complete lack of objects of knowledge.[57] The function of consciousness is to reveal objects. Accordingly, in the absence of objects when there is nothing to reveal, the consciousness remains unmanifest. This, however should not be taken to mean, notes Śaṃkara, that there is a lack of consciousness.[58] The self is the witness of all the three states and underlies them all. The waking state is sublated by the dreaming state, the dreaming by the deep sleep state, which in turn is sublated either by waking or by dreaming. The witness-consciousness persists even in the state of deep sleep, for without it one would not be aware of not-knowing anything during deep sleep (as the followers of Śaṃkara clearly demonstrate); the witness-consciousness is never sublated.

Passage five, from the commentary on II.2.28 of *Brahmasūtra*, contains the most detailed arguments for the notion of witness-consciousness. They are given in the context of refuting the position of Vijñānavādin Buddhists.[59]

Śaṃkara, on behalf of the Vijñānavādins, advances several arguments. These arguments are designed to demonstrate that, for the Vijñānavādins, the external world is not real, and since no object is ever experienced apart from consciousness, object and consciousness are one and the same. The points pertinent from an epistemological perspective are noted below.

1. Our cognitions of objects are similar (*sārūpya*) to the objects of which they are cognitions.[60] Nevertheless, they are differentiated, and such differentiations are the result of the objects that are represented in them, e.g., cognition of a wall, cognition of a pitcher, and so on. This amounts to saying that the form of the object is represented in knowledge or, better yet, knowledge determines the form of the object. Śaṃkara further argues, for the Vijñānavādin Buddhists, that the form of any object can be explained solely on the basis of consciousness, because these forms are contained within consciousness, and concludes that the hypothesis of externally existing objects becomes superfluous.[61]

2. Cognition and content are simultaneous—they are always experienced together (*sahopalambha*), i.e., one is never experienced without the other. This proves that they are identical in nature.[62]

3. The similarity between the cognitions in our waking life and dream cognitions confirms that the external world is not real. In dreams and mirages, external objects appear though there are none. Similarly, our cognitions in waking life are simply ideas, and these ideas themselves appear as external objects.

4. *Saṃskāras* or residual impressions of past ideas account for the variety of ideas, and there is no need to assume a plurality of objects.

Śaṃkara uses his refutation of the Vijñānavādins to substantiate his own position. His goal is to demonstrate and develop his thesis that perception testifies to the existence of external objects: "It is not possible to cognize the nonexistence of external objects. Why? Because they are experienced. The external object is experienced [known] in [its] cognition, just as the pillar, wall, pot, cloth, etc. What is being experienced could not be nonexistent."[63]

Śaṃkara argues that the external world exists; perception testifies to its existence. When we perceive, we perceive external objects like a post, a wall, etc. In response to the Buddhist's argument that consciousness itself appears as external, Śaṃkara says that if there is no external world, how can Buddhists claim that the content of consciousness appears "as if" external? When I perceive an object X, my perception takes the form "this is X" and not "this is like X." Unless there are real snakes, a rope cannot appear as a snake.

He further argues that the simultaneity of our experiences, external objects and ideas does not prove their identity. In our awareness, say, of "knowledge of a pitcher," "knowledge of a cloth," the difference resides in the qualifying (*viśeṣaṇa*)[64] parts, e.g., pitcher and cloth, and not in the cognitions themselves. This proves that the ideas and the objects are distinct. In other words, cognition itself remains constant; differences in external objects account for the differences in cognition, just as when we perceive a black cow and a white cow, the attributes blackness and whiteness differ but cowness remains constant. Thus, there is a difference between external object and cognition.

For Śaṃkara, perception provides a testimony to the existence of external objects. The Vijñānavādins deny external objects because they are not luminous like a lamp. Against such a view, Śaṃkara insists:

> One who admits only cognition [*vijñāna*] has to explain why is it that he does not admit external objects such as pillar and wall. To say that only a cognition is experienced will not do, for it is reasonable to say that external objects also are experienced. It may be objected that a cognition, being like [a] lamp, of the nature of manifestation, experiences itself [or, is itself experienced] while external objects are not like that. To this, one could reply that it would amount to self-contradictory admission that it acts upon itself, like fire burning itself. . . . It cannot be the case that cognition, even if different from objects, experiences itself, for the idea of acting upon itself is contradictory.[65]

Śaṃkara accuses the Vijñānavādins of maintaining that cognitions apprehend themselves and therefore there is no need of a witness to do the apprehending.

> It may be objected that if a cognition apprehends what is other than itself, then that [cognition] is to be apprehended by another, that also by [still] another, leading to an infinite regress. However, one who assumes another knowledge for the [first] knowledge on the ground that knowledge, like [a] lamp, is of the nature of manifestation, cannot account for the relation of manifested and manifesting for the same reason, so that [his] assumption would be pointless. Both are false.[66]

The points that Śaṃkara is trying to make are as follows. If the Buddhists were to argue that a cognition is apprehended by something other than itself, then the second one is apprehended by the third one, and so on, resulting in an infinite regress, so that the only way to avoid the infinite regress is to maintain that an idea is self-luminous like a lamp, then Śaṃkara would say that both these arguments fail because once an idea is apprehended, there is no logical necessity to apprehend the witness of the cognition. The witness-consciousness apprehends the plurality of ideas, requiring no further illumination. The witness that apprehends the ideas, thus, does not require anything else for its own apprehension. Accordingly, the charge of infinite regress does not arise. An idea is apprehended by the witness. Accordingly, an idea is like an object in relation to the witness, the perceiver, the ultimate subject. Śaṃkara concludes that the witness-consciousness is self-evident; its existence is self-proved and it cannot be denied (*svayaṃsiddhasya ca sākṣiṇo' pratyākhyeyatvāt*).

Śaṃkara goes on to argue that when the Buddhists argue that a cognition, like a lamp, manifests itself and does not require another cognition to manifest it, it amounts to saying that knowledge does not require a subject, which is absurd; it is like arguing that a thousand lamps manifest themselves inside an impenetrable rock. If the Buddhists were to contend that by "cognition" they mean consciousness and that since consciousness is also accepted by the Vedāntins, the Advaitins must also accept the view of the Buddhists, then they are wrong because for the Advaitins an idea is like an object that requires the self-luminous witness to make it manifest. An object does not, and cannot, reveal itself, because it is inert. Mental cognitions cannot reveal themselves because they are inert as well. Hence, the need for the self-luminous witness-consciousness to reveal mental cognitions. This witness is an eternal seer whose sight is never destroyed. In short, a cognition points to something beyond it, to a cognizer. All cognitions need a basis, and that basis is the unchanging seer.

Śaṃkara's criticism of the Vijñānavādins underscores the distinctive feature of his own epistemological approach, i.e., that the knower or the subject alone is not real. The knower cannot be the only reality, for that would be to obviate the possibility of there being anything to know. The object of knowledge must be as real as the knower of that object. The position is realistic; but it is not naively realistic, because although equally real, neither the subject nor the object of knowledge is in fact real in its own right. That which is known must be at least as real as that which knows, because both the knower and the known, the subject and the object, are superimpositions on the same reality. However, though appearances of the same reality, neither can be equated with that reality. In talking about *brahman,* it is not a subject or an object, but neither and both; the distinction is not real. Because reality is nondual, the known and the knower come to be recognized as one: *ātman* is *brahman.* In other words, when properly understood, *brahman* and *ātman,* the objective and the subjective poles of experience, are nondifferent.

IV

The above contextual analysis reveals the following points regarding Śaṃkara's notion of *sākṣin.* First, the *sākṣin* is a passive observer as opposed to the doer. Second, it is both the basis of and different from the inner sense. Third, it is self-luminous like the self. Fourth, it is the eternal, unchanging self that fulfills a specific role, as though the self were wearing a different hat.[67] And, fifth, it is an observer and revealer not only of mental cognitions, but also of physical objects. Thus, we may say that, for Śaṃkara, *sākṣin* is a kind of enduring, passive, and unchanging awareness, which observes and reveals mental cognitions and physical objects as well as witnesses all changes and activities that take place due to the intellect, the "I-notion."

The above five points lead me to conclude that there are two basic usages of the term "*sākṣin*" in Śaṃkara: (a) *sākṣin* as simply *ātman* (*śuddhacaitanya*), and (b) *sākṣin* as *ātman* limited by the inner sense. In his commentary on the *Kena Upaniṣad* (KUBh), Śaṃkara makes a distinction between two kinds of knowledge: knowledge of *brahman* and knowledge gained through the mind and the senses.[68] The former is the highest knowledge, knowledge of reality or pure consciousness, beyond the subject-object dichotomy and the substance-attribute relation. It is self-luminous and nonrelational. The latter is modified consciousness; it is a reflection of pure consciousness through a mode of the inner sense (*antaḥkaraṇvṛtti*).[69] It is thus relational knowledge, i.e., it is of the empirical realm, of the phenomenal world where the subject-object dichotomy and the substance-attribute relation occur. Each and every empirical cognition, for Śaṃkara, is a modification of pure consciousness. Empirical knowledge assumes various forms via a mental mode depending on the nature of the external object. External objects, unlike the self, are not self-established. They are known through modifications (*vṛtti*-s)[70] arising from the senses with the assistance of the inner sense.

Of the three aspects of the inner sense—the cognitive, affective, and conative—the cognitive is most fundamental. To explain this aspect, Śaṃkara makes a distinction among four functions of the inner sense:

> [T]he inner sense, which is a limiting adjunct of the self, is also variously called as: *manas* [mind], *buddhi* [intellect], *vijñāna* [cognition], and *citta* [retro-cognition or memory]. Mental modifications account for these functional variations: at times it is called *manas* when it assumes a modification in the form of doubting; *buddhi* when the modification assumes the form of certainty, etc.[71]

These four functions are involved in any and every external perception. When I see an object, say, a table, initially I am aware of it as something (deliberation), recall my past impressions (memory) and identify it as a table (certainty), which gives rise to the knowledge that "I know that this object is a table" (egoism).

These modifications of the inner sense, caused by the forms of the external objects arising with the senses, account for perception. Śaṃkara explains the process of perception with the help of the metaphors of copper and its mold, and of light and its object: "Just as [molten] copper assumes the form of the mold into which it was poured, similarly is certainly experienced the *citta*, pervading [the object's] form-color, [which] appears like it."[72] Again, "just as light, the illuminator, assumes the forms of whatever is illuminated by it, so the intellect assumes the forms of objects, inasmuch as it illuminates all objects."[73]

The intellect acts as an agent insofar as knowledge of diverse objects is concerned. Similarly, *ātman*, when associated with the intellect, is said to be a doer on account of its possessing the I-consciousness. These modifications are instrumental in the perceptual process. They perform specific functions. However, just as pure consciousness, which is neither the I-consciousness nor the intellect, cannot be called an instrument, so also the *ātman* cannot be said to be a doer. It appears to be a doer only on account of its limitor, the intellect.

N. K. Devaraja maintains that "the two elements in the neo-Vedānta theory of perception, namely (1) the going out of the inner sense to the object and (2) the inner sense assuming the form of the object," are not found "in Śaṃkara's discussion of perception."[74] On the basis of the two verses cited above, Mayeda maintains that the first element certainly exists and the second "too is present to a considerable extent."[75]

In his refutation of Vijñānavādins, Śaṃkara describes the witness-consciousness "as apprehending and synthesizing the plurality of ideas."[76] In his commentary on *Bṛhadāraṇyaka Upaniṣad,* he states that the form of the object is first assimilated by the heart (by which he means the mind).[77] But he does not give us any clear indication as to how this synthesis and assimilation takes place. It is worth noting, however, that the verses cited above from *Upadeśasāhasrī* do indeed lend credibility to Mayeda's interpretation. For our present purposes, however, it is enough to note that for Śaṃkara the modifications of the inner sense play a crucial role in the perceptual process. Because in the absence of such an inner sense, there would be either perpetual perception or there would be no perception at all. Śaṃkara himself concedes this: "Unless you admit such an entity (i.e., *antaḥkaraṇa*), there would be permanent experience or lack of experience (i.e., in accordance as the causal conditions of *upalabdhi*—such as the self, sense organ and objects—are proximately available or not). When the causal conditions of perception, viz., the *ātman,* the senses and the objects, are in contiguity, perception takes place."[78] Additionally, if perception does not occur although the three causal conditions of perception are in proximity, constant nonperception will occur. Such constant nonperception would imply that the *ātman* is incapable of modification, or that the senses without any reason have lost their power to cognize an object. Both alternatives were unacceptable to Śaṃkara. Therefore, the inner sense with all its modifications, such as desire, resolve, doubt, etc., is admitted. The self is changeless; it is of the nature of pure awareness. Śaṃkara brings in the inner sense to preserve the integrity of the changeless self, as well as to preserve the possibility of changing perceptions.

If *ātman* is taken to be the perceiver of mental modifications (*vṛtti*-s) assuming the form of external objects, then *ātman* itself would not be free from change. Śaṃkara introduces the concept of semblance (*ābhāsa*) to account for change. In his commentary on *Brahmasūtra,* he makes the point that finite consciousness is a reflection of the pure consciousness like the reflection of the sun in water.[79] Pure consciousness is like the light that assumes the form of whatever it illumines. It illumines the modifications of the intellect and appears as if active when in fact it is not so. There can be no activity in the *ātman*, the light. Thus, the light of the self is said to be *avabhāsaka* or the illuminer (that which manifests the semblance), and the inner sense with its modes is the *avabhāsya* or the illumined (that which is manifested). The apprehension of non-distinction between the two is a fact of life.

In *Upadeśasāhasrī*, Śaṃkara reiterates that when the real self is manifested, on account of its association with the intellect, it is known as *cidābhāsa*, the semblance of pure consciousness or the reflected self: "Just as the properties of a mirror assumed by the reflection of a face in it are attributed to the face, so the properties of the *buddhi* assumed by the reflection of the self are superimposed on the self."[80] Just as the face is different from its reflection in the mirror, similarly, *ātman* is different from its reflection on the intellect (*buddhi*).[81] It is the reflected self identified with the body that is the doer, the experiencer, the agent, rather than the real, transcendental self, the unchanging witness (*sākṣin*) of everything. Accordingly, when it is said that the *ātman* is the doer, what is meant is that the reflected self, the perceiver of external objects, not the real self, is the agent. The real or the transcendental self is immutable; it is the witness (*sākṣin*) of all that occurs.

Thus, witnessing takes place on account of the self's adventitious association with the inner sense—or, better yet, with the intellect—which is responsible for the seeing of objects, not with the pure self, the illuminator of everything. Just as the moon becomes pure and bright by freeing itself from the mouth of Rāhu,[82] similarly, the *ātman* on account of its association with the modifications of the inner sense becomes an I, but by casting off its body it passes into *brahman* again.[83]

Thus, in Śaṃkara one finds the notion of the self as the witness (*sākṣin*) of all knowing, all seeing, all thinking, of cognitions and physical objects. As has been shown, this comes out very clearly in his refutation of the Vijñānavādins. Śaṃkara's theory of *sākṣin*, however, does not contain the epistemological insights of later Advaita. He does not develop the notion of *sākṣin* systematically and in detail. Nor does he bring out the complete ramifications of the notion of a mode of the inner sense (*antaḥkaraṇavṛtti*) that forms the foundation of later Advaitin epistemology. Let me elaborate on these points.

In the first chapter of his commentary on the *Bṛhadāraṇyaka Upaniṣad*, Śaṃkara articulates the self as *dṛṣṭerdṛṣṭā* (the seer of seeing): "The self is the seer of seeing, the hearer of hearing, the thinker of thinking, and the knower of knowledge."[84] It is worth noting that Śaṃkara never uses the term "*sākṣin*" to refer to the seer of seeing; it is simply called the self. Ānandagiri, however, in his commentary on the above text remarks: "The self is to be described as the witness of seeing, etc."[85]

Śaṃkara further makes a distinction between two kinds of seeing: the seeing of the seer and the seeing of the physical objects. He raises the question: What is the difference between whether *ātman* is the seer (*dṛṣtā*) of seeing or of a pitcher? In either case it is a seer.[86] Śaṃkara himself explains that there is a crucial difference. The seeing of the seer is eternal, because it is never the case that there is seeing without a seer. This is not the case, however, with the seeing of a pitcher, because a pitcher may exist without being perceived.[87] Here, once again, Śaṃkara never uses the term "*sākṣin*" to refer to the eternal sight; it is simply called the seer (*dṛṣtā*). At another place, he reiterates: "the seeing of the witness can never be lost."[88] The witness again is said to be "*dṛṣtā*," not "*sākṣin*." Also, it is worth noting that in this passage he does not use the term "*antaḥkaraṇavṛtti*" (mode of the inner sense) to explain the seeing of a pitcher, let alone develop its implications.

Ānandagiri, however, uses the term "*antaḥkaraṇavṛtti*" to explain the difference between the seeing of the seer and the seeing of physical objects: "The seer of a pitcher, who is of the nature of unchanging pure consciousness, becomes subject to change when limited by the inner sense with its modifications; (the seer of pitcher) becomes the seer of modifications of intelligence merely by virtue of proximity alone."[89] A pitcher is perceived by a mental modification, this latter in turn is perceived by the transcendent pure consciousness (*kūṭastha*). Unlike *antaḥkaraṇavṛtti*, the witness-consciousness does not undergo any modification. The seeing of a pitcher changes; the transcendent, unchanging, pure consciousness, however, by its mere presence, manifests these changes.

Śaṃkara again returns to the notion of two kinds of seeing in the fourth chapter of his commentary on the *Bṛhadāraṇyaka Upaniṣad.* This time he does use the expression "*antaḥkaraṇavṛtti.*" He notes: "Ordinary seeing is a function of the contact of the mental mode with the eye; it is an activity and, accordingly, is destructible. However, the seeing that belongs to the self is like the heat and light of fire; it is the essence of the witness/seer; therefore, it is never destroyed."[90] Empirical seeing acquires its meaning and significance only in the context of the eternal seeing.

The question arises: What does the witness-consciousness cognize? Śaṃkara never raises this issue. For later Advaitins, however, anything that does not possess unknown existence (*ajñātasattā*) is revealed by *sākṣin* alone (*kevalasākṣībhāsya*). Conversely, everything that can have unknown existence (i.e., that can be concealed by ignorance) needs a mental mode to mediate the function of the witness-consciousness. Three items fall into the former category: (1) illusory (*prātibhāsika*) objects, (2) mental modifications and subjective mental states, such as pleasure and pain, and (3) ignorance itself.

For objects that do possess unknown existence a mental mode is necessary; its function is to destroy the veil of ignorance that covers the object. A pitcher, for example, may exist without being perceived. Therefore, a pitcher is known through a mode of the inner sense: "Ignorance, in other words, is a necessary presupposition of all knowing. Empirical knowing is always the knowing of the unknown. As a matter of fact, it is only the unknown that really can be known. There can be disclosure in knowledge (*jñāpana*) but only of what has remained concealed (*ajñātā*)."[91] Accordingly, for later Advaitins, all objects—regardless of whether they are known or unknown—are, in the long run, objects of witness-consciousness.

Additionally, for them, witness-consciousness manifests both knowledge (*vidyā*) and ignorance (*avidyā*) alike, pointing to a kind of neutrality between knowledge and ignorance. The idea of neutrality is an important one. Śaṃkara's followers develop this idea and contend that the witness-consciousness does not destroy ignorance, rather a mode of the inner sense does. The witness-consciousness manifests ignorance; they bring in the witness-consciousness for the direct perception of ignorance. Śaṃkara never raises the issue of whether ignorance is mere absence of knowledge (*jñānābhāva*) or a positive entity (*bhāvarūpa*). Later Advaitins, however, make it a positive entity, and it becomes accessible by the witness-consciousness.

Perhaps it is not an exaggeration to say that Śaṃkara brought in the notion of the witness-consciousness in order to preserve his nondualistic thesis, which mandated an explanation of the appearance of the multiplicity of names and forms, as well as the subject-object dichotomy. Accordingly, Śaṃkara's writings do not contain a systematic and detailed treatment of the epistemological ramifications of his theory of witness-consciousness. Śaṃkara does not discuss metaphysical issues such as whether this witness-consciousness is one or many. Nor does he discuss the relationship of the witness-consciousness with *brahman* and God (*Īśvara*). He uses the terms ambiguously. At times this witness is called "*dṛṣṭā*," and at other times "*sākṣin*." At times "*dṛṣṭā*" is used in the sense of an ordinary seer, and at other times to designate the eternal seer. In fact, he uses "*sākṣin*" synonymously with "*Īśvara*," "*brahman*," "*ātman*" and "*dṛṣṭā*," and does not clearly explicate the distinct nuances of these terms. For example, (1) at times, *sākṣin* is said to be the witness of the three states of waking, dreaming, and dreamless sleep,[92] but at other times, *brahman* is articulated as possessing the witnesshood (*sākṣitva*) of all objects;[93] (2) at some places, the *dṛṣṭā* is said to be beyond all qualities and actions,[94] but at other places, *sākṣin* is articulated as beyond qualities, etc.;[95] (3) at several places, the *dṛṣṭā* is said to be the seer of all intellects,[96] but at several other places, *sākṣin* is said to be the seer of all intellects;[97] and (4) in some passages, *sākṣin* is said to be the same as *Īśvara*,[98] whereas in other passages, it is articulated as propertyless (*nirguṇa*) *brahman*.[99]

These ambiguities have given rise to a number of confusions for modern interpreters of Advaita Vedānta. For example, Tara Chatterjee, in her article on the notion of *sākṣin,* notes: "Advaita Vedānta combines in the concept of *sākṣin,* two aspects. As described in the Upaniṣads it is absolutely passive, and as presented by Śaṃkara, it is [a] never-to-be objectified principle of awareness present in every individual."[100] While Dr. Chatterjee is to be commended for distinguishing between the two aspects of the *sākṣin* notion—passivity and nonobjectivity—she misattributes the passivity aspect to the Upaniṣads and nonobjectivity to Śaṃkara. It is indeed true that Advaita Vedānta combines in the theory of *sākṣin* the two senses outlined in her paper. However, the passivity of *sākṣin* is not a motif in the Upaniṣads. First, as pointed out in the second chapter, the theory of *sākṣin* is not clearly articulated in the Upaniṣads. The term "*sākṣin*" does not occur there, although some of the elements embodied in the Advaita notion of *sākṣin*—e.g., the self as the ultimate subject—do occur there. These elements, however, have not yet emerged as a single concept in the Upaniṣads.

Second, the nonobjectivity of the self is repeatedly emphasized in the Upaniṣads, while its passivity is contributed by the Advaitins. The Upaniṣads repeatedly emphasize that self is the ultimate subject; it can never become an object of knowledge. The notion of the self as light in the Upaniṣads provides a clear counterexample to Chatterjee's claim. The light metaphor in the Upaniṣads underscores the freedom, and not the passivity, of the self. It is a way of explaining the unvarying nature and the unrestricted freedom of the self: The self is luminous by its very nature. It is the principle that makes perception and conscious action possible. *Sākṣin,* like the *ātman* of the Upaniṣads, is self-luminous. A light does not require another light to manifest it. Similarly, *sākṣin*—being self-luminous—illumines all: it does not require anything outside of itself to illuminate objects. In Śaṃkara's philosophy, one finds the term "*sākṣin*" in its technical aspect, although only partially. Śaṃkara uses the concept to fulfill a well-defined role in his system. The concept of *sākṣin* provides

Śaṃkara with the much needed epistemological foundation to defend the Upaniṣadic metaphysics.

Metaphysics and epistemology, as they constitute elements in Western philosophy, can be isolated from each other. It is frequently suggested that epistemological conclusions can be arrived at independently of any metaphysical theory. For example, Dryer notes: "Prichard writes, 'Kant's problem is similar to Locke's.' Locke states that his purpose is to inquire into the origin, certainty, and extent of human knowledge.[101] Similarly, Kemp Smith presents the *Critique* as concerned with the theory of knowledge generally, without ever referring to its concerns with metaphysics."[102] Accordingly, these philosophers (Prichard, Kemp Smith) maintain that Kant postulates his theory of the transcendental unity of apperception solely on epistemological grounds. Other interpreters of Kant, notably D. P. Dryer and Martin Heidegger, vehemently disagree with such an epistemological reading of Kant. Dryer further notes that, according to Heidegger: "The aim of the *Critique of Pure Reason* is fundamentally mistaken if this work is interpreted as a 'theory of experience' or as a theory of positive sciences. The *Critique of Pure Reason* has nothing to do with 'theory of knowledge.' "[103]

Whether or not it is true that metaphysics and epistemology can be isolated from each other in the Western context, it certainly is *not* the case in Indian philosophy—especially not in the case of the theory of *sākṣin.* The theory of the witness-consciousness does not require logical justification, it does not require proof, because besides being an epistemological theory, it also reveals the ultimate nature of reality and is, in turn, mandated by that reality. Thus, the obvious conclusion: There is a level of experience wherein knowledge and existence are the same. Hence, it should come as no surprise to the reader that the concept of the witness-consciousness in Advaita is established on epistemological grounds and, accordingly, is called on to perform that function. It would be wrong to assume, however, that this concept is postulated solely on epistemological grounds. One must not lose sight of the fact that the witness-consciousness is grounded in the metaphysical reality as revealed by the scriptures and, therefore, approximates that reality.

I would like to conclude this chapter with one final observation. In the first chapter, I tried to demonstrate that the epistemological foundation of the notion of the witness-consciousness is found in the Upaniṣads. The fact that these ideas are adumberated in the Upaniṣads does not, of course, compel the theory of the witness-consciousness that one finds in Śaṃkara. However, when taken together with the philosophical requirements of his system, they do require a development such as is to be found in his works. The theory of the witness-consciousness forms the epistemological foundation for his metaphysics. It is a natural shaping of the elements to be found in the Upaniṣads into a form that serves his purposes. It is as if Śaṃkara were a midwife assisting in the birth of elements that were gestating in the Upaniṣads.

In this context, it is important to notice that Śaṃkara's theory of the witness-consciousness is not simply a work of exegesis. The Upaniṣads are essentially open texts that allow considerable creativity in their interpretation. Śaṃkara is not simply making clear things that already exist in the Upaniṣads, nor even simply synthesizing the elements that are to be found there. He takes these elements and uses them as a background against which to develop an original theory. Original philosophical work occurs when people bring their own intellectual abilities and accomplishments to the historical corpus of the discipline. The resulting work both represents a historical development of the discipline, even if it radically transforms the discipline, and it also represents a new and fresh way of understanding that corpus. And, of course, once Śaṃkara puts forth a theory of the witness-consciousness, it becomes a part of that corpus and is then available to later philosophers for development and modification. The scholars who have followed Śaṃkara—criticizing, reforming, refining, and developing the theory—provide clear evidence of such a continuity within a tradition. The theory of the witness-consciousness illustrates Śaṃkara's creativity and originality—aspects of his philosophy that are very often underplayed.

4

Sākṣin and Advaita Epistemology

In the previous chapter, I attempted to show that Śaṃkara brings in the notion of witness-consciousness to preserve his nondualistic thesis, which requires that he give an explanation of the multiplicity of names and forms as well as the subject-object dichotomy. However, in his writings he gives only the general guidelines for explaining these issues; he does not provide his readers with a systematic and detailed treatment of the epistemological ramifications of his notion of the witness-consciousness. For example, though Śaṃkara makes a distinction between ordinary seeing and eternal seeing, he nowhere discusses important epistemological issues investigated in detail by his followers, e.g., "What are the objects of the witness-consciousness?" Such issues provide the foci of this chapter. Again, in keeping with his nondualistic thesis, Śaṃkara accepts *brahman* as the only reality and accounts for all empirical distinctions by means of the idea of nescience. However, he never systematically develops the relationship of nescience with *brahman, Īśvara,* and *jīva,* another task taken up by his followers. I will explore this and other related metaphysical issues in the next chapter.

The primary goal of this chapter is to unpack, develop, and evaluate the role played by *sākṣin* in the Advaitin theory of perceiving and specifically the epistemological ramifications of the Advaitin theory of the witness-consciousness. I will do so, first, by discussing the Advaitin theory of perceiving; second, by analyzing the treatment of the objects of *sākṣin* in the post-Śaṃkara tradition; and finally, by examining what is entailed in the claim that all things are objects of *sākṣin* either as known or as unknown. However, before undertaking these analyses, let me pause briefly to review some of the fundamental concepts and distinctions that the Advaitins make and the role they play in Advaita philosophy. Wherever necessary, I will place these distinctions in their historical context, keeping in mind the four most important Advaitin teachers: Sureśvara, his pupil Sarvajñātma Muni, Padmapāda, and Vācaspatimiśra.[1]

I hope that this discussion of some of the fundamental concepts in their historical setting will help my readers correctly understand the basic issues of Advaita epistemology and will, thus, set the stage for the ensuing discussion on the role of the notion of *sākṣin* in Advaita epistemology.

Selected Fundamental Advaita Concepts

Pure Knowledge (*Svarūpajñāna*) and Empirical or Modal Knowledge (*Vṛttijñāna*)

The fundamental principle of Advaita epistemology is pure consciousness; it is the light that reveals the object. Every act of cognition is an expression of pure consciousness through a mental mode. Accordingly, Advaita philosophers make a distinction between pure knowledge and empirical (modal) knowledge. The former is self-luminous, self-established, pure and foundational. The latter is subject to change and appears in relation to particular objects.

All empirical knowledge, in Advaita, must fulfill the following conditions. First, consciousness must be reflected in a mental mode that has the form of the object being cognized; second, consciousness must apperceive what is given to the senses with the help of the intellect; and finally, consciousness must illuminate the object with the aid of the inner sense. Empirical knowledge, in other words, does require differentiations: it necessarily involves a cognizer (*pramātā*), the object known (*prameya*), and the resulting knowledge (*pramiti*) of the object. Since all knowledge is an expression of the radiance of consciousness, the knowledge of an object, like all knowledge, is immediate. From the perspective of pure consciousness, the distinction between immediate and mediate knowledge disappears. The distinction, however, is both relevant and useful from the empirical perspective.

Two Kinds of Mental Modes (*Vṛtti*-s)

The Advaitins make a distinction between two kinds of mental modes. These modes are distinguished according to whether they are transformations of the inner sense (*antaḥkaraṇa*) or of nescience (*avidyā*). Nescience veils the self and transforms itself into different modes. When the activity of the inner sense is present—in the perception of a pitcher, the perception of a chair, etc.—cognition is the result of a modification of the inner sense (*antaḥkaraṇavṛtti*). When the activity of the inner sense is absent and yet there is presence of cognition—in the perception of happiness, the perception of illusory silver, and the like—cognition is due to a mode of nescience (*avidyāvṛtti*). These cognitions result when nescience veils the self and transforms itself into different modes.

Empirical (*Vyāvahārika*) and Illusory (*Prātibhāsika*) Objects

Every cognition, regardless of whether it is valid or erroneous, points to an object. Thus, the question arises: How real are the things that we experience in the phenomenal world? The Advaitins maintain that the multiplicity of names and forms is real as long as the phenomenal world continues for the individual. The real is that which is never contradicted; the unreal never appears. Empirical objects, in other words, are real until they are sublated. All objects of the empirical world, however, do not enjoy the same degree of reality. When one mistakenly perceives silver in a shell, the silver is real to the perceiver only. It is a modification of his ignorance. Therefore, illusory objects are private and limited in their reality; the Advaitins term objects so perceived "illusory" (*prātibhāsika*). On the other hand, empirical (*vyāvahārika*) objects are public in the sense that they may be perceived by several persons simultaneously, e.g., the real silver in the jewelry store. These objects continue to exist until they are sublated with the dawn of pure knowledge.

For the Advaitins, since illusory and empirical objects have different levels of reality, they are cognized differently. The empirical is cognized by the cognizing subject with the help of the inner sense or the mind. In the cognition of illusory objects, on the other hand, no sense contact is involved; the knowledge is produced by a mode of nescience and is cognized by the witness-consciousness.

Two Powers of *Avidyā*

Advaitins make a distinction between two powers or, better yet, two functions of nescience: of veiling or covering or obscuring (*āvaraṇa*) and of projecting or dividing or splitting (*vikṣepa*). Some Advaitins articulate these two powers as the power to delude or create confusion (*mohaśakti*) and the power of construction (*nirmāṇaśakti*). Nescience not only obscures the nature of *brahman*, but also makes it appear as something else, i.e., as the multiplicity of names and forms.

Nescience is said to be constituted of three *guṇas* (qualities): *sattva, rajas,* and *tamas.* In its dynamic function, which is the result of *rajas,* nescience projects the cosmic world. In its static function, which is the result of *tamas,* nescience veils objects. To put it differently, it is in the nature of nescience to veil the underlying reality and project objects on it. Accordingly, there is a veil overlaying each object that nescience projects by means of its veiling capacity. When an object comes into contact with the inner sense via the senses, the inner sense is modified into the form of the object, resulting in the removal of the veil with respect to that object.

The obscuring and projecting functions of nescience account for the appearance of *brahman* in two forms: *Īśvara* and *jīva*. *Īśvara* uses the projecting function to make the world appear; nescience in its projecting function is known as "*māyā*." The obscuring function accounts for the individual's deluded acceptance of the apparent multiplicity of names and forms as real. In other words, the covering function accounts for the self's acting as an agent, a doer, and an enjoyer of pleasures and pains. In this function nescience is called "*avidyā*" or "*ajñāna*."

It is worth noting that Śaṃkara in his writings uses *māyā* and *avidyā* synonymously.[2] *Māyā* signifies a material causal potency that is neither different from nor identical with *brahman*. Following Śaṃkara, Sureśvara and his disciple Sarvajñātman use *māyā* and *avidyā* synonymously.[3] They take *māyā/avidyā* to be *brahman*'s power via which he creates the multiplicity of names and forms. However, most of Śaṃkara's followers make a distinction between the two, *māyā* manifesting as the power of projection and *avidyā* as the power of obscuring.

The Locus (*Āśraya*) and the Object (*Viṣaya*) of *Avidyā*

For the Advaitins, it is because of nescience that the nondual appears as the world. Two important questions arise here: (1) To whom does this nescience belong? In other words, in the multiplicity of names and forms, what is the locus of nescience? It can be argued that since *brahman* is propertyless or without qualities (*nirguṇa*) and undifferentiated (*nirviśeṣa*), it cannot serve as the locus of nescience. (2) What is the object of nescience? In other words, to what kind of object does nescience refer? Can an ever self-luminous entity be the object of nescience?

Regarding the locus of nescience, Śaṃkara's followers are divided. The Vivaraṇa school maintains that nescience belongs to *brahman*. *Brahman* is the locus of nescience in the sense that nescience is manifested by *brahman*. *Jīva* (the individual self) cannot be the locus of nescience, because *jīva*, being the product of nescience, necessarily presupposes nescience. The functional diversity of nescience and the fact that nescience is located in *brahman* do not in any way affect the fundamental nonduality of *brahman*. The Bhāmatī tradition, on the other hand, maintains that the individual self is the locus of nescience. A *jīva* is the locus of its (present) nescience, but is the product of its earlier nescience. Thus, there is a series of *jīva*-s and a series of nesciences. Accordingly, they hold that nescience manifests differently in discrete individual selves. The apparent world originates from *brahman*, the material cause of the world.[4] *Brahman* and *jīva* appear to be different due to nescience; when nescience is removed the two are recognized as nondifferent. Maṇḍana[5] and Vācaspati, the leading exponents of the Bhāmatī school, emphatically declare that the *jīva* is both the locus and the object of nescience.

All the followers of Śaṃkara admit that *brahman* is the object of nescience. Madhusūdana in *Advaitasiddhi* raises the following objection on behalf of the opponents:

> The object of ignorance is pure consciousness alone . . . because the act of covering is impossible with regard to that which, by being self-manifesting, can manifest itself; [it is] not also what is other, for that is a product of ignorance, has no possibility of manifesting itself and, so, the act of concealing is absent.[6]

In response, Madhusūdana argues that only pure consciousness can be the object of nescience, for only pure consciousness can manifest itself. Concealment becomes meaningful only in the context of illumination. Therefore, only pure consciousness, which is self-luminous, needs to be concealed. Conversely, that which is not self-luminous, e.g., a pitcher, needs no concealment.

Against the Advaitins, it has been argued that one and the same entity cannot be both the locus and the object of nescience. Therefore, the locus and the object of nescience should be different. The Advaitin's reply to this objection is based on the self-evident fact of experience manifesting in the forms "I know myself" and "I do not know myself." In both these experiences, say the Advaitins, one and the same "I" is both the locus and the object of knowledge and ignorance, thereby demonstrating that one and the same entity can be both the locus and the object of ignorance. Furthermore, the Advaitins extend this argument and maintain that, from an empirical perspective, this coexistence of locus and object in one entity applies not only to the *jīva*, but also to *brahman*.

Primal Nescience (*Mūlāvidyā*) and Derivative Nesciences (*Tulāvidyā*-s)

Most Advaitins make a distinction between two types of nescience: the first accounts for the appearance of the world, the second for individual illusions. Primal nescience is positive; it does not have a beginning in time, because time is an aspect of it and, so, falls within it. While primal nescience is one, derivative nesciences, being the effects of primal nescience, are many. Derivative nesciences are the impressions left on the minds in the phenomenal world; they have a beginning in time and account for an individual's bondage and freedom. Derivative nescience is removed by a mental mode of the inner sense. Primal nescience, on the other hand, is sublated by the knowledge of *brahman* on the realization of *mokṣa.*

Jīva-s: One or Many

Roughly speaking, there are two basic views concerning the number of *jīva*-s: (1) the view of those who assert the existence of many *jīva*-s (*anekajīvavāda*) and (2) the view of those who regard the *jīva* to be one (*ekajīvavāda*). Although all the Advaitins agree that in the final analysis all three, *Īśvara, jīva,* and *sākṣin,* are nothing but pure consciousness conditioned by nescience; they vary regarding the nature of their relationship to nescience and the variety of nescience to which they are related. For those who believe in many *jīva*-s (*anekajīvavādins*), a *jīva* is pure consciousness reflected or delimited by the inner sense and, since the inner senses are many, *jīva*-s are many. For those who hold that there is only one *jīva* (*ekajīvavādins*), *jīva* is pure consciousness reflected in nescience and, since nescience is one, *jīva* also is one.

Avidyā: One or Many

Whether nescience is held to be one or many in an Advaita school depends, on the one hand, on the view held regarding the locus and the object of nescience; and, on the other hand, on how the distinction between the primal nescience and derivative nesciences is understood.

Vācaspati emphasizes the distinction between primal nescience and derivative nesciences. He explains the appearance of the public world with primal nescience and the appearance of the personal world of illusions in terms of derivative nesciences. Furthermore, he notes that since nescience resides in the *jīva* and since there are a plurality of *jīva*-s, it follows that there is a plurality of nescience. He argues that if nescience is taken to be one, then the liberation of one *jīva* would amount to the liberation of all the *jīva*-s, and that this is absurd. So, he concludes, there are many *jīva*-s.

Sureśvara and his disciple Sarvajñātman reject the distinction between primal and derivative nesciences. In the course of articulating the nature of nescience, Sureśvara explains why nescience is one rather than many. Nescience is regarded as an entity only figuratively; from a metaphysical perspective it is only a property of *brahman.* Thus, *brahman* is the locus of nescience. Nescience appears to be real until *brahman* realization. Although it is one,[7] it wears functionally diverse hats, so to speak: It is "nonapprehension" (*ajñāna*) when it obscures the nature of the given object, "misapprehension" or "erroneous cognition" (*anyathājñāna* or *viparyayajñāna*) when it presents a given object as something that it is not, and "doubt cognition" (*saṃśaya jñāna*) when it presents an object as either this or that.[8] Eventually the position of Sureśvara on nescience became the official position of the Vivaraṇa school.

Following Sureśvara, the Vivaraṇa school takes nescience to be one. Prakāśātman affirms that while there is but one nescience, it veils in different modes. "[They] are different states of the root ignorance; and substrates of silver, etc. cease to be, along with the superimpositions, as a result of knowledge of the shell, etc."[9] The different modes of nescience account for the illusory judgment "this is silver." The followers of this school emphasize the positive nature of nescience and take *brahman* to be both the locus and the object of nescience. Both *Īśvara* and *jīva* are consequential to nescience and, accordingly, can serve neither as its locus nor as the object. Nescience is one; *brahman,* owing to nescience, appears to be bound and, via knowledge, is, so to speak, released.

For the Advaitins, *brahman* is transcendental reality. Accordingly, *brahman* constitutes the condition that makes all knowledge possible. Since *brahman* is the necessary condition of all knowing, it logically precedes all knowing; hence, it comes first ontologically. However, from the epistemological perspective knowledge comes first: *brahman* is that state of being where all subject-object distinctions are obliterated. With the help of the perceiving process, one "perceives" the self-effulgent light (*cit* or *brahman*) that is, logically, a necessary condition for the very possibility of the perceiving process.

Advaita Theory of Perceiving

Objects, regardless of whether they are internal or external, do not have any power of manifestation of their own. They are covered by ignorance prior to being known. In the cognitive process pertaining to the perception of an external object, the object is cognized via its association with the subject-consciousness. *Antaḥkaraṇavṛtti,* a mode of the inner sense, effects such an association. However, a mental mode is inert; so by itself, it cannot illuminate objects. It leads to illumination on account of its association with pure consciousness. In the words of an Advaitin: "Even if consciousness takes up the form of the object via a mental mode, that does not harm the transcendence of consciousness. The mental mode is the relation between the witness-consciousness and the object."[10] Thus, cognition of an object is not possible in the absence of the consciousness that underlies it. Cognition of an object implies the revelation of the consciousness that underlies it.

The multiplicity of names and forms covers pure consciousness. On account of this covering, pure consciousness cannot associate itself with objects of cognition. Instrumentality of the inner sense is required to establish its connection with the object.

> Although the consciousness that is manifested is one, the inner sense, which is the medium of manifestation, has different parts. Consequently, there is a threefold designation: The part of consciousness as limited by the [inner sense's] aspect of agency is [called] the knower. The part of consciousness as limited by the [inner sense's] aspect of operation is [called] the means of knowing. The part of consciousness as limited by the [inner sense's] ability to manifest the object is [called] the true cognition. The possible object of true cognition is nothing but the *brahman*-consciousness residing in the object in a state of unknownness. The same, when known, becomes the fruit of cognition.[11]

Thus, the Advaitins argue that the inner sense is located within the body that is pervaded by it. It is constituted of very fine transparent matter of predominantly *sattva* quality. The purposiveness of the *sattva* material enables it to come in contact with empirical objects through the outer senses and assume their forms. The inner sense is not only material in nature, but is also divided into three parts, so to speak. One part remains inside the body, the second part makes contact with the several objects, and the third part resides between these two making the whole a unit. The interior part is the ego, the intervening part performs the cognitive action, and the part in contact with empirical objects makes them manifest as objects of a cognitive act. The transparency of the inner sense allows pure consciousness to manifest in it and, according to the three parts of the inner sense, it is manifested in three different ways: as the cognizer, the cognitive operation, and the cognition. The nescience that constitutes the inner sense encompasses within itself the activities of the intellect (*buddhi*) and the mind (*manas*). On account of these different activities within the inner sense, one self appears as many. It is by means of the modes of these activities that the veil that had been covering the object is removed, resulting in the cognition of the object. Thus, consciousness, although one, becomes many as a result of different limiting conditions. To be specific, the Advaitins speak of the three modes of consciousness: consciousness conditioned by the object (*viṣayacaitanya*), consciousness conditioned by the means or instruments of right cognition (*pramāṇacaitanya*), and consciousness conditioned by the inner sense (*pramātṛcaitanya*). Consciousness conditioned by an object (say, a pitcher) is the object consciousness, consciousness conditioned by the means of knowledge is the cognitive consciousness, and consciousness conditioned by the inner sense is the cognizer consciousness.[12]

The cognitive process of external visual perception contains the following five steps:

1. The inner sense comes in contact with the organ of vision, reaches out to the object and becomes one with it.
2. The mental mode removes the veil of nescience that had been hiding the object from the perceiver.
3. The consciousness underlying the object, being manifested as a result of the removal of the veil of ignorance, reveals the object.
4. The mind effects an identity between the consciousness conditioned by the object and the consciousness conditioned by the subject.
5. As a result, the cognizer perceives the object.

No object can be cognized without the removal of the veil of nescience that hides the object. The veil of ignorance that hides the object is derivative nescience, a mode of primal nescience that makes possible the projection of the entire world. Removal of individual modes of nescience is necessary in order to manifest what is perceived by a cognizer (*pramātā*) so that the underlying consciousness may become manifest. This explains what is meant by saying that in perception the object is revealed by the cognizer consciousness (*pramātṛcaitanya*). The perceptuality of the cognizer and the perceptibility of the object[13] that is perceived amount to the removal of two modes of nescience. The unperceived remains hidden on account of nescience.

Perception is immediacy of consciousness. By immediate knowledge is meant that knowledge which does not require any sort of intervention by any instrument. The senses do operate, but they simply provide the mechanism for the manifestation of consciousness; they do not generate any new knowledge. Consciousness covered by ignorance requires avenues to manifest, and the perceptual accessories facilitate the removal of the veil. Three conditions must be fulfilled in order for any knowledge to be termed immediate: (1) The object must be directly known, (2) it must exist presently, and (3) the subject and the object must be related intimately. In perceptual knowledge, the inner sense goes out through the senses and assumes the form of the object, with the result that the object and the mind become nondifferent. Perceptual knowledge therefore is said to be direct, immediate knowing. Inferential knowledge, on the other hand, does not fulfill these conditions: it requires the intervention of an instrument, the object need not presently exist, and even if the object exists the subject and the object are not required to be directly related. Therefore, it is said to be mediate or inferential.

The Advaitins give a picturesque description of the process of perception against the setting of the nondifference of consciousness:

> Just as the water of a tank, having come out of an aperture, enters a number of fields through channels assuming like those [fields] a quadrangular or any other form, so also the internal organ, which is characterized by light, goes out [of the body] through the door [sense] of sight, and so on, and [after] reaching the location of the object, say a pitcher, it is modified in the form of the objects like a pitcher. This modification [of the internal organ] is called a mental mode [*vṛtti*]. In the case of inferential cognition, and so on, however, there is no going out of the internal organ to the location of a fire, because the fire, and so on [other inferred objects], are not in contact with the sense of sight, and so on [other sense organs].[14]

The uniqueness of the Advaitin theory of perception lies in its recognition that no object can be cognized without the manifestation of the consciousness that underlies it.

Although all the Advaitins agree that the function of a mental mode is to manifest an object, there is no unanimity among them regarding the way in which an object becomes manifest. These differences are primarily a function of their views on the relation between the knowing self and the object.[15]

Roughly speaking, there are three different views regarding the purpose of the meeting of a mental mode with the object leading to the perception of it: (1) for the sake of associating consciousness with the object (*ciduparāga*); (2) for the sake of removing the veil that covers the object (*āvaraṇābhibhava*); and (3) for the manifestation of the nondifference of consciousness conditioned by the object and consciousness conditioned by the subject (*abhedābhivyakti*).[16] Most Advaitins, however, accept that there are two functions of a mental mode, viz., removal of the veil that covers the object and connecting the object-conditioned-consciousness and the cognizer-conditioned-consciousness.

These two functions comprise the first two views regarding the meeting of mental mode with the object. They agree that a mental mode shines with the reflected light of consciousness and meets the object; the veil of consciousness that covers the object from the cognizer is withdrawn; and the object-conditioned-consciousness becomes manifest through the transparent mental mode, thereby illuminating the object.

Dharmarāja[17] accepts the third view of the functioning of a mental mode; he maintains that the function of a mental mode is to establish nondifference between consciousness conditioned by the object and consciousness conditioned by the mind.

> Thus in the case of perceptual cognitions such as "this is a pitcher," because consciousness conditioned by the pitcher and consciousness conditioned by the mental mode in the form of a pitcher are located in one and the same place [outside the body], the consciousness conditioned by both [the object perceived and the *vṛtti*] is one. This is because the modification of the internal organ and objects like pitchers, although having the capacity of differentiation [between consciousness conditioned by the *vṛtti* and consciousness conditioned by the object], do not give rise to any difference on account of their being located in one and the same place [where the object exists]. For this very reason, ether conditioned by a pitcher in a monastery is not different from ether conditioned by a hall in the monastery [in spite of having two distinct limiting adjuncts].[18]

The basic difference between the first two and the third view is as follows: According to the first two views, the mental mode that leads to the perception of an object only connects the consciousness conditioned by the object and the consciousness conditioned by the subject. They do not become nondifferent, as one finds in the third view.[19]

It must be noted here that knowledge, for the Advaitins, is an event in time. When I apprehend an object, the object undoubtedly is revealed; however, it is not the only thing that is revealed. It is accompanied by an apprehension of apprehension. When I say "this is a chair," I not only know the chair, but also know that I know that this is a chair. The two apprehensions occur simultaneously. "This is a chair" is an instance of perception; however, the perception itself is apprehended by the witness-consciousness. Thus, the Advaitin conception of knowledge is quite different from the Naiyāyika conception of knowledge. For the Naiyāyikas, knowing is a temporal act directed toward an object. It is a property of the self and is expressed in judgments such as "this is a chair." Here, the chair is the object of knowledge. Such a cognition, for them, reveals only the object. It does not reveal either the cognizer or the cognition itself. This is termed "*vyavasāya*" or the primary cognition. This primary cognition, for them, is revealed by a second introspective awareness in the form "I know the chair," or "I have knowledge of the chair." The second cognition or the cognition of the primary cognition is termed "*anuvyavasāya.*" Whereas the object of the primary cognition is the chair, the direct object of the second cognition is the primary cognition, the indirect objects being the self and the object of the primary cognition.

According to the Advaitins, however, consciousness in itself is always self-revealed and self-established. Regardless of the mode of perceiving, whether I am seeing, hearing, etc., there always remains an awareness that is changeless. Consciousness cannot become an object of another consciousness, accordingly there is no consciousness of consciousness. Consciousness is one, without a second, although it manifests objects in its role as the witness-consciousness. External objects are manifested by the witness-consciousness indirectly, with the assistance of the inner sense. It is important to keep in mind in this context that although the object is manifested by the appropriate mental modification, or the *vṛtti,* the mental mode itself is directly manifested by the witness-consciousness: "all modifications of the inner sense, being known by the witness-consciousness, are immediately apprehended."[20] Consciousness is reflected in the mental mode—say, in the perception of a pitcher—and results in a judgment "this is a pitcher." A second mental modification is not required to know the initial modification; when I know an object, I also know that I know that object. The apprehension "I know that I know the object," for the Advaitins, unlike the Naiyāyikas, is not revealed by the finite individual. It is apprehended by the witness-consciousness. Apart from the mental modifications, there are three objects that are only apprehended by the witness-consciousness, the subject matter of the following discussion.

The Objects of *Sākṣin*

For the later Advaitins, three things are revealed by the witness-consciousness *alone*; namely, mental states (cognitive states as well as pleasure, pain, etc.), illusory objects and ignorance itself. At this juncture, one might ask: Why do the Advaitins find it necessary to make *only* these three things the objects of the witness-consciousness? The answer to this question lies in the function of a mental modification itself. Prior to its manifestation, an object enjoys an unknown existence, insofar as it is concealed. A mental modification destroys the cover that conceals the object, thereby making it manifest. So, the Advaitins argue that whatever possesses unknown existence (*ajñātasattā*) is revealed by a means of true cognition (*pramāṇa*); whatever has no unknown existence is revealed directly by the witness-consciousness. Mental states, such as pleasure and pain, illusory objects, and ignorance, do not enjoy unknown existence. Accordingly, they are directly apprehended by the witness-consciousness. There is no need, in their case, for mediation by a mental modification.

Pleasure and Pain

According to Advaita, subjective states of pleasure and pain, and so forth, are revealed by the witness-consciousness. Mental states last as long as they are revealed. Nobody says, "I am happy, but I do not know it." Nor does one say, "I am sad, but I do not know it." I apprehend my happiness directly, as long as it lasts. In other words, my happiness is revealed to me as known. It does not have an unknown existence. Therefore, mental states, such as pleasure, pain and the like, are said by the Advaitins to be apprehended by the witness-consciousness *alone*.

It is worth noting in this context that apprehension by the "witness-consciousness alone" means that the mental states are apprehended unaided by any *pramāṇas*. In other words, mental states are objects of the witness-consciousness directly, i.e., they do not require any mediation by the mind or the sense organs. For the Advaitins, pleasure, pain, and the like are perceptual. If the question is raised as to why this is the case, the Advaitins, in response, would point out that since the witness-consciousness is invariably perceptual, one's introspective cognition of one's state of happiness is always perceptual.

The above discussion regarding consciousness as invariably perceptual and one's introspective cognition of one's mental states also as perceptual raises the issue of the criterion of perceptuality. For the Advaitins, the criterion for perceptuality is the same, irrespective of whether one is talking about a mental state, such as happiness, or a physical object, say, a pitcher:

> [I]n the perception "this is a pitcher," the mental mode, in the form of a pitcher being in contact with the pitcher, the consciousness conditioned by the pitcher and the consciousness conditioned by the mental mode in the form of the pitcher are nondifferent, so for the cognition of the pitcher there is a perceptual character with respect to its form as the pitcher.
>
> Because consciousness conditioned by happiness, pain and so on, and consciousness conditioned by the mental mode in the form of happiness

> and so on, are invariably conditioned by two limiting adjuncts [happiness and the mental mode in the form of happiness] which are located in the same place, the cognitions "I am happy, sad," and so on, are perceptual.[21]

The point that the Advaitins are trying to make is as follows: Identity between consciousness conditioned by the pitcher and consciousness conditioned by the mental mode in the form of the pitcher is required to explain the perceptuality of the cognition of a pitcher. Since this consciousness by its very nature is immediate, it does not require any kind of instrument in order to cognize the pitcher: The cognition of the pitcher is, thus, immediate. The point at issue in this context is the perceptuality of the pure consciousness that serves as the substratum of the object that is superimposed upon it—a pitcher in the example under consideration. Thus, when a pitcher is perceived, what becomes perceptual is consciousness conditioned by the mode of the mind that assumes the form of the pitcher.

Likewise, the cognition "I am happy" expresses the direct experience of the state of happiness on account of the nondifference of the mental mode with it. These states do not have any independent existence; they exist only as states belonging to somebody. They are revealed only as long as they last. My happiness is directly revealed to me; it is revealed without a mental mode. Since my happiness is in direct contact with me, the going out of the mental mode is not involved to make it immediate. An external object is given through a mental mode. But the mental mode is given directly to the witness-consciousness without needing another mental mode.

Before concluding the discussion of this issue, it must be noted that there is a difference of opinion regarding the need for a mental modification in the revelation of mental states. For some Advaitins, pleasure and pain, which appear as modifications of the inner sense superimposed on the witness-consciousness, are directly revealed by the witness-consciousness; hence, there is no need to postulate a mental modification.

Other Advaitins (e.g., Madhusūdana and Brahmānanda) maintain that for the apprehension of internal states a mental modification is required, because these states are later remembered and memory can be caused only by a mental modification. The cognition of happiness lasts only as long as the corresponding mental mode lasts. However, when the mode is destroyed, it leaves behind residual impressions that account for the future recollection of past pain and pleasure, as the statement "I was happiest during the first few years of my married life."

Pleasure, pain, and the like are revealed by the witness-consciousness from the moment of their inception. Thus, Advaitins point out that there is no *āvaraṇa* (concealment) for pleasure, pain and the like. Accordingly, the question of apprehending them by destroying ignorance does not even arise. In other words, since happiness had never been covered at all, there is no need to uncover it. One may, however, be ignorant of the happiness of others. It is known like any external object is known. My friend may be happy, but I may be ignorant of her happiness.

Illusory Objects

Advaitins explain the process of illusory perception, e.g., "this is silver," as follows: Initially, there is contact between the eyes vitiated by *doṣa*-s (faults) resulting in a mental mode in the form of "thisness" with reference to the thing before me. "This" appears divested of its differentia; it appears in its general characteristics as something white and shining. Next, the consciousness (*cit*) conditioned by the "this" is reflected in the mental mode; the three modes of consciousness—the cognizer-consciousness, the consciousness conditioned by the mental mode, and the consciousness conditioned by the "this"—become nondifferent. Finally, the nescience associated with the consciousness on account of some kind of defect—e.g., cataracts, etc.—and the revival of the residual impressions of the past cognition of silver, through similarity, transform themselves into the apparent silver and give rise to the cognition "this is silver."[22]

One can distinguish four components in the illusory perception as described above: a ground or locus (*adhiṣṭhāna*), concealment (*āvaraṇa*), projection (*vikṣepa*), and superimposition (*adhyāsa*). Illusion does not, can not, occur without a locus or substratum. Padmapāda states: "A superimposition without a substratum can not even be conceived, let alone experienced."[23] Vācaspati adds: "Illusion can not occur where the basis of the illusion is clearly apprehended or not apprehended at all."[24] However, a substratum, though necessary, is not sufficient to generate illusory perception. When I perceive silver in a shell, the shell remains concealed from me. It is not only that the shell is not known as the shell, but that it appears as something else, i.e., as the silver. Silver in this case exists only as ascribed to the shell; it does not have any reality of its own.

Advaitins admit two mental modes here: a mode of the inner sense (*antaḥkaraṇavṛtti*) and a mode of nescience (*avidyāvṛtti*), the first one of the form "this" and the second of the form "silver." The two mental modifications coalesce into one, generating the illusory judgment "this is silver." For the Advaitins, while the empirical cognizer perceives the "this" via a mode of the inner sense, the witness-consciousness apprehends the illusory silver. Why? Advaitins answer the question by using the following principle: Whatever possesses unknown existence (*ajñātasattā*) is revealed by a means of true cognition (*pramāṇa*) and so requires a mental mode; but whatever has no unknown existence is revealed directly by the witness-consciousness. An illusory object does not possess unknown existence; it does not exist somewhere out there. Its essence consists in being perceived (*esse est percipi*). The "this," on the other hand, is cognized by the ordinary means of knowing; it is an object of visual perception. It is important to remember here that knowledge for Advaitins consists in the revelation of objects that, though existent, are shrouded by the veil of unknownness, i.e., by nescience. Knowledge does not create the object, it simply manifests the object. *Pramāṇa*-s remove the veil that hides objects and thus makes them manifest. An illusory object is never covered; it never exists as unknown. Objects known via *pramāṇa*-s are covered; *pramāṇa*-s remove the veil that is hiding the objects. Since an illusory object is never hidden, the question of revealing it by removing the veil of unknownness does not arise. Even though some Advaitins admit a mode of nescience in these cases, no *pramāṇa* is necessary for the revelation of an illusory object; no passage is involved from a prior state of unknown existence to its subsequent manifestation.

The Advaitin analysis of illusory perception gives rise to a number of interesting questions. First, the Advaitins themselves point out: "It may be objected that this difference of modifications would contradict the experience of the oneness of cognition."[25] In other words, if the two modifications are different, how can there be experience of the identity of knowledge? Since in every case of illusion there are two separate objects ("this" and the "illusory silver") with their corresponding modes (a mode of the inner sense and a mode of nescience), how is it possible to get one cognition in the form "this is silver"? Second, since the illusory silver is neither internal nor external, how can it be apprehended by the witness-consciousness? Third, when the illusory cognition is sublated by "this is not silver, it is a shell," who makes the sublating judgment? The cognizer-consciousness or the witness-consciousness?

In response to the first question, the Advaitins state:

> Since between the two objects ("this" and "the silver") there is a superimposition of nondifference, so also between the two cognitions. Hence there is one cognition which is only a superimposition. Hence, [there is] no conflict with experience.[26]

Thus, although two different objects are involved, they coalesce with each other in such a fashion that they appear as nondifferent. The two modes, though different, being the products of the inner sense and nescience respectively, are fused together, resulting in the nondifference of the empirically real and the illusorily real silver. So, although there are two objects and two modes, the result is only one judgment, i.e., the manifestation of the object. In other words, both modifications manifest one and the same consciousness—the consciousness conditioned by the object (*viṣayacaitanya*). The result being one, the resulting cognition is, thus, also one.

Regarding the second question raised above, the opponents point out that since silver, unlike happiness, is not an internal state of mind, it cannot be apprehended by introspection. Additionally, since the illusory silver (unlike the empirical silver), does not exist out there, it cannot be known by external cognition; there is no mental mode assuming its form. So they conclude that the witness-consciousness cannot apprehend the illusory silver. In response, the Advaitins first point out that consciousness conditioned by the object is nondifferent from consciousness conditioned by the inner sense, which is the witness-consciousness, and second, that although the silver is superimposed on the consciousness conditioned by the object, it is spoken of as being superimposed on the witness-consciousness.[27] Thus, it follows that the illusory silver can only be apprehended by the witness-consciousness.

They further add that the above also explains why illusory silver, like one's own happiness, cannot be cognized by another person.[28] Since the illusory silver is superimposed on both the consciousness conditioned by the object (the shell) and the witness-consciousness, and since it is revealed by the witness-consciousness and appropriated by an "I," it (the illusory silver) does not reveal itself to another ego at the same time. When I am suffering from the shell-silver illusion, my friend sitting close to me is not suffering from the same illusion. Even if my friend is also perceiving illusory silver, at the same time that I am, her illusory perception is distinct from mine; we may have similar perceptions but her perception of illusory silver is not the same experience as my perception. They differ quantitatively and qualitatively, because we are each distinct individuals who bring different defects and different residual impressions to the cognition.

Finally, although two "agents," the cognizer and the witness-consciousness, are involved, the cognizer appropriates what the witness-consciousness apprehends. Thus, it is the cognizer who makes the sublating judgment correcting the initial error. In illusion, a person mistakes one thing for another; it is a unitary experience, and the appropriation of it by the "I" points to the nondifference of the self that has been stratified. The same silver is superimposed not only on the consciousness conditioned by the object, but also on the witness-consciousness. Psychical states such as mental states and one's own happiness are revealed immediately and, accordingly, they are called *kevalasākṣibhāsya* (revealed by the witness-consciousness alone), unlike objects such as chairs and tables, which are said to be *pramātṛbhāsya* (revealed by the consciousness conditioned by the cognizer) via appropriate mental mode.[29]

Sarvajñātman in this context makes an important distinction between the *adhiṣṭhāna*, the real (the "shell," the knowledge of which cancels the illusion, but which never appears in the illusion), and the *ādhāra*, the support (the "this" that is connected with the illusory silver). When we are perceiving the silver, we are ignorant of the shell, because the knowledge of the shell cancels the illusion. The support functions as the link between the real and the illusory silver. The object of ignorance in this sense is identical with the real basis of illusion.

> The designation of "substrate" [*adhiṣṭhāna*] is well established not in the substance that serves as the locus [*ādhāra*] of the superimposed object, but in the substance that is the object of *avidyā* with its product. . . . In erroneous cognitions . . . only the superimposed object appears. . . . In no case does an object different from the one superimposed appear in the erroneous cognitions.[30]

In "this is silver," the consciousness that underlies the "this" is the substratum, since ignorance of "this" projects the silver, while "this," the shell that appears as related to the superimposed silver, is the support. Sarvajñātman makes a case for the mutual superimposition of the "this" and the silver. The sublating cognition sublates both; however, the shell that is the ground (*adhiṣṭhāna*) is not sublated.

One may argue here that since the illusory silver is a superimposition on the witness-consciousness, the perception should assume the form "I am silver"—like "I am happy."[31] In reply, it is said that the form a cognition assumes depends on the form of the residual impressions (*saṃskāra*-s). Since our previous veridical perception of silver was of the form "this is silver" and not "I am silver," the illusory perception on account of the residual impressions would invariably assume the form "this is silver" and not "I am silver." It is worth noting here that while silver does not belong to the witness-consciousness directly, nescience does. "Silver" is not produced by the witness-consciousness, but by the nescience belonging to the cognizer. "Thisness," as a matter of fact, belongs to the consciousness conditioned by the object, which is nondifferent from the "I" or the consciousness conditioned by the cognizer. The witness-consciousness transforms itself into the object of illusion via the medium of the consciousness conditioned by the object; thus, the transformation is indirect. However, at no time during the genesis of an illusory perception is the association between the illusory object and the objective "this" lost. Therefore, the illusory silver can appear only in the form "this is silver."

Regarding the illusory cognition "this is silver" the question may be asked: Does "thisness" really belong to the silver or to the shell? It does not belong to the silver, because then there would be no sublating cognition "this is a shell." It does not belong to the shell either, because the shell does not appear. Thus, both alternatives are ruled out. Accordingly, the Advaitins maintain that although "thisness" belongs to the shell, it assumes the form of the illusory silver and, since both become nondifferent, the silver is cognized in the place of the shell.[32]

The opponents of the Advaitins may, at this point, raise the following question: Since nescience transforms itself into silver, what is the necessity of a mode of nescience? Even if we assume for the sake of argument that external objects—such as a pitcher—do indeed require a mental mode in the form of a pitcher in order to be related to the witness-consciousness, it does not tell us why we need a mode of nescience to perceive the illusory silver. In fact, since the illusory silver is apprehended directly by the witness-consciousness, there is no need to postulate any kind of a mental mode, let alone a mode of nescience. Additionally, since the witness-consciousness apprehends both the valid and the erroneous cognitions, the illusory silver must also be in contact with the witness-consciousness. Thus, the witness-consciousness may itself be taken to be the manifesting factor of consciousness and, hence, there is no necessity of admitting a mode of nescience in the form of the silver.

In response, Dharmarāja states that a mode of nescience is needed "to establish the immediacy of silver, because the immediacy of an object consists in its not having a level of existence [reality] different from that of the consciousness conditioned by the mental mode which is its own [*sva*] object."[33] Immediacy, as the criterion of the perceptuality of consciousness, implies that the object does not have an independent reality apart from the cognizer.[34] Accordingly, in the perception of an external object, consciousness conditioned by the "this," consciousness conditioned by the inner sense, and consciousness conditioned by the mental mode assuming the form of "this" located in one and the same place are said to be nondifferent. Likewise, in the illusory perception of silver, consciousness conditioned by the "this" element and the silver are said to be nondifferent from the three modes of consciousness mentioned above. This explains why what is superimposed on the cognizer-consciousness is manifested by the witness-consciousness. Additionally, without a mental mode there cannot be the memory of silver. The mental mode leaves behind residual impressions that cause the memory of its object. We do remember the illusory silver; so, we must postulate a mode, in this case a mode of nescience.

It is also important to remember that pure consciousness never comes in direct contact with any quality or characteristic; it only manifests the characters that are presented to it through mental modifications which are transparent. In the illusory perception "this is silver," the mode of "this" does not manifest the illusory silver; accordingly, a separate mode of ignorance must be admitted. A mode of the inner sense receives directly the reflection of pure consciousness and, accordingly, does not require an additional mental mode. The opponents argue:

> But your view is that ignorance itself, depending upon the efficient causality of external faults, gets transformed into the form of silver and the witness-consciousness gets transferred into the seeming-knowledge, having the silver as its limitor; this ignorance, along with its modifications, thereby becomes the object of the witness-consciousness.[35]

The Advaitins point out that in an illusory perception, such as "this is silver," nescience is transformed both as the objective silver and the apparent knowledge of the silver. Both of these transformations are directly the objects of the witness-consciousness.

Thus, we see that illusory objects, like mental modes, are directly apprehended by the witness-consciousness. Neither has unknown existence. However, there is an important difference between the two. In an illusory perception, a claim to objectivity is made, since the illusory silver appears to be "out there" prior to its perception. In the case of internal states, no such claim is made.

Avidyā

Nescience is the pivot around which revolves the entire Advaita philosophy. Advaitins use this concept to vindicate their central thesis: *brahman* is the only reality, the world is false and the individual self is nondifferent from *brahman.* Nescience causes all empirical distinctions by obscuring pure consciousness. Thus, from an epistemological perspective, the distinctions among the subject who knows, the object known, and the resulting knowledge are due to nescience.

The Advaitins articulate nescience as a beginningless, positive entity, removable only by knowledge (*anādibhāvarūpatve sati jñānanivartyāvidyā*).[36] It is beginningless, because when one says "I am ignorant," it does not make sense to ask when your ignorance began.[37] It is positive, although the negative prefix of the term "*avidyā*" ("*a*" = "not" + "*vidyā*" = "knowledge") creates the misleading impression that it is a negative entity, a mere absence of knowledge (*abhāvopādānam ajñānam*).[38] Citsukha explains what is entailed in the claim that nescience is a positive entity; he defines nescience as positive, beginningless, and sublated by the rise of true knowledge.[39] He further adds: "Nescience or ignorance, which is other than the positive and the negative, is taken to be positive as soon as it is said to be other than negation."[40] In other words, nescience is different from both positivity and negativity; however, it is called positive only to indicate that it is not negative. The Advaitins adduce a number of proofs to show its positive nature: To be specific, they contend that perception, inference, and postulation demonstrate the positive nature of nescience. I will return to these proofs shortly.

Nescience is removable by knowledge. "Knowledge" here refers to modal knowledge (*vṛttijñāna*) and not to pure knowledge, the consciousness that is of the nature of the self (*svarūpajñāna*); the latter is not opposed to nescience. Modal knowledge, the knowledge that is generated by means of a mental mode, is opposed to nescience.[41] A mental mode destroys ignorance when reflected through the modification of the means of knowledge. The Advaitins maintain:

> The opposition to ignorance that is experienced in the witness-consciousness is not owing to its being the destroyer of ignorance, but rather owing to the impossibility of its objects, such as desire, etc., being unknown, for they are manifested as long as they exist.[42]

Thus, whereas a mental mode is opposed to ignorance, the witness-consciousness is not. The latter manifests some objects—e.g., pleasure, pain, and the like—directly. Since operation in the form of removing the veil is required in these cases, the witness-consciousness also manifests nescience. For an adequate understanding of Advaita, it is crucial to remember that pure consciousness, in itself, is not opposed to ignorance.

Thus, the Advaitins argue that nescience is *prasiddha*, not *pramāṇa-siddha*, i.e., it is given to us in our experience; it is not, and cannot be, established by any *pramāṇa* (means of true cognition):

> [*A*] *vidyā* cannot be known through the knowledge generated by a *pramāṇa*, for such a knowledge which has to come through a mental mode (*vṛtti*) is opposed to it. Any such attempt to know *avidyā* through *pramāṇa-jñāna* is as futile and absurd as the attempt to see the darkness of a mountain cave by means of a lamp. The light of a lamp will remove darkness. In the same way, *pramāṇa-jñāna*, instead of revealing *avidyā*, will remove it.[43]

Pramāṇa-s give rise to empirical knowledge and make known what was previously unknown.[44] "What is not already known" is another way of saying that it is veiled by nescience. In other words, empirical knowledge, in itself being the result of a mental modification, is by nature opposed to nescience. Accordingly, empirical knowledge accessible via any of the six *pramāṇa*-s accepted by the Advaitins does not, and cannot, reveal nescience. So, the obvious question: How is nescience known?

The Advaitins maintain that nescience is established by the witness-consciousness. For example, Vidyāraṇya[45] and Madhusūdana[46] repeatedly declare that nescience is manifested directly by the witness-conciouness. The witness-consciousness is either pure consciousness that has nescience as its limiting adjunct (*upādhi*) or pure consciousness reflected in the modes of nescience.[47] Nescience cannot hide anything from the witness-consciousness.[48] Since there is no I-consciousness during the sleep state, ignorance is directly experienced and assumes the form "I did not know anything." This experience is accompanied by the knowledge "I know that I did not know," which shows that nescience is established by the witness-consciousness.[49] They further add that nescience is a positive entity and perception provides the most important proof of its positive nature.

The opponents, however, argue that the cognition "I do not know" is not perception of undifferentiated positive nescience, but is rather perception of the negation or absence of knowledge. To substantiate their claim, the opponents point out that the Advaitins themselves, at times, articulate nescience as nonapprehension (*agrahaṇa*). For example, Sureśvara, in *Taittirīyopaniṣad Bhāṣyā-Vārtika*, in speaking about nescience, states: "It does not have a nature other than nonperception of the self. The word '*avidyā*' is to be construed like the word '*amitra*,' then it would be correctly understood."[50] *Agrahaṇa*, a negative component of nescience, remains in a latent form during the state of deep sleep. Therefore, nescience is negative. He also notes: "Only for the deluded mind there is nonperception in the form "I do not know."[51]

It is wrong to conclude from the above, however, that nescience is the absence of knowledge. Ānandagiri in his commentary on the above verse takes the term "*ātmano 'graho*" to mean concealment of the self.[52] The concealing power of nescience accounts for the nonperception of the self. A negative, i.e., a nonexistent, entity cannot conceal. Therefore, nescience must be positive. Thus, it cannot be argued that the perceptual experience that "I do not know" refers to the mere absence of knowledge (*jñānābhāva*) and not to nescience as a positive entity.

The Advaitins press the issue further. They say that even if we assume for the sake of argument that nescience refers to the absence of knowledge, the question still remains: does it refer to the absence of all knowledge or merely to the absence of the knowledge of a particular thing? It does not refer to the former, because in the experience "I do not know," the experiencer is manifested in the form of "I." No one can doubt or deny one's own existence without contradiction. The very experience of not-knowing affirms the existence of a self that does not know. It does not refer to the absence of knowledge of any particular thing, because cognition of negation presupposes knowledge of the thing that is being negated; it cannot be known apart from knowledge of the thing negated (*pratiyogin*) and the substratum (*anuyogin*) of negation. In order for a person to perceive the negation of a pitcher, he must know both the pitcher (*pratiyogin*) and the locus (*anuyogin*) where the absence exists. Knowledge of the absence of knowledge in deep sleep would then require the knowledge of both its locus and its counterpositive—in which case there would be no absence of knowledge. Mind, during the state of deep sleep, is quiescent and therefore cannot have either the knowledge of the locus or of the counterpositive of the absence. To know the absence of the knowledge of X (in "I do not know X") one must already have the knowledge of X—in which case there would be no absence of the knowledge of X. Therefore, what one perceives in "I do not know X" is not absence of the knowledge of X, but a positive ignorance concealing X. So, they conclude that the perceptual experience "I do not know" refers to a positive entity and not to the mere absence of knowledge.[53]

It is important to remember in this context that the Advaitins do not accept antecedent nonexistence. In the experience "the pitcher will come into being," according to the Naiyāyikas, one experiences the prior nonexistence of the pitcher. On the Advaita view, the unreal is nonbeing; it never comes into existence. Its nonexistence is not perceived. What we have rather is the absence of perception. When I say "I do not know the pitcher," I perceive nescience with reference to the pitcher; this is not a perception of the negation of the pitcher. The pitcher is *now*, in some sense, real. Therefore, the arising of knowledge presupposes prior ignorance. A perceptual memory of absence is different from its direct perception. This explains why the Advaitins accept noncognition (*anupalabdhi*) as one of the six means of true cognition. Likewise, the experience "I am ignorant," cannot be taken as perception of a prior absence. This cognition therefore reveals a positive nescience.

For the Advaitins, one experiences pure ignorance in the state of deep sleep, when all the modifications of the inner sense and appearances cease to exist and the self is experienced as devoid of all distinctions. After waking up from deep sleep, an individual recalls, "I did not know anything during sleep." Here a reference to nescience is being made, because it amounts to saying "I was under the influence of nescience, I was not able to comprehend anything." If this were not the case, one would not be able to account for the experience recollected upon waking up expressed as "I did not know anything." During the state of deep sleep, both the inner sense and egoity are enveloped by nescience; only the self and nescience remain. Upon waking up, egoity, as a state of the inner sense, reappears, giving rise to the perception "I did not know anything." Such an argument amounts to a kind of transcendental proof, since one becomes aware of the deep sleep state only retrospectively. The perceptual experience "I am ignorant" is one of the three witness-perceptions (*sākṣī pratyakṣa*-s) that Advaitins, like Madhusūdana, take great pains to explain:

> Now the cognition "I am ignorant," and "I do not know myself and the other," is a perceptual proof of ignorance, the cognition "I do not know what you said" is a specific perceptual proof of ignorance. The cognition "all this time I slept well and did not know anything," which is a perception established by recollection [*parāmarśa*], is also a proof.[54]

These three kinds of witness-perceptions assisted by reasoning demonstrate the existence of positive ignorance, argue the Advaitins.

The First Witness Perception

The perceptual experience "I am ignorant" is possible because both ignorance and the inner sense are superimposed upon consciousness. Both have the same substratum. Through the relation of having the same locus, the inner sense functions as the locus of ignorance.[55] The point that the Advaitins are trying to make is as follows: The real locus is pure consciousness; however, the inner sense is also superimposed on the same consciousness that ignorance tries to conceal. So the inner sense appears to be the locus of ignorance.

For the Advaitins, the perceptual experience "I do not know the pitcher" is not about the absence of the knowledge of the pitcher. Rather, it refers to the fact that consciousness limited by the pitcher is concealed by ignorance. If the consciousness that is the foundation of the pitcher is manifested by a mental mode, then the pitcher stands manifested (being superimposed, by identity, on that consciousness). Just as knowledge is opposed to ignorance, ignorance is likewise opposed to knowledge.

When ignorance is manifested by *sākṣin*, it is manifested as opposed to knowledge.

Now although ignorance is one, owing to difference of limiting adjuncts, it is different. The ignorance belonging to consciousness as limited by the the inner sense is called *pramātṛgata ajñāna* or ignorance belonging to the knower; ignorance belonging to consciousness as limited by the object is called *viṣayagata ajñāna* or ignorance belonging to the object. The former, i.e., the ignorance belonging to the knower, has the power to produce the thought of the nonexistence of the object, the thought "the object does not exist" (*viṣayo nāsti*).[56] Mediate knowledge can destroy this power and can give rise to the cognition "this object exists." The latter, i.e., the ignorance belonging to the object, causes the cognition "the object does not appear." An object that is known by a mediate cognition is known as related to existence, but not as manifesting the object. We may mediately know that atoms exist, but lack perceptual cognition of them. Immediate perceptual cognition removes both kinds of ignorance.

The Advaitins contend that ignorance is directly known by the witness-consciousness. The author of *Nyāyāmṛta* argues that if the witness-consciousness manifests ignorance, how can the former be eternal, while the latter is destroyed by knowledge? In other words, if the witness-consciousness is there, its object, i.e., ignorance, must also be there.

In response, Madhusūdana points out that pleasure, pain, and illusory objects, etc., are manifested by the witness-consciousness. While the witness-consciousness is there, cessation of pleasure, of pain, and of the illusory objects is evidenced by experience. The witness-consciousness is not pure consciousness, but pure consciousness as qualified by the mode of nescience.[57]

It is important to remember in this context that although ignorance is apprehended by the witness-consciousness directly, the distinguishing object of ignorance is known by the witness-consciousness through a mediate relationship (*paramparayā*). Let me give an illustrative example. In the illusory perception "this is silver," the "this" or the shell is not directly apprehended by the witness-consciousness. Both the witness-consciousness and the shell are related to ignorance; however, the witness-consciousness is related to ignorance without any intermediary in the sense that ignorance is directly manifested by the witness. The shell is related to the witness-consciousness indirectly, insofar as ignorance conceals the consciousness that would have manifested the shell. This explains the Advaitin claim that while the witness-consciousness manifests ignorance directly, it manifests the object of that ignorance only indirectly, i.e., by a chain of relation (called *paramparā*) which may be formulated thus: The witness-consciousness manifests the ignorance which, on its part, conceals the consciousness having the shell for its object.

When a true cognition (*pramājñāna*) arises, there is the witness-perception "I know" ("*pramiṇomi*"). In this perception, the true cognition appears as the object and the property of being a true cognition (*pramātva* of that *pramā*) appears as the qualifier. This latter property includes the component property, i.e., "having an object that was hitherto unknown" (*ajñātārtha-viṣayakatva*). To manifest the property of being a true cognition (*pramātva*) one needs the ignorance (implied by "unknown object") to be manifested. But this ignorance *ex hypothesi* has been already removed. Thus, the witness-consciousness of a true cognition manifests the *past* ignorance that has been removed by that cognition. The point that the Advaitins are trying to make is as follows: Let us suppose that I have a true cognition that assumes the form "this is silver." When I know this cognition as true, I know it as possessing the property of being a true cognition. This means that I know it as manifesting a hitherto unknown object, the feature that is apprehended by the witness-consciousness. Knowing it as a previously unknown object in turn implies that its object is now known (*jñātārtha*). Likewise, "I do not know," while manifesting the present ignorance, also manifests the opposition of that ignorance to a true cognition that does not already exist but is yet to be (*bhāvijñāna*). So we can say: The witness of a true cognition manifests *past* ignorance already removed by that true cognition, and the witness of ignorance manifests the *future* true cognition that will remove that ignorance.

The opponents might argue that the ignorance that is perceived is ignorance as qualified by an object, e.g., the pitcher. As a rule, perception of something as qualified presupposes perception of the qualifier. But if the qualifier, i.e., the pitcher in this case, is known, then how can there be ignorance of it? *Advaitasiddhi,* in reply, rejects the Nyāya thesis that knowledge of the qualifier is a condition of the knowledge of the qualified object.[58] Furthermore, since the witness of ignorance is consciousness as qualified by beginningless ignorance, then this witness-consciousness, being beginningless, cannot be caused at all. Therefore, it is not caused by the knowledge of the qualifier.

It must be noted that when the witness-consciousness apprehends ignorance, the qualifier of that ignorance (e.g., the pitcher), the opposition of ignorance to knowledge, and the fact that it has an object (*saviṣayakatva*) cannot all be immediately apprehended by the witness-consciousness. Only the ignorance is directly apprehended. All the others are apprehended in accordance with the principle "an adjective belongs to a substantive, other adjectives belong to that adjective" (*viśeṣye viśeṣaṇaṃ, tatrāpi viśeṣaṇāntaraṃ*), which, in this case, means that the ignorance is directly superimposed upon the witness-consciousness, the object of ignorance qualifies that ignorance and so is known mediately.

The Second Witness Perception

For the Advaitins, "I do not know what you said" (*tvaduktamarthaṃ na jānāmi*) does not mean that the knowledge of what you are talking about is absent in me. The Naiyāyikas, for example, state that the above statement should be taken to mean that I have no direct knowledge of the object you are talking about. Therefore, it establishes the absence of direct knowledge. For the Advaitins, on the other hand, it does not imply that I lack perceptual knowledge of what you talked about. Rather, it refers to positive ignorance and not to the absence of knowledge (*jñānābhāva*). In order to have knowledge of the absence of knowledge, I must have that knowledge (to know an absence, I must know its counterpositive), in which case there would be no absence of that knowledge, thereby resulting in a contradiction.

The point that the Advaitins are trying to make is as follows: Let us suppose that my friend is talking about a certain person and I tell her that I do not know the person about whom she is talking. This does not imply the absence of my knowledge of the person she is talking about because in order for me to have the perceptual knowledge of the absence of the knowledge of that person in me, what is required is that I must have the knowledge of that person, since without knowledge of that person there cannot be the perception of the absence of knowledge of that person in me. In order for me to perceive the absence of an elephant in the room, I must know what an elephant looks like. Thus, if I am to have the perception of the absence of knowledge in me, I must already have that knowledge, which is absurd. If I already had that knowledge there could be no present absence of that knowledge. The simultaneous presence and absence of that knowledge violates the law of noncontradiction and must be false. So, the Advaitins conclude that "I do not know what you said" does not refer to the absence of knowledge but rather establishes positive ignorance.

The opponents point out that when someone says "I do not know what you said," what in effect is being said is as follows: "I know that he said something; however, I do not know what it is. In other words, I have a general idea of the speaker's words, but the details of it are missing." It also implies a hope that in the future the specific objects of the words of the speaker might become known to us. In short, for the opponent, knowledge of ignorance in the example under consideration amounts to ignorance of specific details.

The Advaitins do not accept this interpretation by the opponents. For them, the above example points to an association between ignorance and knowledge, and in it the experience of ignorance may be construed as having a reference to specific details from one perspective. When one says, "I do not know what you said," the ignorance with respect to the statement of the speaker is known directly at the time when the statement is made. They further point out that such a cognition would be inexplicable if the cognition of ignorance did not involve a cognition of the object to be cognized. Therefore, when the object is cognized, its prior ignorance must also be cognized simultaneously, and the object so manifested is perceived by the witness-consciousness.

The difference between the two positions may be summed up as follows: For the opponents, the difference between such a positive ignorance and an absence of knowledge consists in the fact that absence of an object cannot be known without reference to the object whose absence is being cognized. The Advaitins, on the other hand, maintain that perceiving positive ignorance does not need such a knowledge of the counterpositive.

It seems to me that the Advaitins, in the case of the second witness perception, only demonstrate that it does not refer to the absence of knowledge, because such an interpretation, as shown earlier, would lead to a contradiction. They have shown that since ignorance is not the absence of knowledge, it must be a positive entity. There is no other direct argument in favor of this thesis.

The Third Witness Perception

The Advaitins give "I did not so long know of anything" (*etāvantaṃ kālaṃ na kiṃcid avediṣam*) as an instance of the third witness perception. That is, everyone recollects after deep sleep that she slept soundly and did not know anything during deep sleep.

It is important to remember here that in "I slept soundly and I did not know anything," "the not-knowing of anything" is only known upon waking up. Since the subsequent memory would be impossible without the initial experience, it must have been known during the state of sleep itself. Accordingly, for the Advaitins, the not-knowing is a case of memory; it is not and cannot be an instance of inference.

The Naiyāyikas, on the other hand, maintain that it is a case of inference. Although the self exists in deep sleep, it does not know anything then. One becomes aware of such an absence of knowledge by means of reasoning that assumes the following form: The self in deep sleep is characterized by the absence of knowledge because of the nonavailability of the conditions of knowledge (the self, the conjunction of the self with the mind, and the conjunction of the mind with the body). Availability of these means is essential; there must be a conscious experience or the subsequent memory of it would be impossible. Since some of these means (viz., the conjunction of the self with the mind and the conjunction of the mind with the body) are not available, the seeming recollection of not-knowing anything must be a case of inference.

The Naiyāyikas argue that what we have here is actually an inference of the following sort: While I was in deep sleep, I (*pakṣa*, i.e., the subject term of the conclusion and, thus, the minor term of the syllogism)[59] possessed (copula) the absence of knowledge (the *sādhya*, i.e., the predicate term of the conclusion and, thus, the major term), because of either:

> being in a special state, i.e., deep sleep (*avasthāviśeṣavattvāt*)
>
> OR
>
> possessing the absence of the causal conditions necessary for knowledge (*jñānasāmagrīvirahavattvāt*)
>
> OR
>
> not, as a rule, remembering having had any knowledge (*jñānavattayā niyamena asmaryamāṇatvāt*).

The Advaitins provide a refutation of this inference. To begin with, they raise the question: How is the subordinate clause of the conclusion established? That is to say, how is it established that I was in deep sleep? Deep sleep is by definition that state in which there is no cognition. But this precisely is the predicate of the conclusion (*sādhya*) and has to be established. The major term of the inference cannot be the same as the minor term, because the proposition expressed in the conclusion would then become "when I am in deep sleep, I am in deep sleep" or "when I have no cognition, I have no cognition," in which case the conclusion would be a mere tautology and the argument trivial. Also, the first middle term (*hetu*), i.e., being in the state of deep sleep, means "having absence of all cognitions," which is the same as the major term. The inference, therefore, amounts to: I, in the state of deep sleep, possess the absence of all cognition, because I possess the absence of all cognition. Therefore the inference is circular, i.e., the inference commits the fallacy of *petitio principii.*

Likewise, the second middle term—i.e., possessing the absence of some of the causal conditions necessary for knowledge—can only be proved after—not before—proving the predicate (possession of the absence of knowledge). How does one know that the necessary causal conditions for knowledge are not all present? This can be inferred only from the possession of the absence of all knowledge. But the absence of all knowledge is here inferred from the absence of some of the conditions necessary for knowledge. Hence, the inference commits the fallacy of mutual dependence (*anyonyāśraya doṣa*), inasmuch as the establishment of the (second) middle depends upon establishing the major and the establishment of the major upon the (second) middle.

The next question before us is: How is one to know of the nonavailability of the conditions of knowledge during sleep? This can only be established by an appeal to an experience that knows them both. The Advaitins maintain that no such experience is available. The subject of the conclusion (the self in deep sleep) can be said to be in deep sleep only if there is a perception of the possession of the absence of knowledge. No such perception, however, is available in deep sleep. Thus, the argument commits the fallacy of an unproven middle term, because the second middle term, which asserts the nonavailability of the complete set of necessary conditions for knowledge, can be inferred only after the subsequent judgment that "I knew nothing then." Moreover, during deep sleep nescience modifies itself into its own form, and so modified it is manifested by the witness-consciousness, which in itself is consciousness reflected in the modification of nescience. Upon awakening, the modification of ignorance is destroyed and only residual impressions remain. These residual impressions give rise to the recollection of ignorance in the subsequent awakened state, which is expressed by the judgment "I did not know anything," very much like any other memory cognition that we experience.[60]

There is a difference of opinion among the Advaitins regarding the nature of "I did not know anything" (*na kiṃcid avediṣam*) and "I slept happily" (*sukham aham asvāpsam*). These differences are primarily a function of whether one construes the mode of nescience to be indeterminate (*nirvikalpaka*) or determinate (*savikalpaka*). A mode (be it of the inner sense or of nescience) is indeterminate when it is not conceptual and has no linguistic articulation, determinate when it is linguistic and conceptual.

For the Vivaraṇa school, the judgment "I knew nothing and I slept happily," is an instance of recollection resulting from the residual impression of the indeterminate experience during deep sleep. In the state of deep sleep, there is the ignorance, the pleasure (*sukha*), and the witness-consciousness, each with its own mental mode, giving rise to the remembrance (*parāmarśa*) under consideration.[61] In the state of deep sleep everything merges into undifferentiated nescience; the subject-object distinction disappears. Such an ignorance is neither different from nor the same as the witness-consciousness. Since all apperceiving is done by the "I," it alone can remember the subsequent state. The question is:

What is the status of "I" in the state of deep sleep? The "I," or the ego that disappears in sleep, reappears upon waking up. The ego shares quite a few characteristics with the self, e.g., it is subtle like the self and one cannot conceive of the ego as existing apart from the self. Accordingly, the term "I" is used to signify the self.[62]

For Sureśvara, on the other hand, the above recollection is not an instance of memory. Deep sleep, for him, is a state of bare ignorance in which there is no empirical cognition. Such an ever-present ignorance cannot account for the recollection of dreamless sleep upon waking up.

> The cognition, following deep sleep, "I did not know anything" is not memory, [because] the self having no distance in [and so no relation to] space and time [the same is true also of the ignorance belonging to the self]. The self does not perceive the past ignorance. It neither perceives the past time [as past] nor the future time [as future]. All material objects are dependent on the other [i.e., *Brahman*] and so "I did not know anything" must be [not memory but] imagination. [The witness-consciousness perceives it.][63]

Sureśvara argues that since no mental mode is involved in the state of deep sleep, there cannot be any subsequent memory judgment upon waking up. Ignorance, being beginningless, cannot be a cause of anything because a cause must be an event in time. So a person, upon waking, has witness-experience of nescience. Thus, this experience is not indeterminate; it is a determinate experience (*vikalpa*).

Ānandagiri, following the Yoga system, explains *vikalpa* as *śabdajñānānupātī vastuśūnyo vikalpaḥ*: "it is a kind of cognitive consciousness that results from the knowledge generated by words though devoid of corresponding object." The determinate experience of nescience in deep sleep is not mere lack of knowledge, rather it has something positive for its object. Accordingly, Ānandagiri argues that nescience in the deep sleep state possesses the characteristic of determinacy. But how can it be so if there are no words in the deep sleep state?

Madhusūdana, however, contends that these characteristics cannot be experienced in nescience, because there is no "I" (*aham*). Although the self is present, there is no "I" because the "I" is not the self. He gives two inferences to prove that the "I" (*aham*) is not the self (*anātman*):

1. "The object 'I' is not-self, for it is the object of the cognition 'I,' as is the body" (*ahamarthaḥ anātmā, ahaṃpratyayaviṣayatvāt, śarīravat*)."

2. "The object 'I' is other than the self, for it is designated by the word 'I,' as with the designatum of the word "*ahaṃkāra*," i.e., "the ego-

sense" (*ahamarthaḥ ātmānyaḥ, ahaṃśabdābhidheyatvāt, ahaṃkāraśabdābhidheyavat*).[64]

Nyāyāmṛta asks: Is the above recollection "I knew nothing" really an inference or is it an instance of memory? In the former case, what you can infer is only the absence of knowledge, not positive ignorance. In the second case, you cannot explain how memory is possible, because the absence of knowledge cannot leave behind traces necessary for memory.[65]

Madhusūdana in response points out that the recollection under consideration, i.e., "I did not know anything," is not, in all respects, a memory. The "I" is experienced, not remembered. The witness-consciousness has become "I," so to speak. There is no determinate mode (*viśiṣtavṛtti*), because the ego-sense does not persist in deep sleep.[66] Since there is no determinate mode, there cannot be a determinate cognition (*viśiṣtajñāna*). Therefore, the mode of nescience is indeterminate.[67] In order for it to become a determinate cognition, both of its components must be there, which is not available in this case. "I did not know anything" cannot describe a relationship between the "I" and ignorance, because though ignorance is apprehended by the witness during the deep sleep state, the "I" is not. That is why the resulting knowledge cannot be determinate; so it must be indeterminate. The judgment under consideration is memory with respect to its component that is qualified and not so with respect to ignorance as a whole. Brahmānandi further adds: "The same mental mode in one part, i.e., with regard to 'I,' is perceptual, but with regard to what is known by the witness [i.e., 'was happy'] is memory."[68] In other words, the perceptual judgment "I slept happily," for the Advaitins, is a complex cognition containing both presentation and representation; it is presentative insofar as the "I" is concerned; however, when viewed in its aspect of happiness, it is representative.[69]

Laghucandrika, on the other hand, accepts a determinate mode of nescience during the deep sleep state.[70] "[It is] *vikalpa* and not *nirvikalpaka* which is of the nature of memory. . . . The awareness 'I did not know' makes it a *vikalpa.*"[71] On this view, the perceptual experience of ignorance, like the perception of knowledge, has to be determinate. Three different components are manifested in it: the ignorance, its opposition to knowledge and its having an object; the other attributes of ignorance, e.g., the beginninglessness, positivity (*bhāvarupatva*), etc., are not perceived. Nescience is apprehended by the witness-consciousness;[72] its positivity, however, is not perceived but proved by the instruments of knowledge such as inference. A person, upon awakening, remembers the nescience that was perceived. Because it is remembered, its cognition must have been determinate.

According to the Advaitins, what happens is that ignorance is established by the witness. The absence of knowledge is known, nonperceptually, by nonperception (*anupalabdhi*, i.e., by the cognition "if knowledge were present, it would have been perceived"). But the knowledge of nonperception is established by the witness-perception of positive ignorance. To put it differently, the knowledge of ignorance is always associated with the absence of knowledge. Thus, in all instances where there is knowledge of ignorance, the inference to the absence of knowledge would be valid. "Nonperception" as the knowledge of the absence of knowledge can be inferred from positive ignorance.[73] Ignorance is the *vyāpya*[74] of the absence of knowledge: Wherever there is absence of the absence of knowledge, there is absence of ignorance.

In addition to perception, for the Advaitins, inference also proves the positive nature of ignorance. The clearest formulation of this proof is found in the Vivaraṇa tradition, which demonstrates the viability of nescience as a category, as standing for something positive and beginningless. The argument, in a nutshell, states that positive ignorance precedes all knowledge. In other words, a valid act of knowing is preceded by something else that is terminated by it. The reason adduced is that it is an instance of knowledge or knowing. All knowing manifests a thing that was not manifested earlier. A pitcher, previous to its being perceived, was unmanifest, was covered by a veil; perception removes the veil before manifesting it, very much like the light that manifests its object by removing the darkness that existed there earlier.[75]

A form of argument called postulation (*arthāpatti*) also proves that nescience is positive. It is the postulation of a fact to explain a given fact. *Vedānta Paribhāṣā* explains postulation as the process of knowing that renders a given fact meaningful by assuming something else.[76] For example, the Upaniṣads say "*brahman* is bliss." However, this bliss is not manifested at all times, e.g., the individual finite self is not manifested in its nature as bliss.[77] If there were no ignorance, *brahman* would have manifested itself in the full plentitude of its bliss. Nonmanifestation of bliss implies that it is obscured by ignorance. Such an ignorance must be positive in nature.

The Advaitins go to great lengths to show that ignorance is positive in order to underscore its difference from nonbeing. Nonbeing is unreal; it does not have an objective counterpart. It never becomes an object of experience.[78] Ignorance, though false, is not nonbeing. One of the important points that readers must never lose sight of in Advaita is that the appearance of falsity is a fact of experience. Ignorance is the material cause of the phenomenal world; its positive nature lends a degree of reality to it, albeit only empirical.

Before closing this section, I would like to remind my readers that the account of ignorance given above should not be taken to signify that positive ignorance and the absence of knowledge (*jñānābhāva*) are mutually exclusive, i.e., they cannot exist in the same experience. It is indeed true that for the Advaitins the absence of knowledge is known by nonperception (*anupalabdhi*) and ignorance is apprehended by the witness-consciousness. However, experiences, such as "I do not know the pitcher," contain *both* the absence of the knowledge of the pitcher *and* the knowledge of that absence. The former is known by nonperception and the latter by the witness-consciousness. In "I do not know the pitcher," although the consciousness conditioned by the pitcher is concealed, the pitcher is manifested along with the knowledge of its ignorance. For the Advaitins, in order to perceive the absence of the knowledge of a pitcher in me, I must have the knowledge of what constitutes a pitcher. So, there is no absence of the knowledge of a pitcher. In other words, a pitcher is manifested as unknown. Although unknown, it is not entirely unknown. If a pitcher were totally unknown, I could not now have the perceptual experience of the absence of the knowledge of the pitcher. Accordingly, the Advaitins repeatedly point out that the knowing of an object is preceded by the knowing of its previous unknownness[79] and that "everything known or unknown is an object of the witness-consciousness."[80] In other words, the witness-consciousness reveals everything either as known or as unknown.[81] Let us examine what the Advaitins have to say on this issue.

Objects as Known or as Unknown

So far we have seen that the Advaitins hold that, although ultimately an object is a projection of consciousness, it is capable of being known. Knowledge, in their view, simply reveals the object as it is, without constructing or transforming it; knowledge merely manifests its object. All cognition is either direct or indirect. With respect to the witness-consciousness, cognition is always direct. With respect to the object, cognition is either direct or indirect. When the object is directly known, as in "this is a chair," the knowledge of the object (the chair) is immediate. When the object is indirectly known, as in inferring that "the hill has fire because it possesses smoke," the knowledge of the fire is mediated by the perception of smoke. But all knowledge, regardless of whether it is immediate or mediate, is the result of a mental mode. To know an object means some sort of unveiling resulting in its revelation, and this revelation is the end of all epistemic endeavors. As with all our goals, this end may or may not be achieved: the knowledge we obtain of an object may be true or false.

For the Advaitins, there are two conditions that must be fulfilled in order for a thing to become an object of knowledge: a mental mode, through which the mind reaches out to the object, assumes its form, and becomes nondifferent from it, and consciousness reflected in the mental mode. Cognition of an object is not possible in the absence of both of these conditions. On the one hand, the mind, being superimposed on the witness-consciousness, is always related to it, with the result that the mental mode is directly revealed by the witness-consciousness. On the other hand, a cognition always points to an object. In the cognition of a chair, for example, the object of cognition is revealed by the witness-consciousness when the mind reaches out to the chair through the senses, assumes its form, and becomes nondifferent from it. The mental modification unveils the object resulting in its immediate cognition. This is what is meant by saying that an object is revealed by the witness-consciousness as known: specific cognitive acts are the result of the modification of primal nescience and are apprehended directly by the witness-consciousness.[82]

In the case of the cognition of an object,

> the incoming knowledge breaks in upon us as a modification of a dim background. If this position is not accepted, then the object will either be always known without any specific functioning of knowledge, or be always unknown in spite of such a function—neither of which is tangible or even plausible.[83]

This necessitates a consciousness that apprehends objects prior to the origination of a determined cognition. Such a consciousness does not apprehend the absence of a specific cognition prior to the generation of some specific knowledge, but subsequent to this generation such a specific cognition implicitly points to its object's past unknownness. Accordingly, the Advaitins appeal to a common experience that does not explicitly know the unknownness of a particular cognition before its origination, though such explicit unknownness is presupposed by our subsequent implicit knowledge of the previous absence of a specific cognition. Thus, what is initially known implicitly subsequently becomes known explicitly. The case of a blind man illustrates this point: "One who is born blind is not conscious of not seeing. But if such a man comes to see . . . he will have an explicit perception of the previous absence of seeing which will at the same time be re-cognition of the absence as that implicitly cognized during the absence."[84]

Accordingly, prior to my apprehending the object as known, the witness-consciousness apprehends the object as unknown. In the example under consideration, the witness-consciousness reveals the object as having been unknown prior to the perceptual experience of the chair. The Advaitins further claim that such an unknownness is not nonbeing; it is positive. Such a positivity in itself is an undifferentiated state of the perceptual act in question, which eventually gives rise to the perception of the chair. Thus, as long as I am perceiving the chair, the witness-consciousness in me reveals the chair *as known*. However, prior to the occurrence of the perceptual cognitive act, i.e., prior to my apprehending the chair, the chair exists *as unknown*, in the sense that the term "unknown" here, it seems to me, means that which is "inchoately known." In other words, unknownness is an incipient state of knownness. What holds good for this particular chair also holds good for everything else in the world. So, at any particular time t_1, the witness-consciousness knows a particular object or a set of objects as known, and all remaining objects as unknown while all those objects are in an incipient state of unknownness.

Let us further analyze the ramifications of the experience "the chair was not known before." Sureśvara, in this context, raises the following question: "If prior unknownness were established by true cognition, or from some other mark, or intrinsically, how then is knownness to be established?"[85] In other words, the question of "how the unknownness of a thing is established" must be answered. Additionally, three other questions arise: Who is the knower of this cognitive act? What is the nature of this cognition? Finally, what is the form of the unknownness in question?

The Advaitins argue that unknownness is logically prior to the functioning of any *pramāṇa* (means of true cognition), because unknownness can never be established with the help of any such means: "Unknownness is nowhere established by a *pramāṇa*, because it is already known, prior to any such proof [*pramāṇa*]."[86]

None of the causal means of cognition accepted by the Advaitins can apprehend prior unknownness; their function is to make the object known. The past unknownness cannot be revealed by perception because perception needs sense-object contact. Neither can unknownness be said to be the result of inference because there is no middle term by which it could be established. Therefore, there must be a consciousness prior to the origination of a *pramāṇavṛtti* (a mode of the means of true cognition), and this consciousness apprehends nescience without any assistance from a mode of the inner sense. Knowledge of an object through a mental mode and ignorance of that object cannot exist simultaneously; the two states are contradictory to each other. Thus, the object of the knowledge must exist as unknown before it can become an object of a mental mode.

According to the Advaitins, the chair appears to be veiled because pure consciousness, the substratum of the chair, is veiled by ignorance. Thus, the experience of the unknown is not a result of any means of true cognition. Since knowledge destroys ignorance, the chair as qualified by ignorance cannot become an object of a true cognition. Additionally, if unknownness were to be known by a true cognition, then we would be forced to admit prior ignorance of ignorance, thereby leading to infinite regress. There can be no ignorance of ignorance. Thus, it seems that in order to have knowledge of an object, an additional condition, apart from the two outlined at the beginning of this section, must be fulfilled: the witness-consciousness must apprehend the object as unknown. In other words, the witness-consciousness must apprehend ignorance as well as the object attached to it. Because ignorance is apprehended by the witness-consciousness, it is known; because there is no mental modification with respect to it, it is unknown.

The witness-consciousness is impartial; so, it is not equippped to handle the determination of perceived objects. Thus, the witness-consciousness must present the ego with an indeterminate field of perception. Since the function of the "I" is to determine objects in this indeterminate field of perception, it can express the positive homogeneous experience of the witness-consciousness only in negative terms. Therefore, the indeterminate field of perception must be given to the ego by the witness-consciousness before the ego can make any determination of the previously undetermined unknownness from the present knownness of the object it has determined. Ignorance is given to us; it cannot be established by any means of valid knowledge.[87] We have shown that the determinate form must necessarily arise out of an indeterminate object. The statement "I did not know it before" points to the transcendence of the prior unknownness of the object by its subsequent knownness. Regardless of whether an object is known by perception or by inference, the present knownness of a determined object points to its prior indeterminate unknownness.[88]

Prior to the generation of a mental modification, only pure consciousness exists. Hence, since the generation of a mental modification is a necessary condition for the determination of objects, pure consciousness cannot have a determinate object. Prior unknownness cannot have a determinate object either. Only the knowledge resulting from the intellect's subsequent generation of a mental mode can ever possess a determinate content. If this was not the case, it would be difficult to separate prior unknownness from the present knownness of an object.

If the chair were already known prior to its perception, it would not make sense to talk about its prior unknownness. Each and every instance of determinate cognition, in the final analysis, must be an instance of re-cognition by the intellect. This further implies that cognition and re-cognition must refer to the same object. A case can be made that we have instances of indeterminate recognition even at the empirical level. In a dark room, only darkness is known. If I switch on a light in the room, darkness no longer exists there. However, I still acknowledge it to be the room that was previously covered by darkness. This demonstrates that the darkness was previously known as an immediately perceived object. Likewise, the function of ignorance is to cover that which should have been patent and to make its appearance nonexistent.[89]

Additionally, we must keep in mind that knownness and unknownness are not intrinsic characteristics of an object. If that were the case, they would be revealed to everybody along with the object. This leads Murti to argue that "knownness" and "unknownness" are relational properties, generated out of a contrast between two states. "If this is conceded, we should further grant that the two termini of a relation must be known before the relation is known. The 'unknown' has to be apprehended in some way"[90] before "the known" can be known.

The point that the Advaitins are trying to make is as follows: Knowledge of an undifferentiated whole is necessary before the parts can be differentiated and, hence, known. Thus, the statement "I did not know the chair before" contains two components: consciousness (*cit*), which manifests ignorance in its undifferentiated form, and a mode of the inner sense that differentiates a particular object. Thus, knowing involves both omniscience as well as limitation; they are "intertwined in it."[91] An inquiry into the nature of the states that precede a particular cognition and the subsequent states that follow points to an unchanging pure awareness that reveals what is presented to it impartially. Mental modes depend on the pure awareness for their existence; however, the converse is not true. The witness-consciousness manifests both knowledge and ignorance. Both "I know" and "I am ignorant" are revealed by the witness-consciousness. The witness-consciousness is neutral; it manifests both knowledge and ignorance. Thus, it can be argued that it is indeed true that objects are revealed by the witness-consciousness, sometimes as known, other times as unknown. This is especially true of physical objects.

But what about mental states such as pleasure, pain and the like and illusory objects? Do they also, like physical objects, exist both as known and unknown? Or do they exist only as known?

Earlier a case was made to demonstrate that mental states last only as long as they are revealed. Nobody says, "I am happy, but I do not know it." Nor does one say, "I was sad, but I did not know it." I apprehend my happiness directly, as long as it lasts. In other words, my happiness is revealed to me only as known. Thus, it makes no sense to argue that mental states are revealed as unknown. That is, prior to its manifestation, there is no inchoate state or rudimentary form of the state of happiness. We saw earlier that, in the case of physical objects, "revealed as unknown" amounts to revelation through a reflexive cognitive act. However, with respect to feelings of pleasure and pain, it does not make sense to say that they are revealed as unknown. Still, the Advaitin argues that the witness-consciousness is aware of these feelings prior to their origination. It seems to me that by this they mean that the witness-consciousness is aware not only of present feelings of pleasure, pain, etc., but of all psychical states, even those that once existed but have now ceased to exist. In short, mental states at times are revealed actually and at other times are only potentially revealed. Thus, it may be argued that the "knownness" of mental states amounts to their being revealed actually and their "unknownness" points to their potential for revelation even before they arise.

An illusory object, say silver in a conch shell, on the other hand, though cognized, never comes in contact with the sense organ. So, the question arises, in what sense is the illusory silver known or unknown? It is said to be apprehended by a mode of nescience as a result of the contact between the sense organ and the presented datum of experience. Its apprehension consists in its being perceived. In this respect an illusory object is very much like feelings of pleasure and pain. But there is one important difference between the two. Whereas a mental state, such as happiness, is real as long as it lasts, an illusory object does not enjoy even this degree of reality. It only appears to exist. It does not have any existence before or after its appearance. Whereas one can say that the witness-consciousness reveals the illusory object, it , however, reveals the illusory object only as known. One cannot argue that it exists as unknown in either of the two senses outlined above.

The Advaitin analysis of illusory perception gives rise to another important contention: The witness-consciousness does not reveal only what is real; it also reveals what is false. In an illusory perception, consciousness, although one, is reflected in two mental modes: the consciousness conditioned by the "this" and consciousness conditioned by the "snake" (in the case of the illusory perception "this is a snake"). Since, on the one hand, an erroneous perception has a real content for its object and, on the other hand, has a nonreal content—the illusory object—it lacks invariable validity.[92] To put it differently, the witness-consciousness only reveals; *it does not concern itself with either the truth or the falsity of what it reveals.*[93]

Madusūdana raises two very interesting questions in regard to the truth or falsity of what is revealed by the witness-consciousness. He first asks: How can the lack of future contradiction in the case of "falsity" be apprehended, given that "falsity" means the possibility of future contradiction or sublation of an appearance? Second, he asks: Does not the Advaitin theory that all knowledge is intrinsically valid (*svataḥ pramā*) require that the witness-consciousness not only know the present mental modification (*vṛttijñāna*) but also know the future absence of its contradiction? How is the latter possible?

(1) The Vivaraṇa holds that the falsity of an illusory object, e.g., the silver in the seashell, is perceived by the witness-consciousness. In this instance, witness-perception assumes the form "silver appeared falsely" (*mithyā eva rajataṃ abhāt*). The opponents find this claim faulty.[94] They would argue as follows: "Since perception apprehends only what is present now, how can falsity—which is of the nature of 'being the counterpositive of negation for all time in the presented locus'—be perceived?"[95]

To put it differently, the opponent would point out that if to be false means to be what never was, is, or shall be, and since the future is yet to be, then how can the witness-consciousness perceive the future negation? In response, Madhusūdana argues:

> The ignorance located in the witness-consciousness as limited by "this" was transformed into the silver-appearance. When the truth of the locus is perceived, the absence of silverhood [in the shell] is determined by postulation. This negation is perceived by the witness which manifests everything related to it.[96]

The goal of Madhusūdana is to demonstrate that falsity is apprehended by the witness-consciousness. To that end, he points out that when the illusion is removed and one perceives the shell as a shell, he comes to know by "postulation" (*arthāpatti*) that it is not silver. In other words, the absence of silver or, better yet, of silverhood in the shell is known only after he comes to know that the present locus is really a shell. The entire process consists of three steps: first, it is manifested that the object is really a shell; then one determines by "postulation" the absence of silverhood in it; and finally, the knowledge obtained by "postulation" is manifested directly by the witness-consciousness.

The opponent is not yet convinced. He attempts to explain his point with the example of the sky (*ākāśa*) and argues as follows:

> In that case the witness-consciousness, which [as you say] apprehends all times [i.e., past, present, and future], should be able to apprehend the fact that such objects as the sky [which are perceived] cannot be the counterpositive of future negation [i.e., cannot be unreal, contrary to the Advaita position].[97]

The opponent believes that since the sky cannot be negated, it cannot serve as the counterpositive of future negations. Accordingly, it should be classified as ultimately real, which goes against the fundamental Advaitin thesis that *brahman* is the only reality. Madhusūdana in response states: "The witness manifests not everything—but only everything that is present [*vidyamāna*]. The negation of future contradiction is not present, and so cannot be apprehended by the witness."[98] In short, the witness-consciousness does not perceive all possible things; it only perceives that which is actually present. The witness manifests only that which is related to itself (*svasambandha*); it is not that which manifests or illuminates everything (*sarvābhāsaka*). In other words, the witness-consciousness does not apprehend things that have not yet come into being, i.e., the future objects.

(2) In the Advaitin view, the truth of a cognition is apprehended intrinsically. This thesis amounts to: whatever apprehends the locus of truth (*prāmāṇya*) also apprehends the truth. The locus of the truth is the mental modification (*vṛttijñāna*). The latter is apprehended by the witness. Therefore, the witness-consciousness also apprehends the truth. However, argues the opponent, the truth of a cognition cannot be apprehended without apprehending that its object will not be negated in the future. But how can the absence of negation in future be apprehended now?[99]

Madhusūdana, in response, points out that the truth that is said to be apprehended intrinsically (*svataḥ*) is what is needed for *pravṛtti*, i.e., for appropriate practice (*vyavahāra*), which requires that the witness-consciousness apprehend the fact that the object is not contradicted at the time of the practice. That the object cannot be contradicted in future is neither impossible nor can the absence of future contradiction be apprehended now. So, the witness-consciousness apprehends the truth only in the restricted sense of being uncontradicted at the time of practice (*vyavahārakālābādhyatvaṃ*).[100] It thus only apprehends the empirical truth, but not the ultimate truth.

So, the Advaitins conclude: A cognition may be either true or false. A true cognition is a modification of the inner sense; a false cognition is not. For the Advaitins, doubts and errors are due to ignorance and are dependent on the witness-consciousness insofar as ignorance itself is manifested by the latter. Though not accountable in terms of mental modes, they nevertheless need an explanation. The Advaitins maintain that these cognitions can be explained only as products of ignorance, the general cause of everything that appears.

The above analysis of the role of the witness-consciousness highlights the following features of the Advaitin epistemology:

1. Determinate knowledge presupposes ignorance, the homogeneous content presented to a consciousness that is different from the "I."

2. The "I" chooses and rejects. Thus, a distinction must be made between consciousness that chooses and relates, in other words, apperceives, and one that does not apperceive but simply apprehends.

3. The witness-consciousness apprehends, reveals, and illuminates whatever is presented to it.

4. The witness-consciousness is impartial; it reveals truth and falsity alike. It does not reject or choose. It is nonjudgmental and nonrelational.

5. No object is outside the range of consciousness. Everything is revealed by the witness-consciousness either as known or as unknown.

Toward a Reconstruction of the Role of the Witness-Consciousness in the Advaita Epistemology: Concluding Remarks

Before closing this chapter, I will raise and discuss some of the general questions that arise from the account that has been set forth so far: How is the witness-consciousness known? Must we believe in such a consciousness? Why is the concept of ignorance necessary? Is a theory of ignorance necessary for an adequate theory of knowledge? Is identity of cognition and content logically viable? What sense, if any, can we make of the Advaitin thesis that perception involves a "going out" of the inner sense and an assuming of the form of the object? How can a self-luminous entity be the locus of nescience? Additionally, how can ignorance at once reside in consciousness and conceal it? Why does pure consciousness associate itself with the inner sense? Why does it not bypass the inner sense and associate itself directly with the object? Why postulate a modification of the inner sense, and the senses?

I will begin my discussion by analyzing the question as to how we know that the alleged witness-consciousness in fact exists. How is it apprehended?[101] In general, the Advaitins accept six ways of arriving at a true cognition. So, the question before us is: Is there a means of true cognition (*pramāṇa*) by which the witness-consciousness is apprehended?

So far we have seen that the Advaitins maintain that the witness-consciousness is self-manifested or self-manifesting (*svayaṃprakāśa*); accordingly, it cannot be apprehended by any of the means of true cogntion. It cannot be established by perception. Perception belongs to the empirical realm; it is not equipped to prove the existence of a consciousness like the witness-consciousness. As one Advaitin puts it:

> [P]erception is of two kinds: external and internal. External perception cannot get even a glimpse of knowledge, etc., because external perception has no application to the self, and these, i.e., knowledge, etc., are recognized [by the opponent, the Naiyāyikas] as properties of the self. They cannot also be known by mental [i.e., inner] perception, for that would give rise to undesirable consequence.[102]

The undesirable consequence hinted at is, I think, the alleged problem of infinite regress.

The existence of the witness-consciousness cannot be proved by the remaining five means of knowledge either, because the objects known by them presuppose the existence of the self; they cannot be used to prove the existence of the self.

It cannot be known by another consciousness, because such reasoning will lead to an infinite regress of consciousness.

Nor can it be known by itself. The witness-consciousness cannot be an *object* of knowledge; it cannot become the content of true cognition (*pramāviṣaya*). It is the condition of the possibility of knowing anything. It is the seer of seeing and therefore cannot be seen as an object. It illuminates everything and therefore cannot be illumined by anything. Though it is manifested, it is not an object of knowledge. The self is the subject and cannot become both the subject and the object at once. Moreover, the self as the "I" is not the real self. The real self is pure consciousness; it is not consciousness of anything.

So, the Advaitins conclude that the witness-consciousness cannot be apprehended by any means of knowledge. The opponents therefore ask: How then is the witness-consciousness established? The opponents (the Naiyāyikas in this case) make the following point: Since the witness-consciousness is inaccessible to us by any of the recognized means, i.e., it cannot be known by any of the *pramāṇa*-s, it is not established by the scriptures either, for the scriptures do not tell us about anything other than either *jīva* or *brahman*, so it is better to conclude that there is nothing called the witness-consciousness.[103]

Does this imply that there is no witness-consciousness? It needs to be determined: What would happen if there were no witness-consciousness? The Advaitins point out that everyone ought to admit the witness-consciousness, because our experiences are accounted for in light of witness-consciousness. All of us accept mental states such as knowledge, desire, aversion, effort. These cannot be apprehended by any *pramāṇa.* Thus, if there were no witness-consciousness, nothing would be known; nothing would be manifested. Ignorance would not be apprehended, because it is manifested directly by the witness-consciousness. Anything that is directly manifested does not require a proof. Proofs are needed in order to make things that are concealed by ignorance known. If we admit proof for the existence of ignorance, then we must admit that ignorance itself is concealed by another ignorance, resulting in an infinite series of ignorance.

Additionally, in the absence of the witness-consciousness there will be no way to apprehend a cognition. A cognition cannot be said to be known by introspection, because in that case we would require a second cognition to reveal the original cognition, and a third cognition to reveal the second one, resulting in an infinite regress of cognitions.

If it is argued that the earlier cognition, while perishing, establishes the latter cognition, then the question would arise as to what is meant by the "state of perishing."

> Does the state of perishing of a cognition imply its existence or nonexistence, or something which is different from both? If it implies the "existence," then there would be simultaneity of two cognitions; if "nonexistence," then how can a cognition, itself nonexistent, be a perception [of the other]? If "neither existent nor nonexistent," then it will be indescribable, and will not be able to establish any knowledge.[104]

A cognition cannot be known by perception, because it would amount to arguing that the second perception is known by a third perception, and the third again by a fourth, resulting in the the simultaneous origin of an infinite number of cognitions. Such a verdict goes against our experience, which functions temporally.

A cognition cannot be known by inference either. It cannot be inferred either from the behavior of the knower or from the supposed mark of "knownness" in the object known because prior to cognition of the cognition, the behavior is not established. Only if knowledge, like a lamp, removes darkness, can it manifest an object; if the lamp is not manifested, the object also is not manifested. So, prior to achieving knowledge, neither the knownness of the object nor the behavior of the agent can be ascertained. Therefore, a cognition must be able to establish itself.

Thus, our experiences would be impossible if we did not admit a principle that, by being eternal, ubiquitous, and self-manifesting, can simultaneously establish all objects. The very denial of such a self presupposes its existence. All ontological and epistemological inquiries begin with it. The witness-consciousness is the basis of all knowledge. It is discovered regressively; it is that which remains when all knowing ceases to exist. Therefore, the witness-consciousness necessarily exists because in its absence there would be no way of accounting for our experiences. It is the basic presupposition of all knowledge. The very possibility of knowing anything rests on it. It is the necessary condition for the very possibility of judgments such as "I know" and "I do not know."

It may be argued that knowledge is not only a manifestation of its object; it is at the same time a conquest, a victory over ignorance. Just as light removes darkness, or just as when the light extends its scope the darkness recedes, we can say that with the progress of knowledge more and more ignorance is removed. Thus, it makes perfect sense to claim that to know a thing is also to know that prior to this knowledge the very thing was unknown. Accordingly, a thing enjoys unknown existence (*ajñātasattā*) prior to its being known; in other words, "unknown existence" points to the fact that a now manifested object, prior to its manifestation, was covered by ignorance. Thus, knowing implies previous ignorance, i.e., not-knowing.

Ignorance as not-knowing is not unique to Advaita Vedānta. Perhaps Western epistemologists construe ignorance as a simple lack of knowledge. The Naiyāyikas in Indian philosophy certainly construe it in this manner. They maintain that prior to knowing an object, its knowledge was absent, thereby affirming the Western conception of ignorance as simply the absence of knowledge. If one construes ignorance along these lines, then of course there is nothing interesting about ignorance. Accordingly, neither the Western epistemologists nor the Naiyāyikas recognize ignorance as a significant phenomenon.

The Advaita Vedānta school, however, has discovered here something of utmost importance. For them ignorance is not merely an absence of knowledge. It is something positive; it not only conceals the object that is unknown but in certain cases, e.g., in the case of perceptual illusion, it actually projects an illusory object to be superimposed on the real object that is out there. Such a conception of ignorance mandates an answer to the question: How is this positive ignorance known? The Advaitins respond by pointing out that I know my ignorance directly through the witness-consciousness. In other words, no modification of mind is required in the apprehension of ignorance.[105]

If the question "Why ignorance?" is asked, the Advaitins will answer it by appealing directly to our experience with the help of the following two arguments that they repeatedly adduce in its support:

(1) The very attempt of human beings to investigate the nature of ultimate reality presupposes our ignorance about it. The Advaitins call it "*avidyā*" or "*ajñāna.*" We seek to know only that of which we know we are ignorant. Ignorance, like knowledge, acquires its full significance in the context of the object to which it refers and the subject that it characterizes.

(2) Everybody at some time or other experiences ignorance in the form "I do not know," which bears testimony to the fact that ignorance is self-evident in character. When I say "I slept happily and did not know anything," not-knowing here refers to the obscuring of undifferentiated ignorance and not to an absence of all knowledge, because that would amount to equating ignorance with nonbeing. It signifies a unique kind of knowledge removable by the right apprehension, thus pointing to its difference from the negation of knowledge. Hence, ignorance is borne out by experience. Additionally, the experience "I do not know" presupposes that "I know that I do not know." This experience bears testimony to the fact that ignorance manifests consciousness and is, at the same time, manifested by consciousness.

The first argument tells us what ignorance is; the second informs us what ignorance is not. It is necessary to know a thing both ways if we are to know it in its entirety. These two arguments articulate ignorance positively and negatively. It is not merely assumed; it is given to us in our experience. Thus, we can safely conclude that any sound theory of knowledge must have a theory of ignorance; knowing implies previous ignorance.

That the theory of knowledge and the theory of ignorance mutually implicate each other is a most fascinating perspective about knowledge, but one that has been ignored by most epistemologists in the Western tradition with the exception of Plato and Socrates. As soon as one recognizes that knowledge and ignorance mutually implicate each other, one sees the relevance of the witness-consciousness. It is indeed true that certain parts of the Advaitin conception of ignorance require one to believe in certain other parts of their metaphysics, e.g., the thesis, namely, that the inner sense goes out and assumes the form of the object, thereby destroying the positive ignorance. How much of it one can appropriate into one's own thinking is independent of larger metaphysical questions and has no bearing on the fact that ignorance and knowledge indeed presuppose each other.

Before discussing what sense, if any, one can make of the Advaitin thesis that the perceptual process involves a "going out" of the inner sense and its assuming the form of the object, let us discuss briefly whether the Advaitin thesis of the identity of the cognition and the content is viable or coherent.

Regarding the identity of cognition and content, two points must be noted. First, to characterize the position of Advaita in this regard as one of affirmation of the identity of the cognition and the content is not entirely accurate. This is the case because the goal of Advaita is not to affirm the identity of the cognition and the content, but rather to demonstrate the nondifference of the cognizer-consciousness, the consciousness conditioned by the mental mode, and the consciousness conditioned by the object. Second, such identity or nondifference concerns the form, not the material content, of the object. To reiterate, in the perceptual process a mental modification assumes the form of the object. The inner sense, a passive instrument illumined by the witness-consciousness, effects the connection between the mental mode and pure consciousness. In short, the perceptual process takes place as follows: the object is presented; the inner sense goes out and assumes the form of the object; this modification is presented to the witness-consciousness, which in turn illumines it. Thus, it is not consciousness that assumes the form of the object, but rather it is consciousness reflected in the mental mode that gives rise to the cognition of an object. Accordingly, in the perception of a pitcher, for example, consciousness reflected in the mental mode of the pitcher generates the cognition "I know the pitcher."

The question is: Can one meaningfully talk about the Advaitin claim that in the perception of an object the inner sense goes out and assumes the form of the object just as water flows into a field and assumes the form of the field? This claim is a conjunct of two separate assertions: (a) the inner sense goes out, and (b) the inner sense assumes the form of the object. These two assertions are, it seems to me, mutually independent, so it is perfectly plausible to reject (a) without rejecting (b).

I will begin with (a). If it is assumed that the mind, in fact, goes out in the perception of an object, is the "going out" of the mind actual or metaphorical? Since the mind is taken to be a product of matter and structurally participates in the collection of the raw material of perception, it is often taken literally. One Advaita scholar notes: "The Advaitic theory is that it is the function of mind to go out to the object, take on its form, and manifest it. This 'going out' is not metaphorical, but actual, as the mind in Indian thought is a product of the matter."[106] Another Advaita scholar makes the same point when he reiterates: "The function of mind is to go out to the object through the senses and manifest it. It is able to do this because of its capacity to reflect intelligence. Since mind is considered in Indian thought to be a product of primal nature [*prakṛti*] and therefore material, the 'going out' of the mental psychosis[107] is not metaphorical, but actual."[108] It must be noted here that, for the Advaitins, the visual sense organ is capable of working only on reaching/contacting the object (*prāpyakāri*).

The Nyāya school of Indian philosophy believed in a similar theory, except that on their theory the inner sense does not go out, but rather it is the visual sense organ that goes out to meet the object. For them, the going out of the visual sense accounts for its difference from the other sense organs, e.g., the auditory, tactual, gustatory, and olfactory. On the one hand, visual sensation is not produced in the body, but out there in contact with the object. On the other hand, in the case of auditory, gustatory, and olfactory perceptions, the sensations are produced in the body. For example, when I hear a sound, the sound travels in succession and strikes the eardrums. Likewise, in touching, tasting, and smelling, the sensations are produced in the body. Therefore, the Naiyāyikas maintain that only the visual sense goes out to meet the object, other senses do not. The Advaitins, on the other hand, maintain that even in auditory perception the sense goes out to meet the object, because otherwise we would not be able to determine the direction and distance of various sounds. The Nyāya theory cannot account for the direction and distance of various sounds. So, the Advaitins conclude that it makes more sense to say that in auditory perception the sense of hearing goes out and reaches the object.

It must be pointed out that the above conception of the sense organ going out and meeting the object is not unique to Indian philosophy. Before the theories of modern physiology of perception were developed, many Ancient cultures held such a view. The Greeks, for example, held a similar view; they maintained that light rays travel from the object to the visual organ, the visual organ goes out and establishes contact with the object, and sensation is the joint product of those interactions.[109]

Why the Advaitins held the view they did is easy to speculate. Two reasons might be adduced here.

First, the Advaitins were concerned with the question "How is it that the object is there at a distance, yet I am able to see it from here?" What bridges this distance? If the image is produced on my retina as a result of the stimuli traveling from the object to where I am located, then the question would arise: "Why do I perceive the object to be out there and not in my brain?" This is an important issue in the psychology of perception. Thus, the Advaitins had a nice, though scientifically incorrect, answer—

the mind itself goes out there; the form I perceive is not just in my brain but is also out there in the thing perceived.

Second, in the Advaita theory of perception, although both subject and object are necessary for perception, priority is given to the subject; the object is subordinated to the subject. It is indeed true that in the perception of a pitcher, for example, both the pitcher and the perceiving subject become nondifferent. Nondifference in this context should not be taken to signify a literal oneness, but rather that objects qua objects do not have any independent existence apart from the subject. Since objects are superimposed on the consciousness conditioned by them, the existence of objects is none other than the existence of the consciousness that underlies them.[110] This also explains how in the perception of a pitcher, the pitcher is given as "immediate." Thus, notwithstanding the fact that all the referents in a cognitive relation—i.e., the subject, the object and their relation—are nonreal in themselves, from an empirical point of view the subject and the object do not enjoy the same status in a knowledge situation; the subject dominates: "The supreme importance of the *vṛtti* of the mind in perception proves the dominance of the subject-element. But the subject (mind) can pour itself into the object and incorporate it in itself. . . . It is much easier to conceive the *out-going* of the mind intelligized by the conscious self to the object than the *in-coming* of the unconscious object to the mind."[111]

We now know that both the Indian and the Greek conceptions are physiologically incorrect. According to modern science, it is the other way around: visual stimulus travels from the object, hits the retina, and produces an image there, thereby stimulating some portion of the brain, resulting in the perception of the object. This scientific account should not be taken to imply that either the retina or the brain is simply a passive receptor. It is more accurate to say that both actively shape the stimulus.

Assuming that the Western scientific theory is correct, there is still the issue of how to account for the phenomenon of visual perception. If the stimulus produces an image here, inside the brain, how is it that we perceive the thing as being out there? Perhaps there are two kinds of answers that the modern physiologists would adduce: (1) There is the Kantian answer, viz., that the mind imposes the form of space on the sensations, resulting in a form of intuition in which the mind arranges its sensations. This theory, however, is not compatible with strict realism because it implies that the perceived object is partly a construct of the mind. (2) The other account would be that distance is not perceived by any one sense organ, viz., vision, but results from the cooperation of many sense organs—vision together with touch and motion. This was Berkeley's theory—an infant looking up to the moon tries to catch the moon because the infant has not yet developed the ability to integrate visual with tactile and muscular sensations.

It seems to me that even if the inner sense does not travel to the object in perception, the inner sense in perception can assume the form of the object; an image is presented there without the notion of traveling. We find this in the writings of Aristotle as well as in those of Thomas Aquinas. Aristotle categorically declares that in sense perception we receive only the form and not the matter of the object, because a sense

> has the power of receiving into itself the sensible forms of things without the matter. This must be conceived of as taking place in the way in which a piece of wax takes on the impress of a signet ring without the iron or gold; we say that what produces the impression is a signet of bronze or gold, but its particular metallic constitution makes no difference; in a similar way the sense is affected by what is coloured or flavored or sounding, but it is indifferent what in each case the substance is.[112]

Even in the most rudimentary perception, the form (universal) is present to a degree. Intellect is pure potentiality; it takes on the form of the object without taking on its matter.[113]

Aquinas argues along the same lines when he says that sense experience is the primary form of experience. Every material object possesses an intelligible form or structure. The senses facilitate contact between the mind and the object, thereby supplying the mind with material for the ideas.

> Sense is a receptive power, the subject of change by an external principle. This external principle of action is what is directly perceived by sense, and the senses are diversified according to the diversity found there.
>
> There are two sorts of immutation, physiological and psychological. The former comes about by the physical reception of the agent in the patient, the latter according to a certain spiritual reception. Sensation requires, like the latter process, the entrance into the sense organ of a likeness of, or relation to, the sensible thing.[114]

Thus, upon receiving sense impressions, the eye undergoes a physical alteration. However, the process of alteration is not limited to a simple physical change. If physiological immutation alone sufficed, all natural bodies would have sensations when they underwent alteration.[115] In sensation, a sensible form is received. Aquinas calls it "spiritual immutation"; it is a kind of psycho-physical process.

Like Aristotle, he distinguishes between two powers of the mind: active intellect (the *intellectus agens*) and the intellect-able-to-become (*intellectus possibilis*).[116] The first one manifests the images of the object that the senses apprehend. To put it differently, it first illumines the universal element of the image and then abstracts the potential universal element and produces an impression (*specie impressa*) in the *intellectus possibilis*, which reacts to this, resulting in the expression of the universal concept in its entirety (*species expressa*). The mind has universal concepts; it apprehends the forms of things. Accordingly, Aquinas concludes that mind, or what he calls the "intellect," has the power of abstracting from the object a form, that form is the first concept. When I perceive a cow, the mind has abstracted from it a shape, the structure, the first concept of the cow; this is followed by a second abstraction, the definition, the concept in the strict sense.

What is relevant in the context of Advaita is not so much the second abstraction, but rather the notion that the mind has the power of abstracting a form from material content. Thus, the mind possesses the form, not the material content; the matter is out there. If it is maintained that the mind also possesses the matter, then there should actually be a cow in my mind. However, the actual cow is out there; the cognition of the cow is the form that the mind has abstracted from the actual cow. I do not believe that the Advaitins would object to such a rendering of the perceptual process provided we accept that the mind (the mental mode) abstracts the form from the object and transports this form to the inner sense, which then presents the mental mode to the witness-consciousness, which in turn illumines it. Such an account makes the ancient theory plausible by eliminating the old presupposition of the mind traveling out to the object and becoming one with it.[117] Thus, there is no harm in subscribing to the theory that in perception the form of the object is abstracted by the mind or the inner sense, without also subscribing to the Advaita conception that in the perceptual process the inner sense goes out and assumes the form in the same way as water flows into a field and assumes the form of the field.

In response to the objection that it is absurd to suppose that the inner sense assumes the form of the object, Madhusūdana points out that "assuming the form of the object" refers to the capacity of a mental mode to remove the veil of nescience that prevented manifestation of the object.[118] We have seen that a mental mode cannot, by itself, illuminate objects, but that it leads to illumination on account of its association with pure consciousness. Also, it has been established that manifestation occurs only to the cognizer whose mental mode comes in contact with the object. As a result, when an object is revealed to me, it is not necessarily simultaneously revealed to others. The nondifference of the consciousness underlying the cognizer, the mental mode, and the object, *taken together*, constitutes the sufficient condition for manifestation of an object to the perceiver. Mental modes also account for the mediacy of consciousness, in that everything becomes revealed by coming in contact with them. In itself, consciousness is always self-luminous and self-established: one without a second.

One of the questions discussed by the opponents of Vedānta is: How can a self-luminous and self-established consciousness be the locus of ignorance? They point out that it does not make sense to say that ignorance resides in pure consciousness (i.e., in knowledge). In other words, if consciousness is self-luminous and nescience is of the nature of darkness, how can these two things, opposed to each other as light and darkness, coexist? The answer to this question demonstrates the relevance of, and justifies the existence of, the witness-consciousness. The uniqueness of Advaita lies in asserting that ignorance and consciousness are not contradictory to each other. Consciousness appears *as* the witness-consciousness. Ignorance at once manifests the witness-consciousness and is manifested by it.

In this context, one must keep in mind the important distinction that the Advaitins make between *brahman*-knowledge (*svarūpajñāna*) and modal knowledge (*vṛttijñāna*). It is indeed true that, for the Advaitins, knowledge is opposed to ignorance. However, when Advaitins speak of knowledge as opposed to ignorance, they are talking about modal knowledge but *not* about *brahman*-knowledge. "The witness-consciousness, even if it is knowledge of the locus and the counterpositive [of ignorance], does not destroy the positive ignorance, for the witness-consciousness appears as having ignorance for its object."[119] Consciousness in itself is not opposed to ignorance; it rather manifests ignorance. In fact, ignorance is one of the three objects of the witness-consciousness. Therefore, the two are not opposed to each other. The witness-consciousness is self-revealed;[120] the modifications of the inner sense account for variations in knowledge.[121]

Pure consciousness or *brahman* reveals ignorance; therefore, it is not opposed to ignorance. *Brahman* reveals ignorance, but this very revelation amounts to concealment of *brahman*. "The concealing ignorance, even if it covers up the nature of *brahman* does not conceal the witness-consciousness which manifests it. If this were not so, ignorance would be without the witness-consciousness and so could not be established."[122] The concealing ignorance covers up the nature of *brahman* but does not conceal the nature of the witness-consciousness, which manifests that ignorance. For if it did so, then the ignorance, being rendered witness-less, could not be established. *Brahman* is concealed by the very ignorance it reveals.

By an analysis of the object and the locus of ignorance, the Advaitins further elaborate on how ignorance conceals *brahman* or pure consciousness. The question is: What is the object of ignorance? An object, say a pitcher, that is manifested by a valid means of knowledge does not constitute an object of ignorance, because it is manifested as known by a means of true cognition. However, whatever is apprehended by the witness-consciousness as unknown, irrespective of whether it is a pitcher or something else, can constitute the object of ignorance. The witness-consciousness does not destroy ignorance; rather, it establishes ignorance. Thus, ignorance not only resides in the self; it also obscures the self.

Now, what is the locus of ignorance? To whom does the ignorance belong? For the Vivaraṇa school, the object and the locus of ignorance are the same. They draw the attention of their readers to the "audacity of ignorance": ignorance tries to conceal the very thing that proves its existence, i.e., pure consciousness. The question before us is: What is the object of ignorance, i.e., of "not-knowing," in the perceptual experience "I do not know the pitcher"? Is it the pitcher? According to Vivaraṇa, it is not. Why? Because the function of ignorance is to conceal, and only that which can show itself can be meaningfully said to be concealed. A material object, like a pitcher, cannot show itself. The object of ignorance here is consciousness that is conditioned by the pitcher, and not pure consciousness.

The Advaitins explain the dependence of ignorance on *brahman* in a way analogous to the dependence of the demon Rāhu on the moon, which it conceals (during the lunar eclipse according to Hindu mythology), or, alternately, very much like clouds covering the sun. Rāhu tries to conceal the very moon that manifests it and the clouds try to hide the sun that makes them manifest. However, neither of them can totally conceal that which makes perception of them possible to begin with. Likewise, ignorance is manifested by the very same consciousness that it tries to conceal. Does Rāhu completely conceal the moon? Or do the clouds cover the sun completely? They do not, because in that case they themselves would remain unknown. If ignorance completely concealed consciousness, there would be no knowledge of ignorance, and a person would not be able to say "I am ignorant." Ignorance *tries* to conceal consciousness, but in the process is manifested by that very consciousness.

Thus, ignorance accounts for all empirical distinctions; it explains the apparent manyness of pure consciousness (many selves) and, accordingly, is the cause of the distinctions among the knower, the object to be known, and knowledge of that object. Ignorance veils the self and transforms itself into diversity of kinds: "Of these, the transformation of nescience which resides in the body and is called the internal organ, being prompted by merit and demerit, goes out through the channels of the eyes, etc., pervades suitable objects like the pot, and becomes of their respective forms."[123] If the question is asked, "Why does pure consciousness associate itself with the inner sense (the internal organ)?" the Advaitins would point out, in response, that the inner sense is required for the sake of associating consciousness with an object. There cannot be any knowledge without an object. Objects give knowledge its content, which (content) in turn is apprehended by knowledge. In other words, the object conditions the knowledge.

At this juncture, one might wonder: Does not the association of pure consciousness with the object contaminate its purity and, accordingly, make it impure? Why does it associate itself with the inner sense? Why does not pure consciousness bypass the inner sense and associate itself directly with the object? Why postulate the inner sense, the mental mode, the senses, and so on? It must be noted here that self-revealing pure consciousness, as a matter of fact, never becomes the object of any awareness. It does not contain any internal differentiations and diversities. Therefore, it cannot be both the subject and the object at the same time. It only appears to be the object when associated with the modifications of ignorance. Only these modifications have the capacity to become the content of knowledge. Consciousness, on the other hand, is self-certifying. It does not need any proof; it is immediate. The immediacy of consciousness, it must be remembered, differs from the immediacy of a perceptual object. The immedicacy of consciousness, unlike the immediacy of a perceptual object, does not require any mediation; it is ever illumined. An object is not immediate, it is made immediate by the uncovering of the veil of unknownness. Therefore, the immediacy of perceptual objects is conditional, being mediated by a mental mode.

Consciousness manifests everything, including ignorance. However, when the very same consciousness goes through a mental mode, it destroys ignorance. Thus, consciousness in itself does not destroy anything; it is consciousness that is conditioned by the object that destroys ignorance, not the witness-consciousness.

Although the witness-consciousness establishes ignorance, it is not a cognizer (*pramātā*); it is a seer (*dṛṣṭā*). That is why witness-knowledge is not "true cognition" (*pramājñāna*) in its technical sense. The distinction that the Advaitins make between awareness and knowing must be noted in this context. Witness-knowledge is a kind of awareness; cognizer-knowledge is discovery of a hitherto unknown object. A true cognition is ascertainment of a previously unknown object. The witness-consciousness establishes its object, it apprehends the object it establishes, but the object it apprehends is not a previously unknown object. The witness-consciousness does not manifest its object by destroying the ignorance of that object; that is true only of a true cognition. Accordingly, the Advaitins conclude that the witness-consciousness's knowledge is not opposed to ignorance; it is modal knowledge that is opposed to ignorance. This explains the difference between the object established by the witness-consciousness (*sākṣinsiddhavastu*) and the object established by a means of true cognition (*pramāṇasiddhavastu*).

The function of a means of true cognition is to destroy the ignorance of an unknown object and to manifest it. So, Vivaraṇa states: "Everything is an object of the witness-consciousness, either directly or indirectly." In the perceptual experience "this is a table," "this table" is not an object of the witness-consciousness directly; it is directly an object of either knowledge or ignorance. However, both knowledge and ignorance alike are apprehended by the witness-consciousness. So, the Advaitins argue, everything in the world falls into two classes: the known and the unknown. Regardless of whether an object is known or unknown, it is an object of the witness-consciousness. The witness-consciousness manifests an unknown object as unknown, a known object as known. This thesis encapsulates the Advaita idealism. Berkeley was concerned about the status of unknown objects. If everything exists as an idea, then how can unknown objects be accounted for? There are many objects of which I have no awareness whatsoever. Advaita contends that even as unknown, they are the objects of the witness-consciousness. There is no unperceived illusory object. Berkeley's *esse est percipi* applies to illusory objects, say for instance, the illusory silver. It is directly perceived by the witness-consciousness. Empirically real silver is perceived by the cognizer. Unknown objects qua unknown are the objects of the witness-consciousness; known objects qua known are the objects of the witness-consciousness. So everything is an object of the witness-consciousness; however, not everything is an object of a mental mode.

So far, we have seen that the Advaitins provide phenomenological data for admitting the witness-consciousness, over and above the individual cognizer. The nature and essence of such an awareness still remains to be determined. Opponents raise a number of questions regarding the essence of such a consciousness: Is it of the nature of a subject? If it is of the nature of the subject, then is it to be the same as or different from the individual self? From *Īśvara*? From *ātman*? Let us next examine what the Advaitins have to say on these metaphysical issues.

5

Sākṣin and Advaita Metaphysics

Thus far we have seen that the witness-consciousness is a necessary presupposition of all knowing; it makes knowledge possible and forms the starting point of all epistemological inquiries in Advaita Vedānta. The nature of such a consciousness is yet to be determined. Questions immediately arise: What is *sākṣin*? What kind of an entity is it? Is it the same or different from the cognizer? Is it one or many? Additionally, we must assess its relationship with other metaphysical entities that we find in this system, e.g., *Īśvara* (God), *ātman* (self, pure consciousness), and *jīva* (the individual self), and evaluate its status vis-à-vis these metaphysical entities.

Although all Advaitins subscribe to the basic nondualistic thesis of *brahman* as the only reality and agree that *brahman* appears as *Īśvara* and *jīva* on account of nescience, they disagree regarding *brahman*'s exact relation with *Īśvara* and the *jīva*. Śaṃkara makes a distinction between two kinds of seeing: contingent seeing and eternal seeing. The former seeing is attributed to the *jīva* and the latter seeing to the eternal and immutable self—*brahman*. Śaṃkara, however, provides his readers with only general guidelines as to how *brahman* appears as multiple *jīva*-s. He nowhere develops the ramifications of this relationship. He seeks to explain the nature of the *jīva* and its relation to *Īśvara* by means of a number of hypotheses, of which three are worth mentioning: (1) that the *jīva* is consciousness as reflected in the inner sense,[1] (2) that the *jīva* is an appearance,[2] and (3) that the *jīva* is consciousness as *limited* by the inner sense.[3] Śaṃkara himself does not show any preference for any one of these hypotheses. Furthermore, the vague and nonuniform nature of these hypotheses complicates the issue by giving rise to diverse interpretations. The fluid nature of the key concepts—e.g., the concept of nescience around which the entire Advaita system revolves—further compounds the problem of interpretation.

Śaṃkara's followers systematized these diverse interpretations into three different theories corresponding to the three hypotheses given above: (1) *Pratibimbavāda* (the reflection theory), (2) *Ābhāsavāda* (the semblance theory), and (3) *Avacchedavāda* (the limitation theory). What kind of an entity *sākṣin* is, and whether it is one or many, become largely a function of the conceptions of *jīva* and *Īśvara* and of the relation that exists between them in these three theories. I am going to begin my discussion with an analysis of these theories. It seems to me that, although the followers of Śaṃkara clearly bring out the epistemological ramifications of the notion of the witness-consciousness, they do not make the nature and status of this consciousness clear. The question arises: What accounts for this lack of clarity? I will discuss this issue in the concluding section of this chapter.

Sākṣin, *Īśvara*, and *Jīva*

(1) *Pratibimbavāda*: Both Padmapāda and Prakāśātman, in their respective commentaries, *Pañcapādika* and *Pañcapādikāvivaraṇa*, advocate *pratibimbavāda.* They both regard *Īśvara* and the *jīva* as reflections of pure consciousness. They agree that nescience superimposed on *brahman* receives its reflection, like a mirror reflects the image of a face superimposed upon its surface. *Īśvara* is the pure consciousness that serves as the prototype (*bimba*), and *jīva* is the pure consciousness that is reflected (*pratibimba*) in nescience and its modifications. Just as the face reflected in the mirror is the same as the actual face, similarly, the *jīva* reflected in nescience is the same as the prototype. In essence, both the reflected image and the prototype are nondifferent, even though they appear to be different. One realizes that they are nondifferent when one realizes that the *jīva* is only a reflection of pure consciousness. Just as the reflection of the sun or the moon appears to be different depending on whether the water is calm or disturbed, clean or dirty, similarly, the reflection of pure consciousness varies according to the level of nescience in which it is reflected. Thus, they argue that the *jīva,* as the reflected image, is as real as the prototype. Such an interpretation allows the Advaitins to maintain that, being the prototype, *Īśvara* is not influenced by nescience in any manner whatsoever. Accordingly, the defects of nescience are not present in the prototype, but only in the reflected image—the *jīva.* As the reflected image, the *jīva* is under the spell of nescience and is controlled by it. For this group of Advaitins, the witness-consciousness is pure consciousness that is common to both the prototype (*bimba*) and the reflected image (*pratibimba*). It is one, not many.

Sarvajñātman in *Saṃkṣepaśārīraka* explains *pratibimbavāda* slightly differently. He prefers to hold that both *Īśvara* and *jīva* are reflections of pure consciousness. Pure consciousness reflected in nescience is *Īśvara*, while the same pure consciousness reflected in the inner sense is *jīva*.[4] On this account, *Īśvara*, as a reflected image, is subject to the defects of nescience. When characterized by nescience, the self is construed as a witness; when identified with the intellect, it is taken to be the knower.[5] Nescience, the cause of the universe, necessarily imposes the characterization of witnessing with respect to the self when inspired by the reflection of pure consciousness.[6] The supreme self is immutable, but as the witness of everything it apprehends the knower, the knowledge, its means, and the object without any intervention from the sense organs.[7] On account of its association with nescience, the self illumines the superimposed universe and becomes the witness of all.[8] Accordingly, Sarvajñātman concludes that the *sākṣin* is the reflected consciousness, it is one; since there are many inner senses, however, there are many *jīva*-s.

(2) *Ābhāsavāda*: Sureśvara subscribes to this view. This is also a reflection theory; however, the nature of reflection on this account varies from the account that one finds in *pratibimbavāda*. According to *pratibimbavāda*, the reflected image is identical with the prototype and, accordingly, is taken to be as real as the prototype. In *ābhāsavāda*, the reflected image is not identical with the prototype and, so, it is not as real as the prototype. It is neither real nor unreal and, hence, is taken to be indeterminable. On this account, both *Īśvara* and the *jīva* are appearances of pure consciousness. *Īśvara* is the prototype consciousness conditioned by nescience. *Īśvara*, in other words, is the result of reflection of pure consciousness in primal nescience. Since nescience is one, the consciousness reflected in it is also one. *Jīva*, on the other hand, is the reflection of pure consciousness on the product of nescience, i.e., nescience as reflected in the individual inner sense along with residual impressions. Since there are many inner senses, there are many *jīva*-s. The unchangeable self within us cognizes the changes and transformations of the inner sense because the empirical cognizer, as a reflection of consciousness, cannot perceive its own changes.

So, Sureśvara argues that there are two modes of seeing (*dṛk*): *jīva* and *Īśvara*. On this view, *Īśvara* himself is the *sākṣin*.[9] Indeed, *Īśvara* and *sākṣin* are simply two different designations of pure consciousness.[10] *Sākṣin*, like *Īśvara*, is one of the appearances of pure consciousness (*cidābhāsaviśiṣṭāvidyāviśiṣta Īśvaraḥ, tadrśāvidyopahitaḥ sāksitvena sākṣin*). It is the reflection of consciousness in nescience; it is one.

(3) *Avacchedavāda*: This is advocated by Vācaspati in *Bhāmatī*. Vācaspati holds that formless *brahman* is free from any reflection whatsoever.

Pure consciousness as the substratum of nescience is the *jīva*, but pure consciousness as the object of nescience is *Īśvara*. Just as space is one, but on account of limitations appears as divided into specific spaces, like the space in a pitcher and space in a room, similarly, pure consciousness, although one, is taken to be many on account of the limitations—grounded in nescience—that are imposed upon it. *Sākṣin* is *ātman* in its pure nature; it is one. The same consciousness underlies both *jīva* and *Īśvara* in the final analysis.

The above brief overview of these different accounts makes it obvious to the readers that what kind of an entity *sākṣin* is on a particular interpretation hangs on the conception of the nature of *jīva* and of *Īśvara* that one has and on the relationship that one believes exists between the two. Thus, it is not surprising that one finds different accounts of the nature of *sākṣin* among the followers of Śaṃkara.

The Nature of *Sākṣin*

An analysis of some of the major texts of the post-Śaṃkara period reveals that there are at least six different interpretations of the nature of *sākṣin*: (1) *sākṣin* as *ātman*; (2) *sākṣin* as the light of *brahman*; (3) *sākṣin* as *Īśvara* or as an aspect of *Īśvara*; (4) *sākṣin* as *jīva*; (5) *sākṣin* as a consciousness that is neither *Īśvara* nor *jīva*, but rather a consciousness that is common to both; and (6) *sākṣin* as the reflection of consciousness in nescience or in a mode of nescience.

(1) *Sākṣin* as *Ātman*

In the writings of Advaitins immediately following Śaṃkara, such as Padmapāda and Vācaspati, the basic Advaitin epistemological concepts are yet to be crystalized. The notion of *sākṣin* does not yet play a significant role; references to *sākṣin* are few and far between.

Padmapāda articulates *sākṣin* as immediate consciousness: "All negation reaches its limit with that; therefore, that alone has no negation. It itself intrinsically is not experienced [as an object]. All sublation is up to the transcendent, which is immediate and only of the nature of consciousness."[11] In other words, the limit of all negations is the witness-consciousness; it cannot be denied. It is immutable, immediate, and pure consciousness.

He makes a distinction between the I-notion (*ahampratyaya*) and the inner self or the witness of all mental modifications. The inner sense is termed "knowledge" (*pratyayin*), because it undergoes modifications and is superimposed on the witness-consciousness.[12] The pure self appears as the witness-consciousness; it is the same in all finite individuals. This witness-consciousness is not, cannot be, known by any instruments or means of true cognition.[13] In other words, the witness-consciousness is different from the *jīva*-s.

Vācaspati in his commentary on *Brahmasūtrabhāṣya* makes a few references to *sākṣin.* At one place, he explains *sākṣin* as *caitanyodāsīnatā,* i.e., the indifference of consciousness to true and false cognitions. It is said to be different from the inner sense, etc., to which the mental modification, the "I-sense" (*ahaṃpratyayinam*), belongs.[14]

At another place, Vācaspati points out that the individual self, *jīva,* is the object of the "I," the agent, limited by the cause-effect structure. The *jīva*'s witness is the highest self;[15] consciousness in its pure nature is its witness (*śuddhaṃ tu rūpaṃ tasya sākṣin*). In this passage, he seems to identify *paramātman* or the highest self with the *sākṣin*; *paramātman* witnesses the *jīvātman* or the individual self. In the final analysis, the *jīva* and *ātman* are one; the *jīva* is conditioned, whereas *sākṣin* is pure.

At still another place, Vācaspati describes *sākṣiṇ* as the witness of "origin, existence, and dissolution."[16]

Finally, in his *Bhāmatī* on II.2.28, *sākṣin* is said to be immediate and eternal; it realizes experience:

> Just as the cutter, with the help of cutting, cuts the trees, etc., which are to be cut, but does not do cutting by means of another cutting, nor does he cut by cutting, but rather: Devadatta cuts directly, . . . so the knower reaches the objects "blue," etc. by knowledge, but does not have this knowledge through another knowledge, nor is the knowledge itself the knower, but rather the knower knows directly.[17]

The point that Vācaspati is trying to make is as follows: Just as when Devadatta cuts, there is cutting, but this cutting does not depend upon another cutting; so, when I know, there is knowledge but this knowledge does not require another knowledge in order to be known. Hence, there is no infinite regress.[18] Similarly, the witness-consciousness knows directly; it does not need another knowledge in order to know the original knowledge.

Thus, the writings of Padmapāda and Vācaspati emphasize the witness conception of the *sākṣin,* and their understanding of *sākṣin* is not really different from what one finds in Śaṃkara. They basically concur with Śaṃkara that the witness-consciousness is the self that reveals. It is a passive observer, not an active agent. They emphasize the self-luminous nature of *sākṣin.*

(2) *Sākṣin* as the Light of Brahman

Tattvaśuddhi of Jñānaghanapāda articulates *sākṣin* as the light of *brahman,* which appears *as if* it belonged to the empirical individual. In this commentary, an attempt is made to illustrate the nature of *sākṣin* with the help of illusory perceptions. The question is raised whether, in the illusory cognition "this is silver," "thisness" belongs to the silver or to the shell. If it is said to belong to the silver, then there could be no sublating cognition in the form "this is a shell," because the sublating cognition would not only sublate the silver but also the "thisness" that was said to belong to the silver. Nor can the "thisness" belong to the shell, because the shell never appears. Therefore, it makes sense to say that although "thisness" really belongs to the shell, yet on account of its identification with the silver, it also appears with the silver. Likewise, *sākṣin* is *brahman,* but is identified with the *jīva* during bondage.[19]

(3) *Sākṣin* as *Īśvara* or an Aspect of *Īśvara*

Vedānta Kaumudī[20] takes *sākṣin* to be a form of *Īśvara,* a kind of neutral entity devoid of all activities. Rāmadvaya, the author of this text, articulates *sākṣin* as an aspect of *Īśvara.* The question is raised: If the *sākṣin,* as the cognizer of the *jīva*'s ignorance, is proximate to it, whereas *Īśvara,* being omnipotent and omniscient, is remote from the *jīva,* how then can *Īśvara* be said to be the *sākṣin*? In response, it is pointed out that *sākṣin* is not *Īśvara,* but is rather an aspect of *Īśvara.* This allows the *jīva* to act or to refrain from acting at times, but, in itself, it is devoid of all activities; it does not have anything whatsoever to do with the causality of the world. *Īśvara,* although conscious of the activities of the finite individual, is in no way affected by them. It functions through the finite individual and illumines both nescience and its modifications. It is immediate and, as the manifester of an individual's ignorance in the state of dreamless sleep, it is called *prājña*: "Just as he, embraced by the woman he loves, knows nothing outside nor anything within, even so this person, embraced by this *prājña* self, knows nothing outside nor anything within."[21]

Citsukha, in his *Tattvapradīpikā,* explains *sākṣin* as *Īśvara* manifesting itself in all finite individuals. In his analysis of the self, he brings out the significance of *sākṣin.* At the outset, he makes a distinction between the seer (*draṣṭā*) and the cognizer (*pramātā*). The seer is not dependent on any of the instruments of knowing (*pramāṇa*-s). In the state of deep sleep, the witness-consciousness reveals nescience without any such instrumentality. Since the cognizer cognizes via the instruments of knowing, the cognizer and the witness-consciousness are different. This, however, should not be taken to mean that the two are mutually exclusive entities. He provides an inference to support the existence of the witness-consciousness in the *jīva*: "Emotions such as the desire of Caitra are cognized by a direct perception of his which is different from his ephemeral perceptions, because they are directly perceived by him, just as in the case of a pitcher directly perceived."[22] To substantiate his claim, Citsukha points out that desires, being the constituents of the mind, cannot be cognized by the mind. In other words, the mind cannot be both subject and object at the same time. Additionally, the witness-consciousness is necessary to account for the existence of the phenomenon of memory, which necessarily presupposes a continuous consciousness. Thus, we must admit a continuous consciousness that is neither apprehended by the senses nor by the mind, and this is none other than the *sākṣin*. The *sākṣin* is a kind of apprehension that is not characterized by (*viśiṣta*) nescience, nor is nescience a qualification *per accidens* (*upalakṣaṇa*)[23] of the *sākṣin*. Rather, it is that which has nescience as its limiting adjunct (*upādhi*).[24]

The point that Citsukha wishes to make is as follows: The witness-consciousness is different from a cognizer, because even in the absence of the senses in deep sleep it reveals nescience. The witness-consciousness is not *characterized by* nescience (*avidyāviśiṣta*); the self is that consciousness which is known as *sākṣin* because of its relation with the objects to be witnessed (*cidrūpasyaiva ātmanaḥ sākṣyasambandhe sākṣitvena vyavahārāt*).[25] "The pure *brahman* which has become all the inner selves is known to be the witness-consciousness according to differences in finite individual beings."[26] There is but one nescience and just one *jīva*.

(4) *Sākṣin* as *Jīva*

For some Advaitins, only the *jīva* is the witness. Appaya Dīkṣita makes note of this view in his *Siddhāntaleśasaṃgraha*, without identifying the commentator he had in mind:

> Some, however, say thus: The nescience-conditioned *jīva* alone is the witness, because of being directly the spectator; for, in ordinary experience too, the character of being a witness is well known to be spectatorship without agency; and that is directly possible only for the *jīva*, who is of the nature of unattached, indifferent manifestation, since the *jīva*, though subject to the imposition of agency, etc., through getting identified with the internal organ, is in himself indifferent.[27]

Thus, on this view, *jīva* is the *sākṣin,* because it is a passive spectator and not a doer. The false identification of the *jīva* with the inner sense accounts for its agency. To put it differently, there are two aspects of the *jīva,* the real and the apparent. The spectator aspect is real and the agent aspect is only apparent; in its spectator aspect, the *jīva* is *sākṣin.*

(5) *Sākṣin* as Consciousness Common to Both *Īśvara* and *Jīva*

Vidyāraṇya's *Pañcadaśī* (PD) contains an extensive treatment of the nature of *sākṣin.* At the outset of this work, he familiarizes his readers with his understanding of *jīva* and *Īśvara.* In chapter 1, entitled "*Tattvaviveka,*" the reflection of consciousness in *māyā*—in which the *sattva guṇa* predominates—is said to be *Īśvara,* and the reflection of consciousness in *avidyā*—in which *rajas* and *tamas* predominate—is said to be the *jīva. Sākṣin* is *kūṭastha,* i.e., the immutable, unchangeable, eternal light of consciousness in *jīva.* He uses the terms "*sākṣin*" and "*kūṭastha*" interchangeably.[28] *Sākṣin* remains continuous in the three states of waking, dreaming and dreamless sleep. "The consciousness, which is limited by the two bodies (gross and subtle) as locus, is called *kūṭastha* because of its unchanging nature."[29]

Pañcadaśī makes an extensive use of similies to explain the nature of *Īśvara, jīva* and their relation to the witness-consciousness. Of these similies, the three I will discuss are those of: (a) the ether (*ākāśa*), (b) the lamp of the theater, and (c) the sun shining on the wall.

(a) In the sixth chapter entitled "*Citradīp,*" the simile of the space is used to distinguish among four forms of consciousness, viz., *kūṭastha, brahman, jīva,* and *Īśvara.*[30] *Brahman* is like the all-pervasive space. (i) The space conditioned by a pitcher is the limited space within the pitcher (*ghaṭākāśa*); (ii) the space reflected along with the clouds in the water of the pitcher is called "*jalākāśa;*" (iii) the space that is unconditioned is the infinite, unlimited space (*mahākāśa*); and (iv) the space reflected in the particles of water that exists in the clouds is *meghākāśa.* In short, the one space appears to be different when conditioned by different limiting conditions. Similarly, there are four kinds of consciousness: (i) Immutable and unchanging consciousness conditioned by gross and subtle bodies is *kūṭastha;* (ii) that which is reflected in the inner sense on account of its being falsely superimposed on the immutable consciousness is *jīva;* (iii) the unconditioned consciousness is *brahman;* and (iv) that which is reflected in the mental impressions (*dhīvāsanāḥ*) of all creatures is called *Īśvara.* On this account, consciousness reflected in the inner sense is *jīva* and the consciousness reflected in the omnipresent *māyā* tinged with the subtle mental impressions of finite individuals is *Īśvara.*

(b) In the "*Nāṭakadīpa*," the witness is compared to a lamp on a stage in a theater.[31] Although the lamp reveals the director, the actors, the audience, it continues to shine even in their absence. Similarly, while *sākṣin* reveals egoity (*ahaṃkāra*), intellect (*buddhi*), and objects (*viṣaya*), it continues to shine even in their absence.[32] The point is as follows: A lamp on a stage manifests the director, the actress, and the audience; it shines even in the absence of the things it manifests. Similarly, the witness-consciousness reveals agents, actions, external objects, as well as the different cognitions that assume such forms as "I see," "I hear," etc. No knowledge can occur in the absence of its association with these. The witness by its mere presence, since it does not act, effects this association. It envelops all three very much as a light does its surroundings and reveals objects, resulting in their being cognized. Furthermore, the witness-consciousness shines even in the deep sleep state when all modifications of nescience are absent.

(c) At the outset of the chapter entitled "*Kūṭasthadīpa*," the difference between the immutable consciousness (*kūṭastha*) and the *jīva* (the reflection of pure consciousness in the mental mode) is explained through the analogy of the wall and the reflecting mirrors.[33] When several mirrors reflect the light of the sun on a wall that is already illumined by the sun, the spaces between the various reflections are illumined by the light of the sun alone, so that even when the reflections cease, the wall remains illumined. Similarly, during the reflection of pure consciousness in the mental mode (*cidābhāsa*) and during deep sleep (when all reflections are absent), the immutable consciousness remains illumined.

Thus, *sākṣin* is different from both *jīva* and *Īśvara*, because the latter two are products of *māyā*.[34] *Sākṣin*, on the other hand, is nondual, self-luminous, and the supreme good. The ever mobile intellect moves in time and space, while the immutable witness-consciousness, like a lamp, reveals all. The witness reveals not only objects but also their knownness, which is produced by the reflection of consciousness in the intellect (*jīva*). It results in two kinds of knowing, one by the *jīva* and the other by the transcendent self (*kūṭastha*). The former assumes the form "this is a pitcher," while the latter assumes the form "I know this is a pitcher."

The *sākṣin* is different from both the *jīva* and *Īśvara*, since they are subject to change. It is also different from *brahman*, which is pure, unconditioned and beyond superimposition of the world. The *sākṣin* is the changeless consciousness on which the world is superimposed.

(6) *Sākṣin* as the Reflection of Consciousness in *Avidyā* or *Avidyāvṛtti*

Madhusūdana in his works *Siddhāntabindu* and *Advaitasiddhi* discusses *sākṣin*, vis-à-vis *Īśvara* and *jīva*, in detail. In *Siddhāntabindu*—in the process of explaining the distinctions among *Īśvara, jīva*, and *sākṣin*—Madhusūdana also sums up some of the important theories of his predecessors on this issue. Given the importance of Madhusūdana in the post-Śaṃkara tradition, I will try to summarize his main arguments as they appear in *Siddhāntabindu* and *Advaitasiddhi*.

In *Siddhāntabindu*, Madhusūdana begins with the distinction between the seer (*dṛk*) and the seen (*dṛśya*):

> On this view, things are of two kinds: seeing and seen. . . . Seeing is the self, ultimately real and one, always the same, but, according to differences of limiting adjuncts, [the self] is of three kinds: *Īśvara, jīva* and *sākṣin*. *Īśvara* has for its limiting adjunct the root cause ignorance. As limited by the ignorance that is limited by the inner sense and its residual impressions, it is *jīva*. . . . On the alternative that *Īśvara* is the reflection in ignorance, *sākṣin* is the reflected consciousness. On the alternative that *Īśvara* is the reflected consciousness, *sākṣin* is the consciousness common to the *jīva* and *Īśvara*, which recollects all things (just as between a face and its reflection there is the common form of the face). On the view of the author of *Vārtika, Īśvara* is *sākṣin*, so that the seeing consciousness is of two kinds: *jīva* and *Īśvara*.[35]

The seer is pure consciousness; it is one, immediate, and unconditional. However, on account of the limiting adjuncts (*upādhi*-s), it is differentiated into three forms, viz., *Īśvara, jīva*, and *sākṣin*. Pure consciousness conditioned by nescience is *Īśvara*; pure consciousness conditioned by a mode of nescience, i.e., the inner sense, is the *jīva*. If *sākṣin* is taken to signify the original consciousness, then *Īśvara* becomes its reflection in nescience (Sureśvara's view). On the other hand, if *Īśvara* is taken to signify the original consciousness, then *sākṣin* becomes the principle that provides continuity between *Īśvara* and the *jīva* (the Vivaraṇa view). Madhusūdana also notes that for Sureśvara *sākṣin* is only one, and it is not different from *Īśvara*.

Whereas in *Siddhāntabindu*, Madhusūdana focuses on the distinction among *sākṣin, Īśvara*, and *jīva*, in *Advaitasiddhi*, he not only clearly articulates the nature of *sākṣin*, but also informs his readers why *sākṣin* is neither the *jīva* nor *brahman* nor *Īśvara*. Here *sākṣin* is defined as a consciousness that is reflected either in ignorance or in its product.[36] He raises an objection on behalf of the opponents in the following form: Does *sākṣin* belong to the *jīva* or to *brahman* or to a consciousness that is common to both?[37]

> Not the first, because: (i) on the theory that the *jīva* is consciousness having the limiting adjunct *buddhi* and is atomic, and since the object "this" which is known by consciousness and is of the nature of the shell cannot be known by *sākṣin*, there would be the fallacy of circularity and (ii) on the theory that the adjunct of the *jīva* is ignorance and so the *jīva* is ubiquitous, since ignorance is established by *sākṣin*, there would be the fallacy of "mutual dependence."[38]
>
> Not the second [alternative]: for in that case *brahman* and not the *jīva* would possess knowledge of pain, etc., which are known by *sākṣin* and that is the opposite of what should be. Otherwise, the *jīva* would have the nature of being unlimited and have knowledge of bliss. On the view that the *brahman*-consciousness manifests objects such as a pitcher, etc., that consciousness, through manifesting ignorance, is identical with the *jīva*-consciousness, and this identity would be manifested in modifications of the inner sense, but there is no such mode of inner sense [i.e., no mode for pleasure, pain, etc.].[39]
>
> Not the third [alternative]: Even if the *Īśvara*, by pure consciousness, apprehends pain as belonging to the person in bondage, that part [in the person] which is free, i.e., pure consciousness, would be mixed up with pain, etc.[40]

He further adds that if the pure consciousness were taken to be the *sākṣin*, then:

> For Maitra who is asleep, like Maitra's ignorance, etc., as belonging to Maitra, the pain, etc., of Caitra who is awake, as belonging to Caitra, would be presented to Maitra who is asleep, in which case Maitra, on waking up, would say: "So long I did not know the pain, etc."; but Maitra does not say so.[41]
>
> Since we take the witness to be different from both pure *brahman* and the *jīva* having *buddhi* as a limiting adjunct, this objection [pertaining to the third alternative] does not obtain.[42]
>
> And, then, the witness is the consciousness as reflected in modifications of ignorance, the [presence] of modifications of ignorance during deep sleep has previously been asserted.[43]
>
> Although the witness is common to all *jīva*-s, it is presented as nondifferent from each *jīva*-consciousness. Therefore, there is nothing undesirable in the [separate] manifestation of each *jīva*'s pain, etc.[44]

The goal of Madhusūdana, it seems to me, was to demonstrate that pure consciousness becomes a seer on account of its association with nescience and its products. Such a consciousness can be identified neither with the *jīva*, nor with *brahman*, nor with *Īśvara*, nor with a consciousness that is common to both.

Additionally, the witness-consciousness cannot be said to belong to the *jīva*, because such an argument would involve the fallacy of circularity and the fallacy of mutual dependence. To begin with, if the witness-consciousness is said to belong to the *jīva*, there would be no way to apprehend the "this" in an illusory perception. In the illusory perception "this is silver," the "this" is perceived by the "I" and the "silver," being an illusory object, is apprehended by the witness-consciousness. If the witness-consciousness is said to belong to the *jīva*, then the "I" would become the witness-consciousness. However, the witness-consciousness does not, indeed cannot, apprehend the "this" that is out there and is perceived by the sense of sight. According to Madhusūdana, such a conception would involve circular reasoning. Although the justification of this claim is not wholly coherent, he seems to reason that the circularity would result because the conditions of reflection and the seeing function of the seer would be regarded erroneously as identical, resulting in confusion worse confounded. Second, to hold that the witness-consciousness belongs to the *jīva* would commit the fallacy of mutual dependence. It would amount to arguing that, on the one hand, the witness-consciousness belongs to the *jīva*, and that, on the other hand, the *jīva*, which is ignorance, is established by the witness-consciousness. In other words, we would be arguing that the witness-consciousness is established by ignorance and ignorance is established by the witness-consciousness, which is absurd.

The witness-consciousness cannot be said to belong to *brahman* either. Mental states such as pleasure, pain, and the like are the objects of *sākṣin*. *Brahman* does not have pleasure, pain, etc. So, *sākṣin* cannot belong to *brahman*.

Gauḍabrahmānandi, one of the commentators on *Advaitasiddhi*, adds:

> Thus, since there is no concealment of pleasure, etc., there is no need of a mode for their manifestation; therefore the *jīva* can function as the witness-consciousness with regard to a pitcher, etc., through a mental mode, and with regard to pleasure, etc., directly—hence no necessity for witnesshood in *brahman*.[45]

In other words, pleasure, pain and the like are revealed to the individual person without the mediation of any mental mode. Accordingly, the *jīva* can function as *sākṣin* in one case via a mental mode, as in the perception of an external object; in another case it can function without a mental mode, as in the perception of pleasure and pain. There is no need to say that the witness-consciousness belongs to *brahman*, for *brahman* does not have the cognition "I am happy," rather it *is* bliss.

The witness-consciousness cannot be said to belong to *Īśvara* either. If *Īśvara* is taken to be the witness-consciousness, then *Īśvara* would have pure consciousness as a limiting condition. In that case, there would be a mixture (*upaplava*) of both pain (*duḥkha*) and the absence of pain in *Īśvara*. *Īśvara* qua *Īśvara* would apprehend the pain of a person in bondage, and *Īśvara* qua pure consciousness would be free, i.e., there would be absence of pain, thereby leading to a contradiction.

The above argument, Gauḍabrahmānandi points out, is not valid because "'*upaplavo*' is not the mere having of *duḥkha*, etc., as an object; even *Īśvara* has *duḥkha* as an object. But it is having relation to pain, etc., while the falsity of pain, etc., is concealed. This is not true of that part which is free."[46] In short, Gauḍabrahmānandi points out that the contradiction is only apparent and not real. *Īśvara* undoubtedly will apprehend pain as an object, but he will know that the pain is false. This is not true of the part that is pure consciousness, because that part would have no relation to pain.

The objection that if the witness-consciousness were common to all the *jīva*-s Caitra should experience Maitra's pain does not hold good either.

> What is desired is that the pain, etc., of Caitra be manifested as belonging to Caitra. That exists only for Caitra, and cannot be presented to Maitra (who is asleep) as belonging to Caitra. Pain, etc., belonging to one person is concealed for another person and, so, without *pramāṇavṛtti* [a true cognitive mode] cannot be presented to the latter simply by the witness-consciousness.[47]

Gauḍabrahmānandi clarifies the point that although *sākṣin* is common to all the *jīva*-s, in my case, *sākṣin* is presented as nondifferent from me and in your case *sākṣin* is presented as nondifferent from you. That is why my pain is experienced only by me, and not by you. This also explains why Maitra apprehends pain as belonging to Maitra and not to Caitra. There is no concealment of a person's pain in Advaita; accordingly, it is manifested by the *sākṣin*. Maitra, who is asleep, is aware only of nescience, not of nescience as belonging to Maitra. However, the pain of others is covered by ignorance that can only be destroyed by a true cognitive mode.

Thus, the witness-consciousness is one in all cognizers, although it appears *as if* different in each cognizer. This also explains why the experiences of one individual cognizer are apprehended by the witness-consciousness associated with that particular cognizer. Thus, the question of confusing the experiences of different cognizers does not arise when it is maintained that there is only one *sākṣin.*

Advaitasiddhi concludes the discussion by noting: "It is established that *sākṣin* is nondual, eternal, of the nature of knowledge and bliss, and is *brahman.*"[48]

A cursory glance at the above accounts reveals that the witness-consciousness has been variously identified in the post-Śaṃkara tradition. The ramifications of these identifications are yet to be determined. However, before undertaking this task, I will discuss two important issues that the above account raises: What precisely is the relation between the witness-consciousness and a cognizer? Secondly, since cognizers are many, why are there not many *sākṣin*-s? These two issues will form the subject matter of the next two sections. In the final section of this chapter, I will try to come to grips with the ramifications of identifying *sākṣin* with either *Īśvara, brahman,* or the *jīva.*

Sākṣin and *Pramātā*

The most detailed account of the distinction between *sākṣin* and *pramātā* (cognizer) is found in the *Bṛhadāraṇyakopaniṣad Bhāṣya-Vārtika Sāra* (BUBVS). Let us review what this text has to say about this important issue.

> Just as the *pramātā* and its absence are both established by the witness, so if the witness were absent, what will witness its [*pramātā*'s] absence?[49]
>
> The witness of the seer, the seeing and the seen is the self-shining self, which cannot be known by any *pramāṇa.* This is the true nature of the witness.[50]
>
> The eyes cause modifications of the mind, which, in conjunction with the self, manifest color. This modification is called "seeing," and its agent is called by people "seer."[51]
>
> The self is the true nature of all these: means of true cognition, object of true cognition and the cognizer. For it is the witness of the origin and destruction of the cognizer, etc.[52]
>
> If something were not always there in a thing, it could not be its true nature—just as "having an ornament," in relation to a person, [is not a person's true nature]. The witness, however, is never absent.[53]
>
> Just as a person in a boat does not perceive the motion of the boat as a person on the shore does, so a self who is nondifferent from the intellect could not be the witness of the modifications of intellect.[54]

> The modifications of the intellect are superimposed upon the indubitable witness. The knowledge of witness-witnessed is false, and is destroyed by knowledge of the truth.[55]
>
> There are two [kinds of] seeing; one is eternal, the other noneternal. The mental modification is noneternal, the other is witness-consciousness and is eternal.[56]
>
> Although the intellect is unconscious, it becomes the seer owing to reflection of consciousness; hence the usage of the word "sees" in connection with it.[57]
>
> The real seer, whose limiting adjunct is the intellect, does not see in deep sleep. The pure consciousness also does not see, owing to the absence of what is to be seen.[58]
>
> Since consciousness is eternal and has no destruction, the witness is said to see. Since the witness is not an agent and, so, not the agent of the act of seeing, still owing to superimposition of agency, it is said to be an agent.[59]
>
> No absence can be established without the immediate witness perception, not to speak of positive entities in this world. The witness does not depend upon anything else for its establishment.[60]
>
> One who sees, in a dream, the seer, seeing, and the object seen and who sees their absence in deep sleep, is the self. Know this.[61]

All the above passages underscore one basic point: a cognizer and the witness-consciousness are different. Who then is a cognizer? A cognizer is the doer of actions as well as the enjoyer. It is subject to nescience. We have already seen that a modification of the mind, known as "*vṛtti*," is variously characterized as retro-cognition or memory (*citta*), mind (*manas*), intellect (*buddhi*) and the ego-sense (*ahaṃkāra*) by the Advaitins. *Buddhi* functions via the sense organs. However, intellect is inert; it cannot give rise to knownness. On the other hand, consciousness alone is not able to perform this function either. It is reflected in the intellect, thereby producing "I-ness." It is this reflected self that finds expression as the ego and is known as the cognizer (*pramātā*).

Any knowledge situation consists of two factors, the variable and the invariable. Contents of knowledge vary; their true knower does not. The cognizer, the means of true cognition, etc., are all imposed on the witness-consciousness. They are variables; they come and go. *Pramātā*, in other words, is variable; the *sākṣin* is invariable. There are two kinds of seeing: eternal and noneternal.[62] *Sākṣin*'s seeing is eternal and unconditioned. *Sākṣin*, as the revealer of all mental and psychical modifications, is the real self. No activity belongs to it. The seeing of a mental mode, however, is an act of the intellect. *Sākṣin* is a passive observer; it is different from the ever-moving intellect.[63] *Sākṣin* is pure self; it is beyond the cognizer, the means of true cognition and the object of cognition triad. Sureśvara in *Sambandha Vārtika* notes: "Witness/witnessed relationship pertains to a cognizer and not to the self, which is—the seer in the true sense—the *sākṣin*."[64] The relation between the witness and the witnessed operates in the phenomenal realm; it is not operative on the level of pure consciousness. A cognizer requires the witness-consciousness to illumine it. The witness-consciousness, on the other hand, does not require another witness-consciousness to illumine it.

None of the three constituents of the knowledge triad—the cognizer, the cognition and the object cognized—is capable of revealing itself: "The seer, the seeing, and the object seen do not cognize their own being. Nor are they known by one another. Therefore, whether they become objects depends on something that transcends them."[65] That something that transcends them is none other than the witness-consciousness. An external object, such as a chair, is cognized by a cognizer. However, the knowledge of the cognition, i.e., the judgment "the chair is known," is made possible by the witness-consciousness, since all mental modifications are revealed only by the witness-consciousness. In other words, the cognition of a chair is due to both a cognizer and the witness-consiousness; the agency is attributed to the cognizer; however, the knowledge of the agency is on account of the witness-consciousness, the disinterested spectator who observes the activity of the *jīva*.

The importance of the distinction between the two cannot be underscored enough for the Advaitins: the witness-consciousness is not a cognizer; it is only a *dṛṣṭā* (seer). The witness-consciousness simply "establishes" a thing; it does not by itself make the thing known. A cognizer makes things known with the help of a mental modification caused by an instrument or a means of true cogntion (*pramāṇajanyāntaḥkāraṇavṛtti*); the witness-consciousness manifests this mental modification. The witness-consciousness is not opposed to nescience; it reveals nescience. Nescience is dispelled by consciousness reflected in a mode of the inner sense. The knowledge of one's ignorance resulting in judgments such as "I do not know" affirms an identification between a cognizer and the witness-consciousness. Whereas the witness-consciousness apprehends nescience, a cognizer is characterized by the "I-ness" that results from nescience. Modification of nescience gives rise to egoity, i.e., to "I-ness," therefore nescience cannot dispel the notion of "I."[66] Nescience is destroyed by a *pramāṇavṛtti*; "I" is the content of nescience.[67]

If there are different cognizers, their difference is established by the witness-consciousness. In the Advaita thesis of immediacy, all distinctions disappear. Pure consciousness is the only thing that is immediate. Objects of perception, i.e., chairs, pitchers, etc., become immediate when certain conditions are fulfilled, e.g., the contact of the sense organs with the mind and the mind assuming the form of the object it reaches. Perception, inference, etc., are applicable in the conditioned realm, which is governed by cause and effect. The self is unconditional, unrelational; it can only be one. Does this mean that there is but one witness-consciousness? Or is the witness-consciousness many?

Sākṣin: One or Many?

There is no unanimity among the Advaitins on the issue concerning whether *sākṣin* is one or many. Abhyankar, commenting on *Siddhantābindu* of Madhusūdana, refers to two views in this regard.[68] On one view, pure consciousness when adjacent to the residual impressions, etc., is *sākṣin*, but *sākṣin* does not possess any limiting adjuncts; thus, the *sākṣin* is one. This is the view of Sureśvara. Others take pure consciousness itself to be the *sākṣin*. On this view, memory depends upon residual impressions, generated by the inner sense, as well as upon *sākṣin*. They argue that since my recollections of my perceptions are different from your recollections of your perceptions, my *sākṣin* must be different from your *sākṣin*. Accordingly, they conclude that *sākṣin*-s are many. Dharmarāja in his *Vedānta Paribhāṣā* (VP) subscribes to this view. I will begin my discussion of this issue with the latter view, i.e., with an analysis of the account that one finds in *Vedānta Paribhāṣā*.

To explain the manyness of *sākṣin*, Dharmarāja makes an important distinction between the individual-defining consciousness (*jīvasākṣin*) and the God-defining consciousness (*Īśvarasākṣin*): *jīvasākṣin*-s are many; *Īśvarasākṣin* is one.

Before analyzing the nature of *jīvasākṣin* in Advaita, let us review briefly Dharmarāja's understanding of the terms "*jīva*" and "*sākṣin*," the two words that constitute "*jīvasākṣin*." He defines *jīva* as consciousness *conditioned* by the intellect and *sākṣin* as the consciousness that is *associated* with the inner sense.[69] In the former, the inner sense is a qualifying attribute; in the latter, it is an accidental feature. It is important to remember in this context that an accidental feature is not a property of the thing, but only serves to identify it (as in the case of "the house with a crow on the roof").

The inner sense is thus the principle of individuation in Advaita. When the inner sense serves as a qualification (*viśeṣana*) of pure consciousness, pure consciousness is called the *jīva*; when the inner sense serves as a limiting adjunct (*upādhi*), pure consciousness is called the witness-consciousness.

Karl Potter writes:

> The internal organ is . . . by nature unconscious, *jaḍa*, but reflects the light of pure consciousness. Being itself unconscious, the internal organ is not capable in itself of being *about* anything. So the relation between consciousness and internal organ is just that the internal organ residently qualifies consciousness, limiting it in such a way that it *constitutes* what we call the individual self. By contrast when we speak of an individual's self being aware of something or other, we are identifying that self not through its constitutive character—that particular internal organ—but rather through its experiences, the contents it "witnesses," and since these contents are actually the contents of consciousness *per se*, and not the contents of the internal organ which differentiates this self, the witnessing self is being identified through an *upādhi*, through an accidental rather than a resident feature of it.[70]

Thus, the inner sense (or internal organ), being a constitutive element of the finite self, cannot be separated from it. It can, however, be separated from the witness-consciousness, because the inner sense serves as a mere limitation for the witness-consciousness. The finite individual is a knower (*jñātṛ*), a doer (*kartṛ*), and an enjoyer (*bhoktṛ*). The inner sense, being inert, cannot manifest individual consciousness; hence, the need of a witness-consciousness in the individual self.

The point to remember is as follows: The witness-consciousness, although the element of pure awareness in a knowing situation, never appears by itself. It always appears as associated with the inner sense. However, when associated with a particular inner sense it becomes determinate and is then defined in reference to that particular inner sense. This is *jīvasākṣin*. Accordingly, what comes within the purview of experience of one finite individual does not necessarily come within the purview of another finite individual's experience. If this is not accepted, we would be forced to admit that what is cognized by one *jīva* is apprehended by another, which is absurd.

It may be asked: What is to be gained by making a distinction between the *jīva* and the *jīvasākṣin*? In response, it is pointed out that a *jīva* is the cognizer of objects; but there must be a cognizer of the *jīva*, otherwise there would be no unity and coherence of apperception in our cognitions of external objects. The witness-consciousness lends continuity and connectedness to a *jīva*'s cognitions and psychological states.

It is important to remember in this context not just that the witness-consciousness appears only as associated with the inner sense, but also that the converse is true, i.e., no inner sense can be conceived without involving a reference to the witness-consciousness as the principle of awareness. In fact, the witness-consciousness lends knowability to the *jīva* and makes the *jīva* self-conscious. However, it would be erroneous to conclude on this basis that the witness-consciousness can be an object of knowledge, inasmuch as this would presuppose another knowing element, and so on ad infinitum. The distinction between the two may be summed up as follows: "the *jīva* is spirit as immanent in the *antaḥ–karaṇa*, while the *sākṣin* is spirit as transcendent."[71] Accordingly, for Hiriyanna, the witness-consciousness is the transcendental ego, whereas the *jīva* is the empirical ego. The *jīvasākṣin* is the unchanging impartial spectator of all the changes that a *jīva* goes through. It exists in all the three states: waking, dreaming, and dreamless sleep. Given the Advaita position that everything is an object of awareness either as known or as unknown, and since the Advaitins maintain that an existent object is apprehended by the witness-consciousness in its individual determinate mode, it thus makes sense to argue that the undifferentiated plethora of beings can be apprehended only in the context of a "general" or cosmic witness-consciousness. This type of reasoning results in postulating *Īśvarasākṣin*. *Īśvarasākṣin* is a consciousness that is associated with *māyā*. Such an association, however, is accidental (*Īśvarasākṣin tu mayopahitam*). This witness-consciousness is the ground of everything that appears; it is *brahman*. It is said to be one, on account of *māyā* being one. The *jīva*, on the other hand, is different in each individual. So there are many *jīva*-s. Accordingly, there are many *jīvasākṣiñ*-s: "Now, this individual-defining consciousness is different in each individual; for if it were one, then what is cognized by Caitra would also be recollected by Maitra."[72]

Madhusūdana, however, does not find Dharmarāja's arguments persuasive. Madhusūdana argues that there is only one *sākṣin*. The differences in the residual impressions do not lead to differences in *sākṣin*.[73] Individual cognizers possess different inner senses, which accounts for the differences in the perceptions of different cognizers in the waking and dreaming states.[74] The fact that my inner sense is different from your inner sense does not prove that my witness-consciousness is different from your witness-consciousness. In his *Siddhāntabindu*, he quotes Sureśvara to substantiate his position that the *sākṣin* is one, not many. Sureśvara argues that pure consciousness, when adjacent to residual impressions, etc. (i.e., *saṃskārādyupādhi sannihitaḥ*), is *sākṣin*. So *sākṣin* cannot possess any limiting adjuncts. If we include residual impressions in the *sākṣin*, the residual impressions being many, there would be many *sākṣin-s*, which is absurd. Even when the *sākṣin* is adjacent to residual impressions, it is still *cinmātra* (pure consciousness), because of the absence of any limiting adjunct. A red flower near a crystal lends its color to that crystal for the time being; however, the crystal is still a crystal. Just as there are differences in the knowers and in the knowledge possessed by each one of them, while the external object remains the same, so also does the *sākṣin* remain the same; it is called *ātman,* or that which comprehends all things. "Ignorance is everywhere the same, the witness-consciousness does not contain any difference."[75] The point that is being made is as follows: Since the intellect is different in each body according to the differences in the semblance of consciousness in each, consciousness, although one, appears to be different in each. The *jīva* is not many. It, however, appears to be many because of the manyness of the inner organs. Ignorance, however, being nondifferent in all cases, the consciousness reflected in it is also nondifferent; so the witness-consciousness, which is nondifferent from that reflection, is never experienced as different.[76] In other words, one and the same ignorance conditions pure consciousness, which appears to be both the inner ruler (*antaryāmin*) and the material cause of the world (*jagatkāraṇa*) when conditioned by nescience and not distinguished from its own semblance. Accordingly, following Sureśvara, Madhusūdana concludes that the *sākṣin* is one.[77]

Whereas in *Siddhāntabindu* Madhusūdana cites Sureśvara to support his thesis, in his *Advaitasiddhi,* on the other hand, he develops his position systematically and in detail in favor of one *jīva* and one *sākṣin.* He begins his discussion by noting:

> That seer is only one, there being no proof of its manyness. But how can the *jīva* be one, for that would contradict the fact that for each body there is the experience "I am happy," "I am in pain," "I am worldly" and "I slept." Our reply is: That is not so, it is owing to ignorance even *brahman,* though one, [seems to] be involved in the changing world. He is the *jīva.* He has the awareness "I" for each body. The thought "this is happy, this is in pain" with regard to a dream-body, but not the thought about "I," does not relate to the living body. Where there is the "I"-sense, that is alive [has a *jīva*].*
>
> To say that the order of bondage and liberation, etc., prove that there are many *jīva*-s won't do; for those orders, including the order of having a guru or being a disciple, etc., are due, like a dream, to ignorance.
>
> If one *jīva* were asleep, the entire universe would be unknown. This objection won't do, for the primary *jīva,* who knows the entire world, is awake. When that is asleep, at the time of dissolution, the world is not manifest.

That which is limited by the inner sense is merely a seeming-*jīva*; when that is asleep, the world is not manifested to him, not to others, for the limiting adjuncts are not yet dissolved.

The distinction between Caitra and Maitra are due to the limitations of mind and its modifications; hence the uses of "mine," "yours."

But if the *Hiraṇyagarbha*, which imagines all others, is the only *jīva*, and if it is released at the end of a *kalpa*, then all would be released. Yes, that is acceptable to those who worship the determinate *brahman*. (Gauḍabrahmānandī)

The *jīva* is one, although the bodies are many. The different senses of "I" and "you" are due to different inner sense organs being superimposed on the one *jīva*. The same would explain why Caitra's pleasure and pain are not recollected by Maitra. The same explanation is possible of why, when Caitra's illusion is removed by perceiving the shell, Maitra may continue to be perceiving the illusory silver.

Scriptural texts such as "*anādimāyayā supto yadā jīvaḥ prabudhyate*" speak of the *jīva* in the singular. Plurality is explicable by the many inner senses.

But then would not *Īśvara* be the same as the *jīva*, in which case the *jīva* would be omniscient, which contradicts experience? The reply is that the *jīva* which imagines all things is said to be omniscient and agent of all actions.[78]

Basing his position on the above arguments, Madhusūdana concludes that there is one *jīva*, not many; there is one *sākṣin*.[79] *Īśvara* is pure consciousness, having ignorance as its limiting adjunct; the *jīva* is the reflection of *Īśvara* on ignorance. Pure consciousness does not contain any differentiations; however, it appears to be differentiated on account of being conditioned by nescience.

Abhyankar, one of the commentators on *Siddhāntabindu*, also points out the absurdity of the many-*sākṣin* position by drawing our attention to the fact that if the plurality of *sākṣin*-s has a *sākṣin*, then there will be the fallacy of infinite regress. If the plurality of *sākṣin*-s has no *sākṣin*, then it (the plurality) cannot be established.[80]

So, the existence of many *jīva*-s does not prove the existence of many *sākṣin*-s. With this the *Vedāntaparibhāṣā* theory that there are many *sākṣin*-s is rejected. So, Madhusūdana concludes: although there are many *jīva*-s, *sākṣin* is one, remembers all (*sarvānusandhātā*), is present in all (*sarvānugataḥ*), and is called the transcendent (*turīya*).[81]

Articulation of *sākṣin* as "*turīya*" and "*sarvānusandhātā*" gives rise to two very important questions: Is *sākṣin* the same as *turīya*? Does *sākṣin* remember all?

Siddhāntabindu repeatedly affirms that *sākṣin* is beyond the three states of waking, dreaming, and dreamless sleep; it is to be taken as the *turīya* awareness of "I am" (*ahamasmi*).[82] Everything else is false or apparent, not the *sākṣin* itself.[83]

In the waking state, the cognizers vary in the case of each individual. In the state of deep sleep, on the other hand, though the inner sense lapses, the residual impressions continue. When the "I-ness" is reactivated upon waking up, the different cognizers take over.[84] With the analysis of the three states, the Advaitins demonstrate that these states belong to the phenomenal world; beyond these three is the transcendent, i.e., *sākṣin*.

The commentator Abhyankar says: If there is negation of *sākṣin* in the three states, then this negation either has *sākṣin* or has no *sākṣin*. In the former case, we have a contradiction as in saying "I am dumb"; in the latter case, the negation of *sākṣin* is unproven.[85] In other words, if there is negation of *sākṣin*, then that negation would have a *sākṣin*. This would be like a person saying "I cannot speak." That is a contradiction—a pragmatic contradiction, even if not a logical contradiction. Saying "I cannot speak" negates the condition for saying so. It is like the contradiction between someone's being dumb and saying so. It is like saying "I am dead." One cannot say this, because being dead takes away the condition for a person's being able to say so.

Why is the negation of *sākṣin* pertinent to the issue of whether *sākṣin* is one or many? There are different kinds of negation; one kind of negation is mutual negation or difference (*anyonyābhāva*). If there are two *sākṣin*-s, there will be mutual negation between them. If these two *sākṣin*-s are then different, then there must be a witness of that difference as well, thereby giving rise to the view that there is more than one *sākṣin*, a view not acceptable to Madhusūdana. The one and the same self-luminous pure consciousness undergoes the states of waking, dreaming and dreamless sleep on account of ignorance. *Sākṣin* is beyond these three states; it is the witness of everything that appears. Besides the above three, there is a fourth designation, namely, *sākṣin*, which is given to the unchangeable principle that connects the above three states and is present in them all (*sākṣin tu sarvānusandhātā sarvānugatasturīyākhya ekavidha eva*). Although it remains the same, it receives three different designations, namely, *Īśvara, jīva*, and *sākṣin*. So, *sākṣin* is the same as *turīya*.[86]

In the Upaniṣads, nothing is said except that the *turīya* is the fourth. On one interpretation, *turīya* is common to the waking, the dreaming, and the dreamless states. What is common to all is *sākṣin*. On this interpretation, *sākṣin* is the same as *turīya*. On another interpretation, the *turīya* is the fourth; it is beyond the three states. On this interpretation, *sākṣin* and *turīya* are different. The two interpretations are not mutually exclusive. In the *Chāndogya Upaniṣad,* in the Indra and Virocana dialogue, *turīya* is, at once, articulated as the fourth and as that which comprehends all the three. So, there is no difference of *sākṣin* in difference of body (as between Devadatta and Yajñādatta). Also, there is no difference of *sākṣin* in the waking, the dreaming, and the dreamless sleep states. In the state of dreamless sleep, the self is present in its blissful state along with ignorance.[87] On account of the presence of ignorance, it has been described as one of the three states that belong to the phenomenal world; it is then called *prājña* and not pure self.

Siddhāntabindu explains this point further:

> Since the *ātman* is the witness of deep sleep, there is no absence of witness there. Otherwise, the judgment "I am *mudha*" would have been impossible. Although the knower, the knowledge, the causes of knowledge and the object of knowledge are not, at all times, related to the witness, the witness which manifests their absence must be present in all three states.[88]

The self is the witness of deep sleep.[89] The witness is of the nature of intelligence (*citsvabhāvesākṣini*):[90] "It is always the seer, never the object of sight (*sākṣi dṛg eva na tu dṛśyate*)."[91]

The above discussion raises an interesting question regarding the relation between the "I" and the *sākṣin.* The question is: If the *jīva* and the *sākṣin* are different, then how does *sākṣin* remember what the *jīva* perceives? In reply, Madhusūdana points out that being a cognizer includes other limiting adjuncts besides the witness-consciousness. Therefore, recollection by the witness-consciousness is not impossible.[92] Additionally, the question remains: Why is *sākṣin* articulated as the one who remembers all (*sarvānusandhātā*)? To say that *sākṣin* remembers everything amounts to saying that the *sākṣin* is the subject of all our remembrance.[93] This raises an interesting question about the relationship between the *sākṣin* and the residual impressions. How is the witness perception itself remembered if there are no residual impressions? When I have pleasure or pain, I remember it later on. What is the relationship between *sākṣin* and the residual impressions? Additionally, can one remember another person's witness-perception? I can say tomorrow that I had perceived the pitcher yesterday. How is this possible? Although the mental modification in the form of the pitcher is destroyed, it leaves behind residual impressions; these impressions are revived, resulting in my memory judgment.

What about pleasure and pain? The question remains: How can I say I had a witness perception of my pleasure yesterday? Is witness perception subject to destruction like the mental modifications? Does it leave behind residual impressions? *Pañcapādikāvivaraṇa* contains a discussion of this issue; it states that it might be objected that

> since the witness-consciousness which witnesses both ignorance and pleasure is indestructible, and since there is no trace left behind, how can there be memory of all three? The reply is that the reflection of consciousness due to ignorance has an *upādhi* which has an origin, etc. So, the witness-consciousness, ignorance and pleasure, all three, may be said to have origin and destruction and, hence, the possibility of memory.[94]

Two possible answers come to mind: (1) Witness perception in general is not subject to origin and destruction. However, its limiting adjuncts are subject to origination and destruction. Therefore, one can argue that witness perception as associated with ignorance has origin and destruction, which accounts for the residual impressions giving rise to memory. (2) Alternately, it may be replied that residual impressions are not always needed for memory. In other words, although witness perception is eternal, it can also be regarded as coming into being and passing out of being on account of the variable character of the limiting adjuncts that condition it. Commentary *Tattvadīpana* clarifies the point further: "Ignorance transforms into the witness of one's own pleasure; in the so transformed ignorance, reflection of consciousness arises."[95]

Abhyankar points out that it is the witness-consciousness which recollects the pleasure, etc., experienced in deep sleep as belonging to "I-ness" (*ahaṃkāra*).[96] The issue is: To what extent does memory depend on *sākṣin*? Madhusūdana points out that "as a rule, knowledge caused by the instruments of knowledge (*pramāṇa*-s) belongs to "I-ness."[97] However, he reminds his readers of the principle in the Advaita system: "memory, doubt, and error have, as their locus, the witness-consciousness."[98] The reason, notes Abhyankar, is: knowledge that is not *pramā* (a true cognition) is not a modification of the mind (the inner sense), but it is a modification of nescience, and so belongs to the witness-consciousness.[99] Accordingly, *avidyāvṛtti*, or a mode of nescience, accounts for memory. Abhyankar further adds that *sākṣin* is real (although the objects of *sākṣin* are only apparent); it is not the seer, but the seeing.[100] It is interesting to note here that memory is also accounted for in terms of a mental modification of nescience. The Mīmāṃsakas, like the Advaitins, make a distinction between two kinds of cognition: true and false. Memory in their system is false cognition, not because it is false but because its object was known before. The Advaitins, however, do not really explain how the possibility of memory is facilitated by a mental modification of nescience.

Madhusūdana points out that the opponents may ask: "Rejecting the locus of true cognition, you are making the locus of false cognition to be the witness of all and the king among the instruments of knowledge—what sort of a trap is this?"[101] A cognizer that is the locus of true cognitions is not articulated as "the witness of all" (*sarvasākṣin*), but the locus of false cognitions is said to be *sarvasākṣin.* What kind of a trick is it? The question is really interesting. Why do the Advaitins give more prestige to false cognitions? The locus of false cognitions, i.e., *sākṣin,* is also the locus of true cognitions. Without *sākṣin* there is no true cognition. So the locus of false cognition is more comprehensive. It amounts to giving false cognitions a certain priority. Why is this the case? Why is ignorance more important than true cognitions? Madhusūdana reminds his readers that a true cognition is a kind of ignorance, since all instruments of knowing are due to nescience and function in the empirical world. In response to the question, the Advaitins say that "yes, it is a trap, because like a dream it is due to nescience"[102] The question is not really answered. One way of answering the question would be to argue that a true cognition may be defined as that which destroys false cognition, hence the logical and pragmatical priority of false cognition. Truth, in effect, is defined as "not being false."

Before proceeding further, Madhusūdana raises an objection (attributing it to the Prābhākara school): When we admit the knower as the locus of knowledge, then why admit the witness-consciousness as well? Even if the modification of nescience is admitted in the deep sleep state, since the cognizer is already there, why admit *sākṣin*?[103] Madhusūdana points out that "since the knower is experienced as subject to change, the one unchanging, alone, is the witness of all cognition."[104] A cognizer is subject to change (*pariṇāmin*), it is variable; *sākṣin* is *apariṇāmin,* i.e., it is invariable. Whatever is changeable is an object (*dṛśya*) and so needs an unchanging witness. The one unchanging subject is the self, the witness of all things.

Concluding Remarks: Ramifications of Identifying *Sākṣin* with Either *Brahman-Ātman* or *Īśvara* or *Jīva*

So far we have seen that (a) the witness-consciousness is different from a cognizer and (b) for most Advaitins the witness-consciousness is regarded to be one, not many. We have also seen that there is no unanimity in the post-Śaṃkara tradition regarding the nature of the witness-consciousness.

At times "*sākṣin*" is used interchangeably with *brahman-ātman*, at other times with *Īśvara*, and at still other times with *jīva*. Some Advaita scholars do not find this disagreement regarding the nature of the witness-consciousness problematic. For example, Mahadevan notes: "The witness is not what is qualified by nescience . . . it is that which has nescience as its adjunct. The final position of Advaita is that '*Īśvara* who is nondifferent from *brahman* is also nondifferent from the *jīva*.' "[105] So, he concludes that there is no real conflict among the views outlined above, because in the final analysis it does not matter whether the witness-consciousness is identified with *Īśvara* or with the *jīva*.

It is indeed true that, according to the Advaitins, in the final analysis *brahman*, *Īśvara*, and *jīva* are nondifferent. However, I disagree with Mahadevan's thesis that the identification of the witness-consciousness with either *Īśvara* or *jīva* is inconsequential in the system of Advaita. The nature of the witness-consciousness bears significantly on the role that the witness-consciousness plays in their system and, accordingly, has important consequences for their epistemology.

In the system of Advaita, *Īśvara* and *sākṣin* are different concepts, and they have been designed to play different roles. *Īśvara* is creative; the witness-consciousness is not creative but receptive. It is not clear how the two could be the same. Further, it is not certain what is to be gained by identifying the two, because such an identification would amount to stripping *Īśvara* of the very same attributes by which we generally identify her. *Īśvara* and the witness-consciousness could ultimately be the same, but are taken to be different as functioning in different contexts. The point at issue is whether a qualified entity (*viśiṣtavastu*) and an unqualified entity (*vastu*) can be identical. This was debated a great deal in the Nyāya school of Indian philosophy. The question is: assuming that a pitcher is blue, are the "blue pitcher" (qualified entity) and the "pitcher" (unqualified entity) the same? The object that I perceive over there is both a blue pitcher and a pitcher. Similarly, one could argue that pure consciousness (*śuddhacaitanya*) and *sākṣin* (pure consciousness as reflected in nescience or its modes) and *Īśvara* (pure consciousness as conditioned by ignorance as its limiting adjunct) are the same; they are the same *ultimately*, but have different functions in different contexts.

The *jīva* is a knower, a doer, and an enjoyer. The witness-consciousness only apprehends. Accordingly, the witness-consciousness can only be a component of the *jīva*; it cannot be the totality of the *jīva*. The *jīva* is corporeal; it has body. Identification of the witness-consciousness with the *jīva* would make the *jīva* in itself free from agency, and the agency of the *jīva* would then become a function of its identification with the inner sense. Such an identification of the two would result in the manifestation of one person's mental modification to another person, which is absurd.

The witness-consciousness cannot be identified with *brahman* either. The witness-consciousness apprehends mental states, such as pleasure and pain, and the like. *Brahman*, on the other hand, has no pleasure or pain.[106] No kind of distinction in *brahman* is possible; *brahman* is that state of being where the subject-object distinction is obliterated. The witness-consciousness, on the other hand, always appears in a relational context; it makes knowledge possible. It acquires its meaning and significance only in the context of the objects to be witnessed.

In evaluating the relevance and nature of any entity in the system of Advaita, the distinction that the Advaitins make between two levels of reality must be kept in mind: the distinction between the ultimately real (*pāramārthika*) and the empirically real (*vyāvahārika*). This distinction permeates their entire system. These two levels are incommensurable: what is true from one standpoint is not so from another. A confusion between the two partly explains the inconsistencies and the contradictions that one might find in Advaita. From the standpoint of the ultimately real, *Īśvara* and *jīva* are nondifferent from *brahman*, because *brahman* is the only reality. But from the empirical standpoint, *Īśvara* and *jīva* are different; they are real. *Īśvara* accounts for the plurality of names and forms that we perceive in the phenomenal realm: this plurality is only apparent, not ultimately real.

The Advaita thesis, that *brahman* is the only reality, must face the challenge of explaining the concepts of *jīva* and *Īśvara*. Perhaps it is not an exaggeration to say that, from a phenomenological point of view, the theory of *jīva* is more relevant than the theory of *Īśvara*, because without an account of the witness-consciousness one cannot have an account of the *jīva*; I cannot have an account of my consciousness unless I have a place in it for *sākṣin*'s awareness of my mental states, such as happiness and so on.

Advaita is under obligation to provide a plausible account of the self; accordingly, the nature of the *jīva* is not inconsequential in the scheme of Advaita. The task of philosophy is not simply to say what truth is, but it is also called upon to show how it is that some truth, which is such and such, appears to be something different. If someone holds the view that consciousness is one, indivisible, universal, and all-pervasive, etc., then she is under the obligation to provide a satisfactory explanation of why consciousness appears to be individualized. It is the job of the Advaitin to give a satisfactory account of the *jīva*. By the same token, those who believe in *Īśvara* would demand to know what place the concept of *Īśvara* has in the Advaita system; they would demand an explanation of the status of *Īśvara* in Advaita. Additionally, given that the Advaita system has a theory of *Īśvara* and also a theory of the *jīva*, it is imperative to determine the status of the witness-consciousness in such a scheme, i.e., is there a witness belonging to an individual (*jīvasākṣin*)? A witness belonging to God (*Īśvarasākṣin*)?

Thus, Mahadevan's thesis, that it does not really matter whether the witness-consciousness is identified with the *jīva* or *Īśvara*, undermines the role of the witness-consciousness as it functions in the *jīva*; this role is extremely important from a phenomenological point of view. I, in my stage of bondage, can identify and have an immediate grip on the witness-consciousness, insofar as I can empirically—in my own experience—identify the witness-consciousness as it functions in my consciousness. In my consciousness I understand the witness-consciousness only insofar as I perceive/understand my cognitive mental modes, pleasure, pain, etc. Thus, the function of the witness-consciousness has a certain priority. The witness-consciousness also functions in the consciousness that is free, but that does not assume the form of the "I." So, we may say that while the witness-consciousness, as it functions for me, is first in the order of knowledge; the witness-consciousness, as belonging to *brahman-ātman*, is first in the order of being.

Mahadevan's thesis raises an important question about the awareness of the *jiva*-s. The question is whether the cognition of mental modes, modes of nescience, and mental states (e.g., pleasure and pain) is distributive or collective. We must keep in mind that, from an epistemological point of view, one aspect of the awareness of a cognition is that it is distributive, not collective. This explains why I experience only my pleasure and pain and not also yours. The fact that my mental modes, my mode of nescience, and my pleasure and pain are presented only to me and not to another person implies that my witness-consciousness is connected to my "I" or ego in some unique way; it is not, and cannot be, so connected to another person. This also explains why my cognitions and mental states uniformly assume forms such as: "I see this pitcher," "I know," "I do not know," "I am happy," "I am sad." To posit a transcendental "I" that is common to all the small "I's" would create problems. The assumption of a common witness-consciousness, which we all share collectively, would result in making my cognitions and mental states and your cognitions and mental states transparent to each other and to all the other *jīva*-s. We know that such an assertion goes against the verdict of our experience. I only know my own cognitions and mental states and not those of other persons. In other words, to posit a transcendental "I," which is in me as well as in you and to which my mental mode and your mental mode are manifest, would result in my mental modes being manifested to you as well as your mental modes being manifested to me, i.e., when I am perceiving a chair, you would also be having the same perceptual experience, which is, however, absurd.

The issue of the collective vs. distributive awareness of a cognition is very important for the distinction that some Advaitins make between *Īśvarasākṣin* and *jīvasākṣin*. *Īśvara* is a conscious being and, as such, has a witness-consciousness. *Īśvarasākṣin* is only responsible for *Īśvara*, not for me or you. *Īśvara* knows her cognitions and desires, but her witness-consciousness cannot account for my awareness of my cognitions and mental states.

Thus, it seems to me that Mahadevan's thesis undermines the function of the witness-consciousness or, better yet, undermines the function of an aspect of the witness-consciousness, *jīvasākṣin*, i.e., its function in an individual's self. If the witness-consciousness belongs to individuals, then witness-consciousness can be aware only of the states related to that particular individual self, i.e., her mental modes, her mode of nescience, and her pleasure and pain. If the witness-consciousness belongs to God, then that witness-consciousness is aware of my mental mode, mode of nescience, and my pleasure and pain, as well as being aware of your mental mode, your mode of nescience, and your pleasure and pain. This would give rise to unnecessary complications. Because, on this understanding, "I" in a statement such as "I know" (*ahaṃ jānāmi*), would not refer to an empirical "I," but rather to God. This would result in my knowing your awareness, because my awareness and my awareness of your cognition, my desires and your desires would all be presented to a common witness-consciousness, *Īśvarasākṣin*, in such a fashion that I would not only know my desires, but would also know your desires. This, however, is not the case. Moreover, we would be faced with the additional burden of coming up with an explanation for this discrepancy if we accept Mahadevan's thesis.

Before concluding, let us review my thesis that although the Advaitins took great pains to develop the epistemological ramifications of Śaṃkara's theory of the witness-consciousness, they, however, did not take the same care to explicate clearly the nature and status of the witness-consciousness from a metaphysical point of view. That there are as many as six theories regarding the nature of the witness-consciousness provides testimony to the lack of agreement among the Advaitins regarding the nature and status of such a witness-consciousness.

What accounts for this phenomenon? It seems to me that the Advaitins were already committed to an extreme metaphysical position, i.e., that *brahman-ātman* is the only reality. This, in itself, is not problematic;

the problem is how to offer a plausible explanation for other entities while at the same time keeping the *brahman-ātman* thesis intact. So, two questions arise: First, can one subscribe to a distinction between the witness-consciousness that belongs to the individual (*jīvasākṣin*) and the witness-consciousness that belongs to God (*Īśvarasākṣin*) on such an account? And second, given that *sākṣin* is always defined in relation to something that is not real, regardless of whether it is pure consciousness conditioned by a mode of the inner sense (*antaḥkaraṇavaccina caitanya*), or pure consciousness conditioned by a cognizer (*pramātṛacaitanya*), or something else, how can the existence of *sākṣin* be reconciled with the existence of *brahman-ātman*? There is always an adjunct that is not ultimately real. So, when the witness-consciousness is taken to be identical with *ātman* or with *brahman*, the integrity of the metaphysical thesis is preserved, but at the cost of sacrificing some important functions of the notion of the witness-consciousness. For example, *jīvasākṣin* would be lost, because such identification makes participation of witness-consciousness in the empirical realm an impossibility.

As a matter of fact, the witness-consciousness becomes epistemologically significant only when it is not taken to be identical with *brahman-ātman*, when it is in some way differentiated to perform a specific role. Because of their general thesis that the qualified entity (*viśiṣtavastu*) and the pure entity (*śuddhavastu*) are nondifferent, such a differentiation qua role makes the witness-consciousness both identical with and nonidentical with *brahman*. They are both identical and different, but only from different perspectives (strictly speaking, in one sense they are identical, but in another sense they are different). So, the metaphysical status of the witness-consciousness could not be univocally determined, because of the fact that from the metaphysical point of view it has already been determined that the only reality is *ātman*. The Advaitins are involved in a situation in which they cannot ascertain the metaphysical status of the witness-consciousness, because of their unflinching commitment to *brahman-ātman*. Epistemology concerns itself with cognitions; cognitions only make sense in the context of finite individuals. Therefore, all rules of cognition pertain to finite individuals. If "*sākṣin*" is an epistemological concept, then it has to be the same as *ātman* except that it functions only in the epistemological context.

Madhusūdana's definition of the witness-consciousness as consciousness that is reflected either in nescience or in modifications of nescience seems most defensible when viewed in light of the Advaitin nondualistic thesis.

The essence of the witness-consciousness is pure consciousness; however, it is never apprehended in itself, because of the superimposition of "I-ness" upon it. Thus, although the witness-consciousness is real, *sākṣin*-hood (*sākṣitā*) is not, because *sākṣitā* always points to a relationship between the witness-consciousness and inert objects (*sākṣyas*). The witness-consciousness as the principle of revelation does not depend on anything. As the principal element present in experience, it is changeless and does not cease to exist even in deep sleep. During the state of deep sleep, one experiences the self as devoid of all distinctions. All apperception is done by the "I," which alone remembers the states of waking, dreaming, and dreamless sleep. Upon waking up, an individual affirms that she was not aware of anything during the deep sleep state. The mind was quiescent and there was no objective bodily awareness. This, however, does not prove that consciousness was absent during the state of deep sleep. There is no relational knowledge, because the subject, the object, and the resulting knowledge (*tripuṭī*) are absent. The deep sleep state is indeterminate because the individual, upon waking up, says, "I slept." In this state, since the mind is covered by undifferentiated nescience, both ignorance and bliss are revealed by the witness-consciousness. Although pure consciousness is seeing or *dṛk*, in its status as the witness-consciousness it also performs the function of seer. Articulation of the witness-consciousness as a reflection of pure consciousness in nescience makes the role of the witness-consciousness in dreamless sleep, where only undifferentiated nescience exists, plausible; and the witness-consciousness as the reflection of consciousness in modes of nescience—i.e., in modifications of the inner sense—lends credibility to its function in the dreaming and the waking states. In these states the witness-consciousness functions as the reflection of consciousness, assuming the forms of the mental modifications of the inner sense. Whether one construes the finite individual as consciousness conditioned by the inner sense or as ubiquitous consciousness reflected in ignorance, the modifications of the inner sense are necessary for contact with the knower-consciousness and for the destruction of the concealment of the consciousness limited by the object.[107]

So, the witness-consciousness as consciousness *reflected* in the inner sense is different from the cognizer whose nature is *qualified* by the inner sense. Differences in the inner sense, with which the witness-consciousness is associated, leads to many empirically real *jīvasākṣin*-s. The Advaitins bring in *Īśvara* to rescue the world from becoming hopelessly individualized, i.e., relativized to each individual and making possible a cosmic witness-consciousness who believes in the world as *perceived* by the many individual selves. However, consciousness in its ultimate nature bears no relation to the mind nor to any other thing, for there is only one reality. It is important to remember here that not only the objective world of names and forms, but also the subjective realm consisting of experiences, is an appearance. For the Advaitins, pure consciousness, like the revelation of our conscious states, is pure immediacy. Although our apprehensions of objects involve subjective as well as objective factors, their uniqueness lies in their immediacy—which is not only nontemporal but also changeless. Consciousness cannot become an object for another consciousness; accordingly, there is no consciousness *of* consciousness. Consciousness is one, without a second. Regardless of whether I am seeing, hearing, etc., there always remains an awareness that is changeless. The witness-consciousness is such an unchanging awareness; it is the ground of changing knowledge. Thus, it is the necessary precondition of all knowledge, because it not only precedes all cognitions, it also makes them possible. Whereas *brahman* is veiled and projected on account of cosmic ignorance, whereas the *jīva,* in itself being a product of nescience, functions via the inner sense, the awareness of it all is possible because of the witness-consciousness, which is akin to *brahman,* but unlike *brahman* is neither veiled nor projected. It remains detached and functions as a witness, making any knowledge at all possible for finite individuals in this, the apparent world.

6

Sākṣin and Western Phenomenology

The purpose of this chapter is to make the concept of the witness-consciousness accessible to Western philosophers. I will do so by placing this concept in a context familiar to them. I will compare and contrast the notion of the witness-consciousness in Advaita Vedānta with similar ideas in Kant, Husserl, Freud, and Sartre. Wherever necessary, I will also point out the differences among these thinkers. Notwithstanding the fact that a comparison of the Advaitins with Western thinkers is not intrinsically necessary to expound Vedānta, I believe that such a comparison will help Western philosophers gain an access to this central concept around which the entire Advaita epistemology revolves. It seems to me that when one compares the unknown with the known and the unfamiliar with the familiar, the unknown becomes known or at least less unknown, the unfamiliar becomes familiar or at least less unfamiliar. Whereas the Advaitins took great pains to demonstrate the ramifications of this concept and recognized the importance of these ramifications for their theory of knowledge, Western philosophers have only implicitly presupposed this concept and, hence, have not dealt with the implications that arise from its explicit recognition.

There are three questions that one should keep in mind when comparing the Advaitin view of the witness-consciousness with similar ideas in Kant and Husserl. These questions are: (1) How *is* an object known? (2) How do we know *that* we know an object? And (3) how do we know that we do *not* know an object? The third question has not been raised by either Kant or Husserl. As a matter of fact, with the exception of Socrates, no major Western philosopher has raised this issue. We have seen that the notion of ignorance plays an important role in Advaita epistemology. Ignorance is one of the objects of the witness-consciousness; it makes us aware of our ignorance. However, the function of the witness-consciousness is not limited to simply making us aware of ignorance; it goes beyond that. It is also involved in the answers to the other two questions, viz., "How do I know an object?" and "How do I know that I know an object?"

To recall, at the risk of what might appear to be a repetition, on the Advaitin account ignorance is a positive entity. Therefore, something or someone must be responsible for removing the ignorance covering the object that is to be known. The mental mode performs this function. It makes the object known by removing ignorance. However, although the object is manifested by the mental mode, the mental mode cannot perform the function of manifesting the object without the witness-consciousness, insofar as the mental mode must itself be manifested by the witness-consciousness. Thus, we can say that the witness-consciousness is involved directly in manifesting the mental mode and indirectly in making the object known or manifest. With this in mind, I will begin with Kant.

Kant

Kant, unlike the Advaitins, does not have a conception of positive ignorance; in fact the concept of ignorance does not play any part in his theory of knowledge. Although Kant argues that we cannot have any knowledge of metaphysical entities such as God, freedom, and immortality, this lack of knowledge does not result from the fact that these entities are shrouded in ignorance, but rather from the limitations of the human faculties of knowing. Thus, unlike the Vedānta philosophers, he does not hold that to know an object is to remove the ignorance that has been covering it. So the question for Kant is not how ignorance is removed, but rather how an object is known. As pointed out earlier, none of the Western philosophers examined the problem of knowledge from this point of view. This perspective is uniquely Indian, specifically Advaitin.

I think we will better understand the differences between Kant's and the Advaitins' account if we have some idea of what is involved in knowing an object in Kant's theory. We must keep in mind that the differences between the two are not simply a result of the lack of a theory of ignorance in Kant and the importance of this concept in Advaita, but are rather the result of his conception of *a priori* knowledge. In Kant, as in many Western philosophers, we find the peculiarly Western notion that there is a kind of knowledge of an object that is *a priori*. At the outset of the *Critique of Pure Reason*, Kant informs us that although

> all our knowledge begins with experience, it does not follow that it all arises out of experience. For it may well be that even our empirical knowledge is made up of what we receive through impressions and of what our own faculty of knowledge (sensible impressions serving merely as the occasion) supplies from itself.[1]

The contents of our knowledge are derived from experience, argues Kant, but the mind arranges them according to certain *a priori* categories of the understanding. Although he also discusses ordinary empirical knowledge, Kant's main focus was on *a priori* knowledge: "knowledge . . . independent of experience and even of all impressions of the senses."[2] In other words, *a priori* knowledge is not derived through the senses, i.e., by touch, seeing, hearing, etc. *A priori* knowledge, maintains Kant, is derived simply from thinking independent of experience, and it is a means by which we can know certain truths about things, e.g., in mathematics.

He arrived at the conclusion that the mind can know an object *a priori* only if, and to the extent that, the mind is responsible for the formal structure of the object. For example, perception does not, cannot, occur without sensations, e.g., color, sound, and so on. In other words, if I perceive a table lamp in front of me as blue in color, the mind is not responsible for its blue color; the blue color is the content that must be given through the senses. Again, the sensations alone do not constitute knowledge. Sensations only furnish the content of experience; they must be placed in relation to other sensations in the context of space and time. Although our faculties do *not* determine the nature of what exists, they *do* determine the character of what exists insofar as they determine the form that an object has, because an object is thought, understood, and conceived by the understanding in its own peculiar manner. The understanding accomplishes this task according to certain categories or rules that are not derived from experience. Thus, the mind is responsible for knowing what is presented as an object: as a substance; as one, not many; as the effect of a cause; and as satisfying the principles of geometry and physics. These are the features of every object of knowledge for which the human mind is responsible; responsible both for organizing the sensations according to the forms of space and time and for providing a set of concepts by which the sensory impressions are synthesized in the form of representations of an object.

This latter notion, i.e., the notion of synthesis of sensations into the form of representations of an object, brings in Kant's theory of the transcendental unity of self-consciousness. He held that for a synthesis to be possible there must be an identity of the self in time such that the self can run through the various sensory representations that the mind receives. However, an identity of the self across time alone would not do, argues Kant. The self must also be able to organize, synthesize, and conceptualize the material that the mind receives. Thus, the activity of the self is responsible for the possibility of knowledge of the object. Kant further maintains that although we do not know the self as an object, all our experiences presuppose a unitary self-consciousness. All our experiences presuppose a self; philosophical reflection makes the self and its activities explicit. So Kant's position amounts to this: Not only are there sense impressions, there is also an internal mental activity—a transcendental unity of self-consciousness—which is responsible for the overall unification and organization of the object of knowledge. It is because of this transcendental unity that we know whatever we know, and it is this internal mental activity of which we have an implicit awareness that can be made explicit. So, as a result, Kant's position is that no object is known, or for that matter can be known, save through the activity of the transcendental unity of self-consciousness. The transcendental unity of self-consciousness itself is known to us directly: we have a reflective awareness of it that is not the same as our knowledge of an object.

Keeping the above in mind, let me now compare Kant's transcendental unity of self-consciousness to the Advaitin notion of the witness-consciousness. Both the witness-consciousness and the Kantian unity of self-consciousness serve to make possible the knowledge of the object as well as the knowledge of such knowledge. For Kant, the unity of apperception is also the unity of self-consciousness. He calls it consciousness because the unity of apperception is aware of itself, of its functioning, and is also aware of the object of knowledge. Likewise, not only is the witness-consciousness the awareness of our knowing ("knowing" taken in the sense of an inner mental process, a mental mode in Advaita epistemology), but it also makes knowledge of the object possible. The witness-consciousness, however, is not an active principle that constitutes an object. All constitution of the object is ascribed to the principle of ignorance, and therein lies the important and decisive difference between the Kantian and the Advaitin positions.

The Kantian unity of apperception makes the object and the knowledge of the object possible by the activity of synthesis. So one could say that the unity of apperception is a necessary condition for the possibility of the representation of the object. There could be no knowledge of the object otherwise. Kant is both an empirical realist and a transcendental idealist. He holds that there are unknown things—that things exist independently of our knowledge of them. But our knowledge of the object is made possible by functions exercised by the transcendental unity of apperception. So, the unity of apperception is an activity that shapes our representations of the object. It is responsible for the possibility of knowing the object. The witness-consciousness does not have any such function. It is a passive principle of manifestation in the sense that it only receives impressions from without, rather than an active principle that either creates or shapes the object via the imposition of categories. It is an absolutely impartial spectator "who does not identify himself with a point, with a particular position in space [and hence] cannot make divisions in space relative to that or to any point."[3] Since it does not identify itself with a particular position, it has no Archimedean point from which to orient itself in any relational mode of cognition. In other words, the witness-consciousness is totally receptive; it is not creative. The only way an object is made possible by the witness-consciousness is that the witness-consciousness may be construed as the substratum on which the object is superimposed.[4] Insofar as the superimposed object is made possible by the substratum, all objects of knowledge presuppose the witness-consciousness. It, however, does not give shape to them; it does not give form to them, manufacture them, or construct them in any way. What makes objects possible in Advaita metaphysics is not the activity of the self but rather ignorance.

The witness-consciousness, however, is much broader in its functioning scope than the Kantian unity of apperception, inasmuch as it goes beyond the general Kantian position. For Kant, the transcendental unity of apperception is responsible not only for the knowledge of an object but also for the knowledge of our knowledge. The witness-consciousness, on the other hand, is responsible not only for the knowledge of knowledge but also for the knowledge of all other mental states, like desire, pleasure, and pain, etc. So the Advaita position is that all inner states (or what Kant would call modifications of the inner sense, including sensory representations and thoughts and states of feeling and willing) are revealed to us immediately by the witness-consciousness.

Additionally, in the Advaita philosophy there is no distinction, the kind that arises as a result of philosophical reflection in Kant, between an implicit and explicit witness-consciousness. Kant writes:

> For this unitary consciousness is what combines the manifold, successively intuited, and thereupon also reproduced, into one representation. This consciousness may often be only faint, so that we do not connect it with the act itself, that is, not in any direct manner with the *generation* of the representation, but only with the outcome [that which is thereby represented]. But notwithstanding these variations, such consciousness, however indistinct, must always be present; without it, concepts, and therewith knowledge of objects, are altogether impossible.[5]

Again, he affirms that "the manifold representations . . . are . . . my representations (even if I am not conscious of them as such)."[6] Finally, he asserts that "consciousness itself has always a degree, which always allows of diminution."[7] In these passages, Kant makes a distinction between a faint consciousness and a clear and distinct reflective consciousness, which may be construed as a distinction between implicit and explicit consciousness. Implicit, however indistinct, is not unconscious. Even if I am not aware of my representations as my representations, I can be made conscious of them via philosophical reflections, thereby making them explicit. That the object of cognition or the cognition itself is the result of an act of synthesis is discovered on my part by an act of reflection. In this context we must remember that for Kant there is a pre-reflective awareness, no matter how indistinct, of this act. Consciousness of the act of synthesis may be very indistinct, because one always connects it to the outcome; accordingly, I may not be consciously aware that I have performed an act of synthesis.

Thus, Kant argues that we have an implicit awareness of the unity of apperception, which can be made explicit via philosophical reflection:

> It must be possible for the "I think" to accompany all my representations; for otherwise something would be represented in me which could not be thought at all, and that is equivalent to saying that the representation would be impossible, or at least would be nothing to me. That representation which can be given prior to all thought is entitled intuition. All the manifold of intuition has, therefore, a necessary relation to the "I think" in the same subject in which this manifold is found.[8]

In the above passage, Kant clearly affirms the necessity of the possibility that the "I think" accompanies all our representations. What Kant meant is as follows: When I see a table lamp, I do not usually say that I see the table lamp, but I say that the table lamp is blue. So "I think" is a blanket expression for "I see," "I know," etc. The "I think" *can* be attached to the original judgment about the object, but not contingently. It is not as if in some cases the cognitive state can and in other cases cannot be so ascribed; in all cases it can transform the original judgment "it is blue" to the reflective judgment "I see that it is blue," or "I know that it is blue." Unless I am able do that, representations like "it is blue," etc., would not be mine; if they are not mine, they would not belong to my consciousness, so they would be nothing to me. So, in a certain way Kant, in the above passage, comes very close to needing something like the Advaitin notion of the witness-consciousness. After all, if the mental mode is not accompanied by or manifested by the witness-consciousness, then it would be nothing for me, I would not be aware of it; and if I am not aware of it, i.e., if the mental mode itself remained unknown, then it could not function as the manifester of its object. Kant seems to have some such view; unless I could say "I see," "I perceive," "I think," the representations that I am having would not belong to me, they would not be my representations; if they are not my representations, then I would not have any knowledge of the represented object.

One must, of course, ask whether the Kantian "I" is a self-conscious "I." When one explicitly describes one's representations, the description always assumes the form "I think," "I perceive," "I know"; the "I" is always there. Although the "I" accompanies all our representations, we are not intuitively aware of the "I." In Kant's view it is always a thought—an intellectual representation—that we intuit. Allison, in his analysis of Kant's unity of apperception, notes: "The Kantian conception of self-consciousness as it is presented in the doctrine of apperception, concerns the thought of the 'I' as the subject of thought."[9] Self-consciousness in Kant simply amounts to the ability to determine what experiences we are having and who is having these experiences. The unity of apperception is the unity of self-consciousness, but it is not necessarily a consciousness of self-consciousness, paradoxical as this may sound. Thus, we can say that the Kantian "I," although a necessary accompaniment of all of our experiences, is not necessarily a self-conscious "I."

Analogously, it is necessary to ask whether the witness-consciousness is a self-conscious "I." The witness-consciousness in Advaita is certainly not a self-conscious "I"; it is not essentially individuated. To put it differently, it is individuated contingently, i.e., there are differences in the mental modes that the witness-consciousness manifests; however, merely as the function of manifestation, it is not individuated. In reviewing the Advaita literature, one finds two senses of the "I":

> In the cognition "I," there is a component "not-this" which is of the sole nature of consciousness. In that component the referent of "you," imagined to be "man," manifested by that consciousness's own power, appears as identical with it. That is "superimposition."[10]

The two senses are the "I" (1) as pure consciousness or pure intelligence and (2) as *ahaṃkāra*, the ego-sense or the subjectivity revealed by pure consciousness that results in such judgments as "I am" or "I am a man." Subjectivity, the "I" of which one is self-conscious, is not absolutely real; it is only empirically real. Something more basic, more fundamental is required; this is none other than pure consciousness. In Advaita, pure consciousness in reality is not individuated; it does not belong to anybody.

It is *nirāśraya*, i.e., it does not have any locus. It is *sui generis*; it remains self-identical regardless of the changes it undergoes. However, on account of ignorance that resides in the pure self, the true nature of the self is not revealed; nevertheless it appears as a self that is a perceiver, actor, and enjoyer of experiences in the empirical world. For the Advaitins, it is the self-shining light of consciousness that accounts for the knowledge of an object; regardless of how finite, determinate, and individualized consciousness may *seem* to be, it never loses its transcendence.

In Kant, on the other hand, the "I" is really the individuating principle; there is no universal consciousness except in the sense that the forms or the concepts of the understanding are common to all rational beings. Otherwise, any act of thinking is my act of thinking, or your act of thinking. So, for Kant, the "I" is essentially individual. The concepts that the "I" employs in thinking, however, are universal. They are shared by all rational beings. Thus, neither of the two Advaita senses of the "I" outlined above—the "I" as pure consciousness limited by ignorance or as subjectivity revealed by pure consciousness—are found in Kant.

Before concluding the section on Kant, I would like to note that there is a discussion in the Advaita literature concerning whether the witness-consciousness is one or many; the notion of *jīvasākṣin* or the thesis that each individual has its own witness-consciousness, implying, thereby, that the witness-consciousness is not one, that it is many, would be relevant in this regard.[11] Likewise, the question may be raised whether the Kantian unity of apperception is one or many. If one believes that the unity of apperception is a function that is the same in every knowing individual, and that there is no way of distinguishing between my unity of apperception and your unity of apperception, because the function of the unity of apperception is simply to organize and systematize the representations in accordance with the categories of the understanding that are shared by all rational beings, then the unity of apperception is one, not many. This means that even though you and I are different, we are not different with respect to the unity of self-consciousness. We are the same in the respect that our consciousness is structurally identical. So, on this interpretation, the unity of apperception can be said to be only one. Similarly, there are Advaita scholars who maintain that the function of the witness-consciousness is simply to manifest the object; the differences in perception are due to the inner sense with which it is associated. For these scholars, the witness-consciousness is one, not many.

It seems to me that whether one takes the unity of apperception or the witness-consciousness to be one or many depends on one's understanding of the terms "one" and "many." For Kant, the rules that we each use in synthesizing our sensory experiences are identical. Perceptions must take place in something; they cannot simply float in the air. My perceptions happen in me, yours in you, and his in him. There is a type-token distinction here. All of us are human beings; so my unity of apperception, your unity of apperception, and his unity of apperception are the same in the sense that they conform to the same general rules. That is also the condition under which objectivity is possible since the rules that I use to synthesize my perceptions are the rules that you use to synthesize your perceptions. My perceptions occur in my apperception in the same way that your perceptions occur in your apperception. So, even if the unity of apperception in one sense is one and not many, in another sense every subject has a distinct unity of apperception, and these apperceptions are many, i.e., many numerically and not qualitatively. Thus, the unity of apperception is one when viewed qualitatively, many when viewed numerically. On similar grounds, one could argue that the witness-consciousness is one insofar as its function of manifesting the object is concerned; it is many when viewed in light of the differences in the inner senses with which it is associated.

Husserl

Besides Kant, another philosopher in whose writings one can find something similar to the Advaitin concept of the witness-consciousness is Husserl. In order to determine in what sense, if any, Husserl can be said to have something similar to the concept of the witness-consciousness, I will begin by discussing what Husserl means by the transcendental ego or the transcendental "I."

In seeking to understand Husserl's notion of the transcendental ego or the transcendental "I," the following important features of Husserl's thinking must be kept in mind. First, the idea of the transcendental ego is reached by a conscious reflective methodological move that is known as the transcendental reduction or *epoché*. It involves complete suspension of all presuppositions about the world by the knowing mind:

> By phenomenological *epoché* I reduce my natural human ego and my psychic life . . . to my transcendental-phenomenological Ego, the realm of *transcendental-phenomenological self-experience*. The Objective world, the world that exists for me, that always has and always will exist for me—this world with all its objects, I said, derives its whole sense and its existential status, which it has for me, from me myself, *from me as the transcendental Ego*, the Ego who comes to the fore only with transcendental-phenomenological *epoché*.[12]

This deliberately chosen attitude involves a "bracketing," i.e., a setting aside of all beliefs about oneself and the spatio-temporal world. Such an attitude, maintains Husserl, avoids the possibility of doubt, which is a consequence of naturalism, and establishes truths independently of the existence of the world.

For Husserl, consciousness is intentional; it is always consciousness of something. Every act of consciousness must have an object. Indeed, he even goes so far as to assert that a certain type of intentional act corresponds to each type of object. J. N. Mohanty explains this Husserlian position as a conjunction of two separate propositions:

> On the one hand, there is, for Husserl, a correlation between types of objects and types of intentional reference in the sense that to each type of object there corresponds a certain mode of givenness. In fact the mode of givenness characteristic of a certain type of object may be used to bring out the phenomenological distinctiveness of that type. In the second place, to each particular object there corresponds a whole series of actual and possible intentional acts which have precisely that object as their intentional object. Two typically Husserlian notions arise out of this latter situation: the notion of noesis-noema correlation and that of the constitution of objects in the acts.[13]

The point that is being made is as follows: If we succeed in bracketing all presuppositions of our natural conception of the world and of consciousness as a part of the world, then there would result an experience of our own consciousness that is no longer understood as a part of nature in the sense of belonging to this body, or person, or psychophysical organism. Husserl calls consciousness so experienced "purified consciousness" or "transcendental consciousness." This transcendental consciousness contains a subject pole as well as an object pole; he terms the subject pole the "transcendental 'I,' " the object pole the "*noema.*" So the structure that comes into view has the transcendental "I," the noetic act, and its *noematic* correlate, the ego, the *cogito* and the *cogitatum.* My immediate interest is in the transcendental "I." Is it something like the witness-consciousness of the Advaitins?

To find in Husserl's thinking an access to something like a witness-consciousness, I would introduce what Fink calls the paradox of the three egos. Fink describes the *epoché* thus: It

> is not a "direct" refraining from belief paralleling the believing life of the thematic experience of the world which directly enacts its beliefs, but—and this cannot be overemphasized—is a structural moment of

> transcendental reflection. The *epoché* is a reflexive *epoché*, it is a refraining from belief on the part of the reflective observer, who looks on the belief in the world in the actuality of its live performance *without taking part in it.*[14]

Fink's point is as follows: Transcendental reflection is different from the natural reflective attitude. Prior to transcendental reflection, a human ego's reflection upon himself is confined to human self-apperception, and it moves within the parameters of the natural attitude. Bracketing of the world implicitly implies that, for the first time, an attempt is made to establish a reflective ego that is outside human apperception from the very beginning:

> This ego knowingly directs itself toward the universal world apperception as its theme. The disconnection of the world, however, not only makes possible the formation of a nonworldly reflecting-self, but . . . also makes possible the discovery of the true subject of the belief in the world: the transcendental subjectivity which accepts the world.[15]

Accordingly, he argues that there are three egos in Husserl's thinking:

> 1. the ego which is preoccupied with the world (I, the human being as a unity of acceptance, together with my intramundane life of experience); 2. the transcendental ego for whom the world is pregiven in the flow of the universal apperception and who accepts it; 3. the "onlooker" who performs the *epoché.*[16]

In other words, when one applies the method of reduction to the empirical ego, i.e., to an empirical consciousness as directed toward the empirical world, the result is a transcendental ego with its *noetic* act and *noematic* correlate. This gives rise to the question: Who is it that makes the distinction between the empirical ego and the transcendental ego? Do we need a third ego to make this distinction? It is here that we find something like the notion of the witness-consciousness. It is possible for me as a reflecting philosopher to distinguish within me between the empirical "I" and the transcendental "I." The empirical "I" is a part of the world, is subject to natural principles of causality, and belongs to an empirical psycho-physical organism; the transcendental ego is the same "I" but purified of all natural presuppositions. It must be possible for me, however, to observe the distinction between the empirical "I" and the transcendental "I," and this observer who apprehends the distinction must be a pure disinterested spectator or observer, or what the Advaitins call the witness-consciousness.

We must keep in mind in this context that the transcendental "I," as distinguished from the empirical "I," is not a mere disinterested spectator, because the transcendental "I," on Husserl's account, also constitutes the world. This implies that consciousness does not simply find the object and then adapt itself to it, but rather that, insofar as acts of consciousness are acts of conferring meaning, they are constitutive of the object. In the words of Kockelmans, in Husserl's philosophy:

> the object appears as essentially determined by the structure of thinking itself; this thinking itself first gives meaning to the object and then continues to orient itself to the pole of identity which it itself has created. When Husserl speaks of transcendence, he does not begin with the reality of the object but always with the meaning of the object. Hence the intentional analyses ultimately always become constitutive analyses, i.e., analyses which do not indicate how meaning is found in the primordial experiences, but which want to explain how the meaning of things is primarily constituted in and through consciousness.[17]

Thus, the transcendental ego, for Husserl, is not a disinterested spectator; it is a constitutive ego. The witness-consciousness, on the other hand, does not and cannot be said to constitute the world. In this respect the transcendental "I" is closer to the Kantian unity of apperception. In Kant's case, the transcendental unity of apperception constructs or, better yet, is responsible for the construction of the representation of the object as well as the knowledge of the object. Additionally, inasmuch as the unity of apperception is the principle of self-consciousness, it is also responsible for the knowledge of knowledge. Similarly, in Husserl, the world derives its structure, meaning and form from the transcendental ego. There are important differences between Kant's unity of apperception and Husserl's transcendental "I," but those differences do not concern us here. What is decisive is that Husserl's transcendental "I" is not merely a spectator; it is not a witness-consciousness.

Husserl's phenomenological method entailed describing how things are, i.e., how consciousness constitutes the world. This necessitated his positing a level of consciousness that observes and describes and that must be different from both the empirical ego and the constituting transcendental ego; this consciousness is none other than a disinterested spectator. Accordingly, Husserl argues that both the world and its constitution in transcendental consciousness are subject matters of phenomenological description. However, the idea of a descriptive philosophy already presupposes a moment of consciousness or a dimension of consciousness to which all descriptive data are presented. This dimension of consciousness is none other than the disinterested spectator.

Moreover, we also know that Husserl's phenomenology was interpreted by Heidegger as construing the "I" or the ego as a pure disinterested spectator. For example, Kockelmans notes:

> Heidegger chose to see intentionality as a relating to that which is, as a relation to the world. This is directly evident from his description of *Dasein* as Being-in-the-world. With this in mind we can easily understand that Heidegger's intentional analysis can never take the form of a constitutive analysis as we find in Husserl. This is also the reason why Heidegger will have nothing to do with a phenomenological or transcendental subjectivity, with a theory of the ego as a "disinterested observer," or with a complete and universal reflection.[18]

This interpretation is true, but only partially. It is true insofar as a descriptive phenomenology does indeed require that at some level consciousness must be simply a witness-consciousness; it is not true insofar as Husserl's transcendental ego is a *constituting*, and not a merely observing, subjectivity.

Finally, in the preface to the article in which Fink introduces the notion of disinterested spectator, Husserl himself acknowledges that he agrees with Fink's interpretation of his philosophy. Husserl writes: "I am happy to be able to state that it contains no sentence which I could not completely accept [as] my own or openly acknowledge as my own conviction."[19] Therefore, we can assert without any hesitation that Husserl, indeed, accepted the notion of a disinterested spectator. So, Husserl has to recognize three egos: the empirical, the transcendental, and the disinterested observer. In a very peculiar way, within my empirical consciousness, as I experience it in my everyday life before I begin to philosophize, these three are intertwined; they are not distinguished. The goal of phenomenology, at least of the Husserlian kind, consists in separating out these dimensions of consciousness and making their respective objects clear.

It seems, although it is difficult to determine with certainty, that Husserl held the view that consciousness is always implicitly aware of itself. Reflection, however, reveals or helps us recognize that we were aware of our own experiences all along. But he does not seem to have posited a disinterested spectator or witness-consciousness for this purpose, i.e., to account for the implicit self-awareness of pre-reflective and reflective consciousness. For him, the disinterested spectator is necessary, however, for the purpose of a phenomenologically descriptive philosophy, because the very possibility of phenomenological description implies that experiences must be given to a consciousness that describes what it finds. Husserl's disinterested spectator is not the same sort of consciousness that Sartre articulates; it does not require what Sartre calls pre-reflective transparency of all consciousness. For Sartre, as we shall see shortly, all pre-reflective consciousness is transparent to itself; it has a nonpositional awareness of itself. Thus, regarding the notion of transparency of consciousness, Husserl takes up a position that is not as strong as Sartre's.

Sartre

For Sartre, there are two species of being: "being-in-itself" (*en-soi*) and "being-for-itself" (*pour-soi*). "Being-in-itself" is the being of phenomena; it refers to the being of things, the objects of intention. "Being-for-itself" is the being of persons; it is consciousness and, for Sartre as for Husserl, consciousness is intentional, i.e., consciousness is consciousness of something. Incompleteness and lack of any determinate structure characterize being-for-itself. As pure intentionality, it is nothingness; it is not conditioned by any essence. This explains why consciousness is always for-itself. Whereas things are complete in themselves, human beings are incomplete insofar as they are open toward the future. Choices that an agent makes fill up the empty future. Emptiness of the future forces the agent to confront not only Heideggerian anxiety but also Sartrean nausea.

Since consciousness is transparent, nothing is hidden from it. Sartre notes:

> Indeed, the existence of consciousness is an absolute because consciousness is consciousness of itself. . . . And consciousness is aware of itself insofar as it is consciousness of a transcendent object. All is therefore clear and lucid in consciousness: the object with its characteristic opacity is before consciousness, but consciousness is purely and simply consciousness of being consciousness of that object. . . . consciousness of consciousness—except in the case of reflective consciousness . . . [it] is not positional, which is to say that consciousness is not for itself its own object. Its object is by nature outside of it, and that is why consciousness posits and grasps the object in the same act. Consciousness knows itself only as absolute inwardness. We shall call such a consciousness: consciousness in the first degree, or unreflected consciousness.[20]

He further adds:

> Insofar as my reflective consciousness is consciousness of itself, it is non-positional consciousness. It becomes positional only by directing itself upon the reflected consciousness which itself was not positional consciousness of itself before being reflected.[21]

Consciousness thus forms the starting point of his philosophy. There are two modes of consciousness: pre-reflective consciousness (non-thetic or nonpositional consciousness) and reflective consciousness (thetic consciousness or positional self-consciousness). The following example would explain the difference between the two. Let us assume that I am counting the number of students that showed up for my Indian philosophy class today. As I am counting, I am aware of counting, but not of reflecting *that* I am counting. This latter is pre-reflective consciousness. However, if one of my students were to ask me what I was doing, I would become aware of the act of counting via reflection. This consciousness of consciousness is what Sartre calls reflective consciousness. In other words, my counting is known by a positing consciousness, i.e., a consciousness that has an object; however, even before I reflect on my counting I am *aware* of my counting nonpositionally.

This is Sartre's general position. One immediately notices several similarities between Sartre's account of the transparency of consciousness and the Advaita account of the witness-consciousness. However, before discussing these similarities, I would like to note, even at the risk of what might appear to be a digression, two pertinent points in this regard: (1) what Hegel has to say regarding the transparency of consciousness, and (2) a philosophical objection that might be raised against Sartre's notion of the transparency of consciousness.

(1) It is worth noting that Hegel was perhaps the first major philosopher to question the transparency of consciousness. Consciousness, maintains Hegel, is always aware of itself. One cannot compare consciousness to anything else. Consciousness is its own criterion, it is its own comparison; it has its own object within itself, one cannot apply any external criterion to it. This implies that one cannot get out of consciousness and set it over against some other external standard. The point that is relevant here is the general Hegelian perspective in the *Phenomenology* that even if consciousness is aware of itself, it is not always aware of its own truth. This implies that a consciousness may have a certain understanding of itself that is not true or correct. A consciousness may be laboring under self-deception as to what it really is about. This is, in a way, the beginning of a fundamental departure from the classical tradition according to

which consciousness, like light, always shows itself, that it is transparent. Hegel believed that even if we do not go outside the overall sphere of consciousness, we can still find that a particular form of consciousness can be criticized and shown not to be fully aware of its own truth, leading to another level of consciousness, although one is still within the field of consciousness. For example, as Hegel shows, perceptual consciousness which believes that it knows, that it apprehends, takes in, and perceives material objects around it, really does not know its own truth. Hegel attempts to demonstrate that we do not really perceive simple physical objects around us. There are conceptual problems about perception, and these problems show that we really do not understand what is happening. Hence, his critique of perception leads to physics, because physics attempts to explain what perception cannot. All this for Hegel implies that consciousness is not a static phenomenon, but rather a developing process: from elementary sensation where it begins, consciousness develops as a process to the level that Hegel calls absolute knowledge. At this developed level, consciousness would be wholly transparent and would know its own truth. This is the Hegelian ideal of philosophical cognition. Thus, although Hegel believed that consciousness is an autonomous domain, he is far from saying that consciousness at all levels is fully cognizant of its own nature, of its own truth. This, however, requires that consciousness always moves on to higher levels. However, he accepts the classical philosophical position that philosophical cognition would eventually be fully aware of its own truth. Modern philosophers, or rather postmodern philosophers, really want to deny this. Derrida, for example, totally denies that consciousness can at any level of philosophical thinking be fully aware of all its presuppositions, which means that there would always be something that is out of its reach about itself. In other words, for postmodern philosophers complete self-knowledge is never possible. Hegel, on the other hand, believed that complete self-knowledge is possible; he calls it absolute knowledge. Vedāntins think that it is possible; they go a step further and maintain that it is also actual in a certain sense: It is always there; only it is concealed by ignorance. However, one must remember that, for them, one has awareness—even of ignorance.

(2) One might object that whereas it makes perfect sense to say "I know" in the context of a cognition that is manifested immediately, one cannot make the same claim for emotions, feelings, and desires, because there may be emotions, feelings, and desires that one might have and not be aware of consciously. Freud, Jung, and the depth psychologists, for example, argue that I may indeed have a desire, but I may not be conscious of that desire. A person suffers from a neurosis[22] and sees a psychoanalyst. Long therapy reveals that he had a hatred for

his father; this emotion of hatred was repressed, i.e., it was "covered up." According to psychoanalysis, one is not consciously aware of one's repressed emotions. Both Sartre and the Advaitin would find this general psychoanalytic thesis unacceptable. If psychoanalysis has yielded true insight, then both Sartre and the Advaitin would be wrong: Sartre in holding that consciousness is always transparent, that there is nothing hidden from it; the Advaitin in holding that there is no unknown emotion, that emotions exist only as revealed. However, it seems to me that whereas Sartre (in *Being and Nothingness*) would find the Freudian account totally unacceptable, the Advaitin would find it only partially unacceptable.

Sartre rejects Freudian psychoanalytic theory because of his unflinching commitment to the thesis that consciousness is completely transparent to itself. He uses the intentional form of consciousness to reject the Freudian theory of emotions. Freud and Jung took the unconscious to be the abode of desires and emotions. Accordingly, they characterize emotions as intrusions from the unconscious. Freud cautions his readers against confounding conscious and unconscious mental processes in the following words:

> In psycho-analysis there is no choice for us but to assert that mental processes are in themselves unconscious, and to liken the perception of them by means of consciousness to the perception of the external world by means of sense-organs. . . . Just as Kant warned us not to overlook the fact that our perceptions are subjectively conditioned and must not be regarded as identical with what is perceived though unknowable, so psycho-analysis warns us not to equate perception by means of consciousness with the unconscious mental processes which are their object. Like the physical, the psychical is not necessarily in reality what it appears to us to be.[23]

Jung notes that "the unconscious produces dreams, visions, fantasies, emotions, grotesque ideas, and so forth."[24] And he further observes that "one is inclined to think that ego-consciousness is capable of assimilating the unconscious, at least one hopes that such a solution is possible. But unfortunately the unconscious really is unconscious; in other words, it is unknown."[25] Freud and Jung provide evidence from cases of amnesia and split personality, and from dream interpretation, for their thesis that the unconscious in fact exists, and is unknown.

Sartre maintains, on the contrary, that all these cases involve conscious behavior. He replaced the notion of the unconscious with his concept of bad faith (*mauvaise foi*). Sartre contends that all things happen for consciousness; bad faith is denial by consciousness of what it implicitly knows. Accordingly, Sartre argues that emotions are for consciousness, never in consciousness. They are intentional and so must be explained in the context of their intentional objects, i.e., they must be explained as directed toward an object of consciousness:

> Emotion is not an accident. It is a mode of existence of consciousness, one of the ways in which it *understands* its "being-in-the-world." . . . A reflective consciousness can always direct itself upon emotion. In this case emotion appears as a structure of consciousness.[26]

Emotions belong to consciousness; they are manifested for a purpose and accordingly cannot be accounted for in terms of the unconscious. No id, ego, and superego are needed here. The followers of Freudian psychoanalysis argue that if I really hated my father, I would know it, although I might not admit it to myself, i.e., I might repress my consciousness of that emotion. Sartre argues that consciousness always knows, even if nonpositionally, what is happening in consciousness. Our behavior is conscious, although sometimes we are in bad faith. In bad faith "consciousness instead of directing its negation outward turns it toward itself."[27] In *Being and Nothingness,* one of the examples he gives to explain bad faith is that of a woman who agrees to go out on a date with a man who she is aware has a sexual interest in her.[28] She knows that sooner or later she will have to make a decision about his intentions; however, she postpones making that decision as long as she can. She lives in the present and does not want to confront the future. Sartre argues that this woman is a paradigm instance of bad faith, insofar as she knows her situation but refuses to admit it to herself. No activity of the unconscious is required here.

> [O]ne who practices bad faith is hiding a displeasing truth or presenting as truth a pleasing untruth. Bad faith then has in appearance the structure of falsehood. Only what changes everything is the fact that in bad faith it is from myself that I am hiding the truth. Thus the duality of the deceiver and the deceived does not exist here. Bad faith on the contrary implies in essence the unity of a *single* consciousness.[29]

In other words, in bad faith, although I do not want to deal with the truth, I am not really unaware of the fact that I am so inclined:

> I must know the truth very exactly in order to conceal it more carefully. . . . That which effects itself with bad faith must be conscious [of] its bad faith since the being of consciousness is consciousness of being. It appears then

> that I must be in good faith, at least to the extent that I am conscious of my bad faith.[30]

Thus, Sartre holds that consciousness is fully transparent. It may be ambiguous, but in that case it is transparent as ambiguous. In other words, a transparent consciousness is not necessarily clear; it may be clouded by ambiguity.

The Advaitins would, in general, welcome the ideas of covering and projecting that one finds in Freudian psychology. Freud talks about the covering up of one's mental states, one's states of willing. For example, a son's erotic feeling for his mother is socially unacceptable, so he covers it up. He could never admit it to himself, because it is not acceptable to society. For Freud, covering it up means that the superego knows that none of these despicable feelings should be manifested. So, it allows them to manifest only if they are sufficiently symbolized in a form in which they are not recognized. The symbolized feeling is what shows up in your dreams. "All dreams" for Freud "represent the fulfillment of wishes," and "the functioning of dreams provides systematic evidence of the unconscious. . . . Dreams occur during sleep—when the conscious part of the personality is most relaxed and off-guard. . . . The wish is often . . . well hidden, disguised and distorted. . . . The latent content of the dream . . . is only allowed to appear if it is disguised as manifest content."[31] This is the general Freudian theory, which contains within its fold both concealment (*āvaraṇa*) and projection (*vikṣepa*): concealment of the original emotion and projection of it in the form of the symbols in which it is clothed and allowed to reappear—generally in one's dreams and perhaps, once in a while, during waking experience, e.g., in a slip of the tongue. This is an interesting account of ignorance that one finds in Freud; something is covered up and something else, i.e., the symbol, is created. Although the Advaitins would find the general Freudian thesis of covering and projecting plausible when viewed in the context of cognitive experiences, they would not, however, accept the psychoanalytical thesis that one's emotions are also covered, that one might not know anything about one's emotions. For the Advaitins emotions can exist only as revealed; they do not, and cannot, exist as unrevealed.

It seems to me that Sartre's account of the transparency of consciousness is similar to the witness-consciousness theory, insofar as any mental state (e.g., love, desire, anger, pleasure, cognition, pain) is immediately known to a person. An emotion, argues Sartre, exists only as consciousness of that emotion. For both Sartre and the Advaitins, there are no unmanifested emotions. However, there is an important difference between the two: For Sartre, unlike the Advaitins, no witness-consciousness is needed to manifest these emotions; for him, any conscious state is known as soon as it occurs, but not as an objective awareness.

Although the function of ignorance is not found in Sartre, two modes of consciousness, the positional and the nonpositional, play an important role in his theory of consciousness. It would not be an exaggeration to say that the witness-consciousness's awareness of mental modes is also a nonpositional awareness, given that a mental mode is not manifested by the witness-consciousness *as an object.* The Advaitins, as we have seen, repeatedly make a distinction between two kinds of awareness: an objective awareness, in which the subject and the object are different, and an awareness of my own knowing, which is a nonobjective awareness. Such a nonobjective awareness implies that there is an identity of that which knows and that which is known whereby they are both one. So there is a nonpositional transparency of consciousness for the Advaitin. This is precisely Sartre's view. Sartre's distinction between positing and nonpositing consciousness implies that in the perception of a lamp on a table, for example, the table lamp is known by a positing consciousness (a consciousness that has an object), but my perceiving is known nonpositionally, i.e., it is known, but not as an object, although I am aware of it. I can know it by reflection, thereby making it an object; but even before I reflect on my perceiving, I am aware of my perceiving nonpositionally.

Sartre's original nonpositing, nonobjective transparent consciousness is not an "I"; it is not an ego. "Every positional consciousness of an object is at the same time a non-positional consciousness of itself."[32] He makes a distinction between a pre-reflective and a reflective *cogito.* In *The Transcendence of the Ego,* Sartre repeatedly states that the original awareness of my consciousness does not include the "I think." Here he is arguing against both Husserl and Kant. The question arises: What is this original awareness? Let us suppose that a person is standing outside waiting for a bus. He sees the bus coming—there is an original, nonpositional transparent consciousness. How does he describe this original consciousness? He does not say "I see the bus coming," which would entail reflection on his part, but rather says that "the bus is coming," an assertion that really describes the structure of the world. That is why Sartre calls the original consciousness "nothingness." The original consciousness, he argues, is so totally absorbed in the world that to describe it is to describe the world. The point that Sartre is trying to make is as follows: In pre-reflective consciousness there is no room for an "I." Pre-reflective consciousness is directed toward the object. The very structure of consciousness entails that there is a pre-reflective consciousness within it. In a similar fashion, the Advaitins also argue that the witness-consciousness is not an *aham,* it is not an "I." One does not articulate the witness-consciousness; it is implicitly present. Thus, for both Sartre and the Advaitin, the "I" is not a component of the original pre-reflective consciousness.

Pre-reflective consciousness precedes all knowing in both accounts. Such a consciousness is a necessary precondition of all knowing for both Sartre and the Advaitin. In the absence of such a consciousness, says Sartre, the consciousness could only be reflective, thereby necessitating the positing of a third consciousness and so on ad infinitum:

> All reflecting consciousness is, indeed, in itself being unreflected, and a new act of the third degree is necessary in order to posit it. Moreover, there is no infinite regress involved here, since consciousness has no need at all of a reflective consciousness in order to be conscious of itself. It simply does not posit itself as an object.[33]

An object with its opacity is simply presented to consciousness, for Sartre. However, reflective consciousness is more complex; it is consciousness of the consciousness of that object. So, consciousness is known, although not as an object is known. There is no knower-known dualism in the pre-reflective apprehension of consciousness. Pre-reflective consciousness, thus, is not constituted by its object; the object is something external to it: "All consciousness is positional in that it transcends itself in order to reach an object, and it exhausts itself in this same positing."[34] Sartre further expounds: "A pure consciousness is an absolute quite simply because it is consciousness of itself. It remains therefore a 'phenomenon' in the very special sense in which 'to be' and 'to appear' are one. It is all lightness, all translucence."[35] The very nature of consciousness is such that for it to be and to be aware of itself are one and the same. So, for Sartre, all consciousness is intrinsically aware of itself.

However, not all consciousness is knowledge, because in order for consciousness to be knowing, consciousness must be aware of itself as knowing. Thus, he argues that the essential character of being-for-itself is to negate itself; it is not and cannot become being-in-itself. From the perspective of the in-itself, the for-itself is incomplete and not the foundation of its being. The for-itself strives toward authenticity. Consciousness is not static; it is dynamic. It transcends itself, i.e., it reaches beyond what it is in order to eliminate its lack of being. It reaches out to the other—other objects and other persons. Consciousness is the ground of nothingness because nothingness arises in being. Freedom, so Sartre argues, is the nothingness of being.

Once again, Sartre reminds us of the Advaitins, who articulate consciousness as immediately revealing itself. If Sartre is right, then consciousness in all its states is transparent. His description of consciousness as absolute inwardness, and the object as something external has Advaitin overtones. The Advaitins, like Sartre, describe consciousness as wholly light and translucent; in Sartrean style, they argue that there is no need to postulate a knower to know consciousness, thereby requiring a third entity to know the knower and so on ad infinitum. However, notwithstanding the similarities that one finds in the two accounts, I must make note of two important and decisive differences between them before concluding this discussion. Whereas for Sartre freedom is the nothingness of being, for the Advaitins freedom is that state of being in which all subject-object distinctions are obliterated; it is a state of bliss. Again, for Sartre, consciousness is intrinsically temporal and ever changing, but for the Advaitins it is permanent and eternal. Thus, although both articulate consciousness as translucent, they arrive at entirely different conclusions. How and why this happens provides the subject matter for another study.

Awareness and Knowing

Before closing, I would like to say a few words about the distinction between awareness and knowing that permeates both Western and Indian thinking. Notwithstanding the fact that they both make this distinction, there are important differences between the two traditions on this issue.

Western philosophers do recognize this distinction. David Smith in *The Circle of Acquaintance* states:

> For when I am consciously thinking something, I am aware of my own thinking, and by virtue of that awareness I know that I am consciously so thinking. This awareness—whatever its analysis—is not the same as knowledge (which consists in true belief with adequate justification, appropriate causal history, etc.), but having this awareness is the normal ground for knowing that I am so thinking. . . . Indeed, our concerns are the structure of consciousness and the direct awareness it brings of oneself and one's experience; claims about knowledge are a different matter.[36]

Thus, Western scholars do allow a distinction between knowing and awareness of knowing. There are many things one may know, but one is not always aware that he knows those things. Western psychologists articulate a belief in what they call unconscious knowing; they talk about unconscious inference. I may see someone from a distance and say, "I think I see my friend coming." In this instance, I did not actually see my friend, rather I inferred it. Inference here is unconscious, i.e., I infer, but I do not know that I am inferring.

This distinction between awareness and knowledge is based on what is termed "unconscious knowledge" in the Western context. A computer provides an illustrative example. It solves mathematical problems, but while it solves the problems it is not aware of solving them. People say, "The computer knows it; it will solve the problem." A computer, however, is not aware—the computer does not have the capacity for cognition. Does it know? Knowing presupposes the possibility of unconscious cognition. Many people believe in it; they believe that many cognitions of which we are unaware occur in the mind. Unconscious cognition is not merely limited to a machine's cognition. When driving an automobile one makes many decisions in the stretch of one block, but one is not aware of all of them. A child knows a lot of material at the age of six, but is not consciously aware of all that he knows. In his linguistic theory, Noam Chomsky demonstrates that when a child first learns language he learns a few words, then a few sentences. Give him a string of words that is not well formed, a sentence that does not make sense because the structure is incomplete or renders the meaning ambiguous, and he will be puzzled; he will recognize that something is wrong. Give him a well-constructed sentence, and he will say he does not understand it, but he will not be puzzled. How does one account for the fact that a child, who knows only a few sentences and has a very limited vocabulary, is able to recognize that the sentence he has been given is neither right nor wrong? Chomsky's hypothesis is that there is an unconscious linguistic cognition in the human mind; it is a kind of genetic or innate competence that is there:

> [T]his theory is now called "universal grammar" (UG), adapting a traditional term to a new context of inquiry. UG may be regarded as a characterization of the genetically determined language faculty. One may think of this faculty as a "language acquisition device," an innate component of the human mind that yields a particular language through interaction with presented experience, a device that converts experience into a system of knowledge attained: knowledge of one or another language.[37]

For Chomsky, there is a grammarian, so to speak, sitting in your brain who can figure out what is syntactically correct and what is not. There is linguistic cognition, but there is no awareness of scanning a string of words. There is no conscious awareness of whether or not the sentence obeys the rules of syntax. So, there is knowledge without awareness; we know far more than we are aware of consciously.

The Advaitins, like Western scholars, make a distinction between knowing and awareness. However, there are important differences between the two distinctions: First, in the Advaitin context the awareness is not only of knowing but also of not-knowing, of desiring, of pleasure, in other words, of all the mental states; and second, the Advaitins do not recognize unconscious cognition. Knownness in Advaita presupposes unknownness. When we know an object, we also know its previous unknownness. Thus, paradoxical as it may sound, knowing an object presupposes knownness and unknownness. Awareness of not-knowing in the Advaitin context assumes the form "I do not know." It is given to us in our experience. It implies that "I know that I do not know"; this is knowledge of ignorance. It is like trying to see darkness by the light of a lamp. There should be some mode of seeing the darkness without the help of light. There must be some mode of being aware of not-knowing that is an awareness, but which in itself is not the knowing by means of which the not-knowing could be removed. The fact that I know that I do not know demonstrates that there is no pure and simple ignorance; ignorance is revealed by a consciousness, and that consciousness, for the Advaitins, is the witness-consciousness.

The second important difference between the Advaitin and Western analysis has to do with unconscious cognition; it is not allowed for in the Vedāntic context.[38] Whatever one knows is also presented to the witness-consciousness; the witness-consciousness is ubiquitous, it is everywhere. This explains why their theory of error takes a peculiar form. Let us take the instance of the rope-snake illusion. Is this illusion perceptual or inferential? What do I see? Is it real? Is it not real? Western psychologists would say it is a case of unconscious inference, i.e., I see the rope and infer a snake. The Advaitin would say I am seeing a snake; I am not inferring it. Indian epistemologists generally accept the verdict of consciousness. If my consciousness tells me that I am seeing, then I am seeing. But the Western epistemologists hold that if one's consciousness tells one that he is seeing "X," he might not be actually seeing "X," he might be mistaken, he might be making an erroneous inference. The Advaitin notion of the witness-consciousness is very comprehensive, insofar as it encompasses within its fold (1) all cognitions, (2) all mental modes, and (3) all noncognitive mental states. But it does not allow for unconscious inference. One may or may not accept the Advaita theory with regard to all three of these. The Advaitins clearly succeed in demonstrating that one's awareness is not only limited to knowing; it also includes not-knowing. Therein lies their uniqueness and their fundamental difference from Western epistemologists.

Notes

Chapter 1. Introduction

1. Eliot Deutsch, *Advaita Vedānta: A Philosophical Reconstruction* (Honolulu: University Press of Hawaii, 1973), p. 81.

2. *Ātman* is usually translated as "self." In the Western philosophico-religious traditions, the term "self" generally connotes a subject, the referent of "I." *Ātman,* however, is not the empirical self. It is pure consciousness, a kind of trans-empirical consciousness that is at once different from and forms the basis of empirical consciousness. Although the Sanskrit term "*cit*" translates literally as consciousness, in this work, I will use "self," "consciousness," "pure consciousness," "real self," and "pure self" interchangeably to connote *ātman* as distinguished from the finite self, the empirical self (*jīva*).

3. The best available current resource on the notion of the *sākṣin* is A. K. Chatterjee and R. R. Dravid's monograph *The Concept of Sākṣin in Advaita Vedānta* (Banaras: Banaras Hindu University, 1979). This short monograph has helped me to focus on some of the important issues surrounding the notion of *sākṣin.* While making some useful points, the monograph at times uses technical terms with insufficient precision, and at other times uses them without English equivalents. As a result, the significance and ramifications of these terms are not clear to the readers.

4. *sākṣiṇaḥ sadā'sandigdhāviparyastasya nityasākṣātkāratā'nāgantukaprakāśatva. . . . Bhāṣyabhāvaprakāśikā* on *Brahmasūtrabhāṣya,* in *Brahmasūtra-Śāṃkara-Bhāṣyam* (BSB) with Nine Commentaries, ed. Anantakrishna Śastri (Calcutta: Metropolitan Printing and Publishing House, Calcutta, 1933), II.2.28, p. 57. Henceforth this edition will be cited as *Nine Commentaries.*

5. *antaḥkaraṇavṛttyupahitamadhyastaṃ caitanyameva śabalitaṃ sākṣīti. Pradīpaḥ* on Śaṃkara's "Adhyāsbhāṣyam," ibid., p. 293.

6. *sākṣiṇo nāvaraṇaṃ. Ṛjuvivaraṇaṃ,* ibid., p. 364.

7. *sākṣicaitanyasya ca ajñānāvabhāsakatvāt. Pañcapādikāvivaraṇam,* ibid., p. 265.

8. *sākṣādeva bhāsayati, sākṣī. Tattvadīpana,* ibid., p. 478.

9. The sentence "*yasya bhāsā sarvaṃ idaṃ vibhāti*" (i.e., by whose light, all this is illuminated) really means being witness of all things ("*sarva sākṣitvāt*"). *Vārtika* on BSB, I.2.23, ibid., p. 198.

10. Debabrata Sinha, *The Idealist Standpoint: A Study in the Vedāntic Metaphysic of Experience* (Visva Bharati, Centre of Advanced Study in Philosophy, 1965), p. 73.

11. Edmund Husserl, "Second Meditation," *Cartesian Meditations: An Introduction to Phenomenology*, trans. Dorian Cairns (The Hague: Martinus Nijhoff, 1973), p. 35.

12. Even Hegel recognizes it when he writes that the new object "which offers itself to consciousness without consciousness knowing how it comes by it—that to us, who watch the process is to be seen going on, so to say, behind its back." G. W. F. Hegel, *The Phenomenology of Mind*, ed. and trans. J. B. Baillie (New York: Harper Torchbook, 1967), p. 144. Again: "true knowledge lies rather in the seeming inactivity which merely watches" (p. 804).

13. See Chapter 6. The notion of a disinterested spectator is present in Husserl, but Heidegger criticizes this notion at many places. For Heidegger, there is nothing like a disinterested spectator. Such a notion belongs to a certain tradition in Western thinking in which the cognitive subject is taken simply to observe and contemplate the nature of objects, taking no active role in dealing with the object. The idea of a pure disinterested spectator who simply observes what is going on in the universe, but does not in any way interfere, roughly corresponds to the distinction between theory and practice in the Western tradition. The idea of pure theory in the Greek tradition, however, presupposes the idea of a disinterested spectator. *Theoria* literally means observing the sport taking place in the stadium without taking part in it. For the Greeks, knowing the truth presupposes a disinterested spectator very much like the witness-consciousness of the Advaitins.

14. J. Kockelmans, "What Is Phenomenology?" in *Phenomenology*, ed. J. Kockelmans (Garden City, N.Y.: Doubleday, 1967), p. 27. See also "Philosophy as a Rigorous Science," in Edmund Husserl's *Phenomenology and the Crisis of Philosophy*, trans. Quentin Lauer (New York: Harper Torchbook, 1965), pp. 71–148.

15. Edmund Husserl, "The Idea of Phenomenology," in *Readings in Twentieth-Century Philosophy*, ed. William P. Alaston and George Nakhnikian (London: Free Press of Glencoe, 1963), p. 627.

16. Marvin Farber, *Foundations of Phenomenology* (Cambridge, Mass: Harvard University Press, 1943), p. 527.

17. False (*mithyā*), argue the Advaitins, is other than the real (*sadviviktatvaṃ vā mithyātvaṃ*). To say that X is false should not be taken to mean that it has no reality; the false is empirically real. There is a kind of temporality about it insofar as it is transcended; it is an object of experience, for example, the rope-snake. Thus, it is different from the unreal or nonbeing, which is never an object of experience, true or false. In fact the concept of the unreal is reserved for self-contradictory concepts, for example, the son of a barren woman. A clear understanding of the logical and ontological distinction between the false and the unreal is essential for a proper understanding of the Advaita system.

18. Kalidas Bhattacharyya, *A Modern Understanding of Advaita* (Ahmedabad: L. D. Institute of Indology, 1975), pp. 4–5.

19. Ibid., pp. 1–2.

20. "*Ajñāna*" or "*Avidyā*" is ignorance; it is nescience. In the Advaita view, ignorance is not a mere absence of knowledge; it is positive and is removed upon *brahman* realization. The same ignorance, in its cosmic aspect known as "*māyā*," explains why one *brahman* appears as many individual selves and the empirical world. Although "*māyā*," "*ajñāna*" and "*avidyā*" at times have been used interchangeably, in matters of individual bondage, "*avidyā*" or "*ajñāna*" has been accorded precedence over "*māyā*." In other words, the denotation of these three is nescience or ignorance. Śaṃkara notes: "By that element of plurality which is the fiction of Nescience, which is characterized by name and form, which is evolved as well as nonevolved, which is not to be defined either as the Existing or the Nonexisting, *brahman* becomes the basis of this entire apparent world with its changes, and so on, while in its true and real nature it at the same time remains unchanged, lifted above the phenomenal universe." *The Vedānta-Sūtras of Bādarāyaṇa with the Commentary by Śaṃkara*, trans. George Thibaut (New York: Dover Publications, 1970), II.1 27, p. 352.

21. Husserl, "The Idea of Phenomenology," p. 14.

22. Ibid., p. 19.

23. Pierre Thèvenaz, *What Is Phenomenology*? (Chicago: Quadrangle Books, Inc., 1962), pp. 90–91.

Chapter 2. The Advaita Notion of *Sākṣin* (Witness-Consciousness)

An earlier version of this chapter was presented at the 25th anniversary meetings of the Society for Asian and Comparative Philosophy, Hancock, Mass., July–August, 1993. That version appeared in *Indian Philosophical Quarterly* (October 1995).

1. Madhusūdana in *Advaitasiddhi*, in the context of explaining the nature of witness perception, clearly points out that pure consciousness becomes a witness on account of a certain limiting adjunct. He raises and answers the following question: *nanu—sākṣipratyakṣaṃ na bādhyaṃ, doṣājanyatvāt, pratyuta śrutijanitādvaitajñānameva bādhyam. . . . ceti na, caitanyasya svarūpato doṣājanyatve'pi tadavacchedakāyā avidyāvṛtterdoṣajanyatvāt, tatpratiphalitacaitanyasyaiva sākṣipadārthatvāt.* (If it be objected that the witness-perception not being caused by a fault is not capable of being contradicted, while the knowledge of nonduality caused by *śruti* is, we reply: No. Although consciousness is, in its true nature, not caused by a fault, its limiting adjunct—i.e., modification of ignorance—is caused by a fault, and witness is consciousness as reflected in that modification.) *Advaitasiddhi* (Delhi: Parimal Publications, 1988), p. 395. Henceforth this edition will be cited as AS.

Madhusūdana clarifies the issue further by raising yet another question: *nanu—kathaṃ dṛgrūpasya brahmaṇaḥ sākṣādṛṣṭṛtvarūpaṃ sākṣitvam?* . . .

dṛgrupasyāpi upādhinā dṛṣṭṛtvam. (If it is asked, how can *brahman,* which is of the nature of seeing, be the witness, which is of the nature of the immediate seer? . . . [we reply] although it is of the nature of seeing, it becomes seer owing to its limiting adjunct.) Ibid., pp. 753–54.

Prakāśātman in his *Pañcapādikāvivaraṇa* makes the same point: *sarvagatamapi caitanyam avidyāvṛtatvāt svayamapi tāvan na prakāśate.* (Although consciousness is ubiquitous, it does not appear to be so because of being covered up by ignorance.) Prakāśātman, *Pañcapādikāvivaraṇa,* ed. S. Srirama Sastri and S. R. Krishnamurthi Sastri (Madras: Madras Government Manuscripts Library, 1958), p. 310. Hereafter this edition will be cited as PPV.

2. M. Hiriyanna, *Outlines of Indian Philosophy* (London: Allen and Unwin, 1967), p. 343. Hereafter this book will be cited as *Outlines.*

3. Any scholar working on Advaita is well aware that although the Upaniṣads are not systematic philosophical treatises, they nevertheless, without doubt, remain the foundation on which the entire edifice of Advaita metaphysics and epistemology rests. Almost every later theoretical development of the Advaita Vedānta of Śaṃkara can, with some propriety, be looked upon as exegesis of some fragmentary and admittedly obscure Upaniṣadic passage. The important Advaitin concept of *sākṣin* provides an excellent example of such an exegesis.

If the question should arise as to why I am concerned only with the Upaniṣads, the reply is that Upaniṣadic texts were Śaṃkara's concern. I am not so much interested in the historical development as I am in the conceptual development of the notion of *sākṣin.* I believe that I can adequately explicate the conceptual development of *sākṣin* in Advaita without concerning myself with other sources, such as the *Mahābhārata* and *Sāṃkhyakārikā*—the literatures necessary for an historical analysis of this notion. I am appealing to the Upaniṣads because Śaṃkara found them to be authoritative, and he did not believe that he needed any other foundation for his analysis.

4. BU, III.4.2.

5. Ibid., III.7.23.

6. Ibid., IV.3.6.

7. Ibid., IV.3.9.

8. As a philosophical concept, *sākṣin* is found in the later Upaniṣads such as *Śvetāśvatara* (VI.11) and *Maitrī* (VI.16). It also occurs in the *Sāṃkhyakārikā* (19), in which the *puruṣa* is said to be the witness of *prakṛti*; it is neutral and it is not an agent (*mādhyasthyam draṣṭṛtvamakartṛtvam* . . .).

Śaṃkara makes the same point when he says: "*athavā—yaḥ prakṛtah paramātmādhyātmamadhidaivataṃ ca puruṣavidhatvopādhiḥ, tasya yat kevalaṃ sākṣirūpaṃ tadabhiprāyeṇa idam ucyate—'puruṣe'ntaḥ pratiṣṭhitaṃ veda iti.*" (When it is said "*puruṣe'ntaḥ pratiṣṭhitaṃ veda*" what is intended is to denote only his [of the *paramātmā*] witness form.) BSBh, I.2.28.

Vārtikam on the above aphorism clarifies the point further: "*antaḥpratiṣṭhā = madhyasthatā* (= neutrality). *tathā ca sākṣitvam lakṣayati.*" (Therefore "witness-hood" is intended.)

9. *Kaṭha,* II. 3.2 (see Śaṃkara's commentary on it).

10. *Muṇḍaka Upaniṣad*, III.1.1 (see Śaṃkara's commentary on it).

11. Yājñavalkya appears twice in BU, first in a verbal contest with other brahmins and subsequently in a dialogue with King Janaka of Videha.

12. *na dṛṣṭer draṣṭāram paśyeh na śruteḥ śrotāraṃ śṛṇuyāḥ, na mater mantāraṃ manvīthāḥ, na vijñāter vijñātāraṃ vijānīyāḥ.* BU, III.4.2.

13. *sākṣāddraṣṭari saṃjñāyāṃ. Pāṇini*, V. 2.91.

14. *sa eṣa iha praviṣṭa ānakhāgrebhyaḥ yathā, kṣuraḥ kṣuradhāne'vahitaḥ syāt, viśvambharo vā viśvambharakulāye, taṃ na paśyanti. akṛtsno hi saḥ. . . . tad etat padanīyam asya sarvasya yad ayam ātmā, anena hyetat sarvaṃ veda yathā ha vai padenānuvindet evaṃ.* BU, I.4.7.

15. *yasyāmatam tasya mataṃ mataṃ yasya na veda saḥ*
avijñātaṃ vijānatām vijñātamavijānatām. Kena, II.3.

16. TU, II. 9. 1.

17. *naiva vācā na manasā prāptuṃ śakyo na cakṣuṣā*
astīti bruvato'nyatra kathaṃ tad upalabhyate. Kaṭha, VI.12.

18. *adṛṣṭo draṣṭā aśrutaḥ śrotā, amato mantā, avijñatā vijñāto. nānyo'to'sti dṛṣṭā, nānyo'to'sti śrotā, nānyo'to'sti mantā, nanyo'to'sti vijñātā: esa ta ātmāntaryāmy amṛtaḥ: ato'nyad ārtam.* BU, III.7.23

19. Ibid., III.4.1.

20. Ibid., I.4.10.

21. *ātmaivāsya jyotir bhavati, ātmanaivāyam jyotiṣāste, palyayate, karma kurūte, vipalyeti iti.* Ibid., IV.3.6. Also see *Kaṭha*, II.2.15: "He shining, everything shines after him"; CU, III.4.12: "His form is light."

22. BU, IV.3.7.

23. Ibid.

24. Ibid. The *Bṛhadāraṇyaka Upaniṣad with the Commentary of Śaṃkarācārya*, trans. Swami Madhvananda (Madras: Advaita Ashrama, 1941). Hereafter this work will be cited as Madhvananda's BUBh.

25. CU, VIII. 7–12.

26. Ibid., VIII.11.1.

27. Ibid., VIII.12.1.

28. *sa yatra prasvapiti, asya lokasya sarvāvato mātrām apādāya, svayaṃ vihatya, svayaṃ nirmāya, svena bhāsā, svena jyotiṣā prasvapiti; atrāyam puruṣaḥ svayaṃjyotir bhavati.* BU, IV.3.9.

29. Ibid., IV.3.18.

30. Ibid., IV.3.19.

31. *yad vai tan na paśyati, paśyan vai tan na paśyati; na hi draṣṭur dṛṣṭer viparilopo vidyate, avināśitvāt; na tu tad dvitīyam asti, tato'nyad vibhaktam yat paśyet.* Ibid., IV.3.23.

32. Bina Gupta, *Perceiving in Advaita Vedānta: Epistemological Analysis and Interpretation* (Lewisburg, Pa: Bucknell University Press, 1991), p. 56. Hereafter this book will be cited as *Perceiving in Advaita Vedānta.*

33. *jāgaritasthāno bahiṣprajñaḥ saptāṅga ekonaviṃśatimukhaḥ sthūlabhugvaiśvānaraḥ prathamaḥ pādaḥ.* MAU, 3.

svapnasthāno'ntaḥprājñaḥ saptāṅga ekonaviṃśatimukhaḥ praviviktabhuk taijaso dvitīyaḥ pādaḥ. Ibid., 4.

yatra supto na kaṃcana kāmaṃ kāmayate, na kaṃcana svapnaṃ paśyati, tat suṣuptam. suṣuptasthāna ekībhūtaḥ prajñānaghana evānandamayo hyānandabhuk cetomukhaḥ prājñastṛtīyaḥ pādaḥ. Ibid., 5.

34. CU, V.18.2. provides a description of the seven limbs:

tasya ha vā etasyātmano vaiśvānarasya mūrdhaiva sutejāḥ, cakṣur viśva-rūpaḥ, prāṇaḥ pṛthagvartmātmā, saṃdeho bahulaḥ, bastir eva rayiḥ, pṛthivy eva pādāv ura eva vediḥ, lomāni barhiḥ, hṛdayaṃ gārhapatyaḥ, mano'nvāhārya-pacanaḥ, āsyam āhavanīyaḥ. (Of this universal self, the head is the intense light, the eye is the universal form, the breath is [the air] of diverse courses, the trunk is the vast, the bladder is the wealth, the feet are the earth, the chest is the altar, the heart is the sacred grass, the heart is the *gārhapatya* fire, the mind is the *anvāhārya pacana* fire and the mouth is the *āhavanīya* fire.)

The passage elucidates an essential one-on-one correspondence between the microcosm and the macrocosm—just as there is a consciousness that animates our physical body, similarly, there is a consciousness that animates the physical universe. This consciousness resides in all beings. It is called *vaiśvānara* (*viśva* = the cosmos + *nara* = man), the cosmic man. There is one man or one consciousness that is immanent in everything, conscious and unconscious. It is important to remember in this context that in saying that the consciousness has seven limbs, one is only giving the rough contours of his personality. Perhaps it is more accurate to say that this consciousness has infinite limbs, rather than seven limbs.

35. The nineteen mouths are concerned with the microcosmic aspect of the consciousness, the state of I-ness. They are: the five organs of sense (hearing, touch, sight, taste, and smell), the five organs of action (speech, hands, locomotion, generation, and excretion), the five vital breaths, the mind (*manas*), the intellect (*buddhi*), the ego-sense (*ahaṃkāra*), and the mind-stuff (*citta*). The nineteen mouths thus pertain to the multiple functions of the self and depict the self as a finite individual different from the real self. We consume things via the mouth that are assimilated in our bodies, so to speak. The five organs of sense, the five organs of action, and the five vital breaths refer to the outer core of the individual's activity. The remaining four—the mind, the intellect, the ego-sense, and the mind-stuff—refer to the inner core of the individual.

36. Hiriyanna, *Outlines*, p. 71.

37. *bahiṣprajño vibhurviśvo hyantaḥgprajñastu taijasaḥ*
ghanaprajñastathā prājña eka eva tridhā smṛtaḥ. Māṇḍūkyakārikā, 1.

For a readable translation of *Gauḍapāda's Kārikā*, readers might wish to consult *The Māṇḍūkyopaniṣad with Gauḍapāda's Kārikā and Śaṃkara's Commentary*, trans. Swami Nikhilananda (Mysore: Sri Ramakrishna Ashrama, 1974).

38. *dakṣiṇākṣimukhe viśvo manasyantastu taijasaḥ*
ākāśe ca hṛdi prājñastridhā dehe vyavasthitaḥ. Ibid., 2.

39. *kāryakāraṇabaddhautāvisyeteviśvataijasau*
prājñaḥ kāraṇabaddhastu dvau tau turye na sidhyataḥ. Ibid., 11.

40. Śaṃkara's commentary on *Māṇḍūkyakārikā,* 11.
41. *nātmānaṃ na parāṃścaiva na satyaṃ nāpi cānṛtam prājñaḥ kiṃcana saṃvetti turīyaṃ tat sarvadṛk sadā.* Ibid., 12.
42. *dvaitasyāgrahaṇaṃ tulyamubhayoḥ prājñaturyayoḥ bījanidrāyutaḥ prājñaḥ sā ca turye na vidyate.* Ibid., 13.
43. Ibid.,12.
44. Ibid., VII. 13.
45. Ibid., I.1.
46. *Perceiving in Advaita Vedānta,* p. 57.
47. *Kaṭha Upaniṣad,* I.3.4.
48. It is not an exaggeration to say that we may have here in an obscure form an anticipation of *Īśvara-Sākṣin* (God-defining-consciousness), a later doctrine. See *Vedānta Paribhāṣā* (VP) passages 37–41 in *Perceiving in Advaita Vedānta.* "Consciousness conditioned by *māyā* is *Īśvara* or the supreme lord. When *māyā* is a qualifying attribute, it is the state of being a God (*Īśvaratva*); and when it is a limiting adjunct there is the state of being a witness (*sākṣitva*). Such is the difference between the state of being a God (*Īśvaratva*) and the state of being a witness (*sākṣitva*), and not between God and the witness-consciousness possessing these attributes." *Perceiving in Advaita Vedānta,* p. 71.
49. *Māṇḍūkyakārikā,* VII.12.
50. *tadyatraitatsuptaḥ samastaḥ samprasannaḥ svapnaṃ na vijānātyeṣaātmeti hovācaitadamṛtamabhayametadbrahmeti.* CU, VIII.11.1
51. *tadvā asyaitadaticchando'pahatapāpmābhayaṃ rūpam. tadyathā priyayā striyā sampariṣvakto na bāhyaṃ kiṃcana veda nāntaram, evamevāyam puruṣah prājñenātmanā sampariṣvakto na bāhyaṃ kiṃcana veda nāntaram; tadvā asyaitadāptakāmam ātmakāmam akāmaṃ rūpaṃ śokāntaram.* BU, IV.3.21
52. Ibid., IV. 3. 2.
53. Ibid., II.4.14.
54. This analysis of the notion of *prājña,* and the relationship among the three states, raises a number of questions. What role, if any, does the *prājña* play during dreaming, or, for that matter, during the waking state? Is *prājña* different in different individuals? Or is there one *prājña* in all individuals? Equation of *sākṣin* with God only confuses the issue further (see *Muṇḍaka Upaniṣad* [MU], III.1.1, and Śaṃkara's commentary on it). On the one hand, we have a principle associated with body, the experiencer of pleasure and pain, and on the other hand, pure consciousness, the observer of both the enjoyer and the enjoyed. Some of these issues will be dealt with in the following chapters.
55. BU, III.4.2.
56. See VP, 2.11, in *Perceiving in Advaita Vedānta,* p. 139.

Chapter 3. Śaṃkara on *Sākṣin*

1. It is very difficult to say with certainty how many books and commentaries were actually authored by Śaṃkara. It is generally believed that he wrote

commentaries (*bhāṣya*-s) on the *Brahmasūtra* (BS), the *Bhagavadgītā*, the *Upadeśasāhasrī* (*Upadeśa*), and the ten principal Upaniṣads: *Īśā, Kena, Kaṭha, Praśna, Muṇḍaka, Māṇḍūkya, Aitareya, Taittirīya* (TUBh), *Chāndogya* (CUBh), and *Bṛhadāraṇyaka* (BUBh), I have made use of these commentaries in this study. I have also cited passages from *Śvetāśvatara Upaniṣadbhāṣya* (*Svetā.* UBh), *Ātmajñānopadeshavidhi* (AV), *Viveka Cūḍāmaṇi* (VC) and *Vākyavṛtti* (VV). The authenticity of these four has been questioned by some Western scholars, for example, see S. Mayeda (tr.), *A Thousand Teachings: The Upadeśasāhasrī of Śaṅkara* (Tokyo: University of Tokyo Press, 1979), p. 6. Indian scholars, on the other hand, generally take all or at least some of these works to be genuine, for example, see S. N. Dasgupta's *A History of Indian Philosophy* (Delhi: Motilal Banarsidass, 1975), vol. 3, pp. 77–82. Also see Karl Potter, ed., *Advaita Vedānta up to Śaṃkara and His Pupils* (Princeton, N.J.: Princeton University Press, 1981), p. 217. For my present purposes, it is not necessary to enter into a debate regarding this issue. Suffice it to say that since there does not seem to be any conclusive evidence in favor of either view, I have decided to use these works in my study.

Mayeda notes: "Penetrating insight, analytical skill, and lucid style characterize Śaṅkara's works. He cannot be called a particularly original philosopher . . . in India it is not originality but fidelity to tradition which is of great virtue. He was an excellent exegete, with an approach to truth which was psychological and religious rather than philosophical. He was really not so much a philosopher as a pre-eminent religious leader and a most successful religious teacher." Ibid. I do not agree with Mayeda's assessment of Śaṃkara. It seems to me that Śaṃkara was not only an excellent exegete, he was also a creative and original thinker, as his theory of *sākṣin* illustrates.

2. BSBh, I.3.22. In this aphorism, Śaṃkara also quotes several BU texts to substantiate this claim, for example, "it is on account of the light of the self that one sits, goes out, walks and returns" (*ātmaivāsya jyotir bhavati, ātmanaivāyam jyotiṣaste, palyāyate, ātmanaivāyam jyotiṣāte, palyayate, karma kurute, vipalyeti iti*). BU, IV.3.6.

3. BSBh, II.2.28.

4. Ibid., II.3.40.

5. *agṛhyaḥ, nahi gṛhyate.* BUBh, III.9.26.

6. *na cāgneriva ātmā ātmano viṣayo na cāviṣaye jñāturjñānamupapadyate,* BUBh, II.4.14

7. *na hi niravayavasya yugapajjñeyajñātṛtvopapattiḥ.* TUBh, II.1.

8. BUBh, IV.3.23.

9. *kuṭasthanitya evāyaṃ vijñānaghana ātmā.* BSBh I.4.22. Also see *Upadeśa,* XV:18.

10. BUBh, III.4.2.

11. *anyadeva tadviditādatho aviditādadhi. . . .* KUBh, I.3.

12. Paul Hacker provides an interesting corroboration of the same point from an entirely different orientation when he writes: "At the root of all our experiences and all our reflections, we find, then, a being which immediately recognizes itself, because it is its knowledge both of itself and of all things, and

which knows its own existence, not by observation and as a given fact, nor by inference from any idea of itself, but through direct contact with that existence. Self-consciousness is the very being of mind in action. The act whereby I am conscious of something must itself be apprehended at the very moment at which it is carried out, otherwise it would collapse." Hacker, "Śaṃkara's Conception of Man," *Kleine Schriften* (Wiesbaden: F. Steiner, 1978), p. 128.

13. Madhavananda's BUBh, IV.4.20, p. 746.

14. *evaṃ ahaṃpratyayinamaśeṣasvapracārasākṣiṇi pratyagātmanyadhyasya, taṃ ca pratyagātmānaṃ, sarvasākṣiṇaṃ tadviparyayeṇa antaḥkaraṇādiṣvadhyasyati.* BSBh in "*Adhyāsabhāṣyaṃ.*"

15. *nanvātmā'haṃpratyaviṣayatvādupaniṣatsveva vijñāyata ityanupapannam. na, tatsākṣitvena pratyuktatvāt. nahyahaṃpratyayaviṣayakartṛvyatirekeṇa tatsākṣī.* Ibid., I.1.4.

Bhāmatī, commenting on the above text, notes that although the *jīvātmā* and the *paramātmā* are metaphysically (ultimately) identical, nevertheless the highest self as limited is the *jīva*, while in its pure nature it is the witness. This cannot be known by any other source of knowledge; it is known only by the Upaniṣads.

16. *avidyāvasthāyām kāryakāraṇasaṃghātāvivekadarśino jīvasyāvidyātimirāndhasya sataḥ parasmādātmanaḥ karmādhyakṣātsarvabhūtādhivāsātsākṣiṇaścetayitur Īśvarāt tadanujñayā kartṛtvabhoktṛtvalakṣaṇasya saṃsārasya siddhiḥ. . . .* Ibid., II.3.41.

17. *yathāca svapnadṛgekaḥ svapnadarśanamāyayā na saṃspṛśyate, prabodhasaṃprasādayorananvāgatatvāt, evamavasthātrayasākṣyeko 'vyabhicāryavasthātrayeṇa vyabhicāriṇā na saṃspṛśyate.* Ibid., II.1.9

18. *vijñānagrahaṇamātra eva vijñānasākṣi grahaṇākāṅkṣānutpādādanavasthāśankānupapatteḥ. sākṣipratyayayośca svabhāvavaiṣamyādupalabdhṛūpalabhyabhāvopapatteḥ svayamsiddhasya ca sākṣino'pratyākhyeyatvāt.* Ibid., II.2.28.

19. *yathātmabuddhicārāṇāṃ sākṣī tadvatpareṣvapi*
naivāpoḍhuṃ na vādātuṃ śakyastasmātparo hyahaṃ. Upadeśa, II.7.2

20. *vikāritvamaśuddhatvaṃ bhautikatvaṃ na cātmaṇa*
aśeṣabuddhisāk sitvādbuddhivaccālpavedanā. Ibid., II.7.3

21. *vyomavatsarvabhūtasthobhūtadoṣairvivarjitaḥ*
sākṣī cetā'guṇah suddho brahmaivāsmīti kevalaḥ. Ibid., II.11.6

22. *draṣṭuścānyadbhaveddṛśyaṃdṛśyatvādghaṭavatsadā*
dṛśyāddraṣṭā'sajātīyo na dhīvatsākṣitānyathā. Ibid., II.15.4

23. *sarvapratyayasākṣitvādavikārī ca sarvagaḥ*
vikriyeta yadi dṛṣṭā buddhyādīvālpavidbhavet. Ibid., II.15.17

24. *upalabdhiḥ svayaṃjyotidṛśiḥ pratyaksadakriyaḥ*
sākṣātsarvāntaraḥ sākṣī cetā nityo'guno 'dvayaḥ. Ibid., II.18.26.

25. *buddhyārūdhaṃ sadā sarvaṃ sāhaṃkartrā ca sākṣiṇaḥ*
tasmātsarvāvabhāso jñaḥ kincidapyaspṛśansadā. Ibid., II.18.94.

26. *daśamastvamasītyevaṃtattvamasyādivākyataḥ*
svamātmānaṃ vijānātikṛtsnāntaḥkaraṇekṣaṇam. Ibid., II.18.176.

27. *prakṛtivikṛtibhinnaḥ śuddhabodhasvabhāvaḥ*

sadasadidamaśeṣam bhāsayannirviśeṣah
vilasati paramātmā jāgradādiṣvavasthāsvaha—
mahamiti sākṣātsākṣīrupeṇa buddheḥ. VC, 135

28. *pañcānāmapi kośānām niṣedhe yuktitaḥ śrutaḥ*
tanniṣedhāvadhī sākṣī bodharūpo'vaśiṣyate. Ibid., 210.

29. *yo'yamātmā svayaṃjyotiḥ pañcakośavilakṣaṇaḥ*
avasthātrayasākṣī sannirvikāro nirañjanaḥ
sadānandaḥ sa vijñeyaḥ svātmatvena vipaśicata. Ibid., 211.

30. *tatsākṣikaṃbhavettattadyadyādyenānubhūyate.*
kasyāpyananubhūtārthe sākṣitvaṃ nopayujyate. Ibid., 215

31. *asau svasākṣiko bhāvo yataḥ svenānubhūyate*
ataḥ paraṃ svayaṃ sākṣātpratyagātmā na cetaraḥ. Ibid., 216.

32. *vācaṃ niyacchātmani taṃ niyaccha*
buddhau dhiyaṃ yaccha ca buddhisākṣiṇi
tam cāpi pūrṇātmani nirvikalpe
vilāpya śāntiṃ paramāṃ bhajasva. Ibid., 369.

33. *antaḥkaraṇatadvṛttisākṣicaitanyavigrahaḥ*
ānandarūpaḥ satyaḥ san kiṃ nātmānaṃ pradadyase. VV, 11.

34. *satyānandasvarūpam dhisākṣiṇaṃ bodhavigrahaṃ*
cintayātmatayā nityaṃ tyaktvā dehādigāṃ dhiyam. Ibid., 12.

35. *yaḥ sākṣilakṣaṇo bodhastvaṃpadārthaḥ sa ucyate*
sākṣitvamapiboddhṛtvamavikārityātmanaḥ. Ibid., 26.

36. *sarvavikriyāviśeṣarahitasyātmano dṛgrūpasya caitanyasvarupeṇa vyatiriktena sarvapratyaya sākṣiṇo dṛśyasannidhimātreṇa drastṛtvamupacaryate buddhyādi—dṛśyābhivyaktyapekṣayā'nyathādraṣṭṛtvābhāvāt.* AV, II.12.

37. *tadubhayasākṣiṇaḥ kālākāśādivat sarvagatasya niravayavasyāvikriyasya dṛgrūpaśyātmano.* Ibid., III.7.

38. *astikaścitsvayaṃnityamahampratyayālambanaḥ*
avasthātrayasākṣīsaṇaḥpañcakośavilakṣaṇaḥ. VC, 125

39. *dehataddharmatatkarmatadavasthādisākṣiṇah*
sata eva svataḥsiddhaṃ tadvailakṣaṇyamātmanaḥ. Ibid., 157.

40. *yastu punarvidyāvidye īśate niyamayati, sa tābhyāmanyastatsākṣitvāt. Svetā.* UBh, 5.1.

41. *sarveṣām bhūtānām sākṣī sarvadṛṣṭā.*
sākṣāddraṣṭari samjñāyāmiti smaraṇāt.

In his commentary on *Svetā* U, 6.11, Śaṃkara says: "He is the witness, consciousness, alone and without attribute," (. . . *sākṣī cetā kevalo nirguṇaśca*).

42. *śarvo hi ātmopādhilakṣaṇaḥ para eva jale sūryādivat iha praviṣto dehe sarvabuddhipratyaya sākṣitayā.* MUBh, II. 2.4.

43. *tat hi paraṃ jyotiryadanyānavabhāsyamātmajyotista dyadātmavidaḥ ātmānaṃ svaṃ śabdādiviṣayabuddhipratyayasākṣiṇāṃ ye vivekino vidurvijānanti ta ātmavidastadvidurātmapratyayānusāriṇaḥ.* Ibid., II.2.9.

44. Padampāda, Śaṃkara's youngest contemporary and his student, started a tradition of interpretation and understanding of Śaṃkara. Several commentators belong to this tradition, including Prakāśātman, who wrote a commentary called

Vivaraṇa, the name by which this school of Advaita is known. The views expressed in *Vivaraṇa* and Padampāda's significant work, *Pañcapādikā,* have come to be known as the tenets of the Vivaraṇa tradition. The views of Maṇḍana Miśra, another contemporary of Śaṃkara, were developed in considerable detail by Vācaspati Miśra (ninth century C.E.). He incorporated Maṇḍana's ideas in his interpretation of Śaṃkara, which came to be identified as the tenets of the Bhāmatī tradition.

45. The Sanskrit term "*bādha*" can be translated as "sublation" or "subration." Etymologically, it means "contradiction" or "cancellation": "It is the mental process whereby one disvalues some previously appraised object or content of consciousness because of being contradicted by a new experience. . . . It is an axio-noetic process that involves, psychologically, a withdrawal of attention from an object as it was originally judged to be and the fastening of attention either to the same object as reappraised or to another object that replaces the first object as a content of consciousness; and the placing of a higher value upon the content of the new judgment." Eliot Deutsch, *Advaita Vedānta: A Philosophical Reconstruction,* pp. 15–16. In short, subration or sublation involves three things: initially, a judgment is made about some object or content of consciousness; the initial judgment is recognized as faulty in the light of a new judgment that is incompatible with the first judgment; and finally the new judgment is accepted as valid.

Śaṃkara uses the criterion of *bādha* to arrive at his ontological hierarchy. Anything that is in principle negated has a lesser degree of reality than that which replaces it. Given this, to say that the experience of reality itself cannot be sublated amounts to saying that the experience of reality cannot be denied or disvalued by anything else.

In Śaṃkara's writings, one finds three levels: *pāramārthika,* the level of reality; *vyavahārika,* the level of appearance; and *prātibhāsika,* the level of illusory objects. Reality is that which cannot be sublated by any other experience. Appearance is sublated only by direct knowledge of *brahman.* Illusory objects can be sublated by all other types of experience.

The term "level" in this context should not be construed in terms of its spatial connotations. These levels differ because reason cannot establish any causal relation among them. Professor Deutsch brings out the ontological, epistemological and logical characteristics pertaining to a level of being: "The term 'level' seems to function in discourse primarily as a spatial metaphor: in common language it connotes 'aboves' and 'belows'—one forms an image of 'levels' by thinking of one thing as being above or below another thing or of one thing as being 'deeper' than another thing, as in the expression 'level of meaning.' The term 'level,' however, for purposes of ontology, can be given a more precise conceptual meaning. Two orders of being can be said to be on different levels: (1) when, epistemologically, because of differences in kind between them (temporal, qualitative, and so on), relations cannot be established rationally between them; (2) when, logically, assertions made about one of the orders from the standpoint of the other may legitimately violate the formal requirements that govern the thought of the one order when confined to itself (for example, assertions about the Godhead or Absolute in religious literature made from the empirical standpoint may legitimately violate—and they frequently do—the law of contradiction); and (3) when, axiologically, different grades of value are ascribed to the orders." Ibid., 25–26.

46. In the preamble to his commentary on *Brahmasūtra*, Śaṃkara defines superimposition as the "apparent presentation (to consciousness) in the form of remembrance of something previously experienced in something else." In the rope-snake example, the rope, the immediate datum of consciousness, is taken as a snake because the qualities of snakes perceived in the past are erroneously attributed to it. The point to note here is that the illusory judgment "this is a snake" is the result of a confusion between that which is remembered and that which is perceived.

47. Although Śaṃkara discusses the inner sense (*antaḥkaraṇa*) at various places in his writings, he never makes his own position on this important concept very clear. The question is generally raised whether he believed in one inner sense or more than one. At one place, Śaṃkara uses the expression "*antaḥkaraṇadvaya*" (twofold inner senses), which leads one to believe that he recognizes two inner senses rather than one, although one is never told what those two might be (*Upadeśa*, I. 3.116). At another place, Śaṃkara also articulates *ātman* as the witness of all *antaḥkaraṇa*-s (*kṛstnāntaḥkaraṇekṣaṇa*), which suggests that there are more than two *antaḥkaraṇa*-s (*Upadeśa*, I.18.176). Mayeda suggests that "each of the modifications of the *antaḥkaraṇa* such as *manas, vijñāna,* and *citta* is called *antaḥkaraṇa*: these *antaḥkaraṇa*-s may be represented by the two words *buddhi* and *manas*." Ibid. Deussen suggests that for Śaṃkara *antaḥkaraṇa* and *manas* are "completely interchangeable." P. Deussen, *The System of the Vedānta* (New York: Dover Publications, 1973), p. 330.

Although it is true that Śaṃkara at times uses *buddhi* and *manas* interchangeably, I do not concur with Deussen that they are "completely interchangeable." *Kaṭha*, III.10, takes *buddhi* to be superior to the *manas* (. . . *manasaś ca parā buddhir* . . .). Śaṃkara in his commentary on this verse states that *buddhi* is "more subtle" (*parā sukshmatarā*) than the *manas*. He reiterates the same point in his commentary on the *Bhagavadgītā*: "similarly, higher is *buddhi* which is determination or resolution" (*tathā manasastu parā buddhir niścāyatmikā*, III. 42). I believe it was more important for Śaṃkara's purposes to show that *antaḥkaraṇa* exists, rather than to worry about whether it is one or many.

48. BSBh, II.3.7.

49. *na cedṛśasya nirākaraṇaṃ saṃbhavati. āgantukaṃ hi vastu nirākriyate, na svarūpam. ya eva hi nirākartā tadeva tasya svarūpam. na hyagnerauṣṇyamagniṇā nirākriyate.* Ibid.

50. Chatterjee and Dravid maintain that *pratyagātman* refers "to the individual self (*jīva*) for Śaṅkara." *The Concept of Sākṣin*, p. 13. However, I do not concur with them. *Pratyagātman* refers to the inmost self, the indwelling self, rather than the finite individual self. It is said to be opposed to the "*ahaṃ*

pratyayin" or "*asmatpratyaya*," i.e., the individual denoted by the "I." The Advaitins repeatedly affirm this:

"*asmadarthaścidātmā sākṣitayā pratīyate pratibimbate asmin*" explains "*asmatpratyaya*" i.e., the "I" is that in which the self as consciousness (denoted by "I") appears as witness, and is reflected. *Bhāṣyabhāvaprakāśikā* on "Adhyāsabhāṣyaṃ."

Vārtika on the above states: *tatra ahamākārāntaḥkaraṇavṛttirdvividhā—ekā tāvat "tattvamasyā'divākyajanyā niṣkṛṣṭāhamkārasuddhacinmātraviṣayā jīvanmuktānām, anyā tu cidābhāsaviśiṣṭāhamkāraviṣayā saṃsāriṇām. iyamca yadyapi sākṣāt na ātmaviṣayā, tathāpyappātramiva ādityaviṣayaṃ, ādarśa iva mukhaviṣayaścidābhāscidvārā tadviṣayā bhavati.*" (The modification of the inner sense into the form "I" is of two kinds: One of these is that of the living-free, a state whose object is only the pure consciousness free from the ego-sense, and which is produced by sentences such as "thou are that"; the other is that of the worldly persons, whose object is the ego-sense as qualified by the reflection of the pure consciousness. This latter, although its direct object is not the self, yet comes to have that as its object—just as a bowl of water comes to reflect the sun or the mirror comes to contain a face, so it also comes to have the self as its object through the reflection of the self.)

Vārtika further explains that the use of "I" is of two kinds: *ekaḥ sudhātmaviṣayo'nubhavināṃ, anyaḥ sarveṣām cidābhāsaviśiṣṭāhaṃkāraviṣayaḥ, parantu prathamo lakṣaṇayā, dvitīyaḥ śakyā iti bhedaḥ.* (One is that of those who experience the pure self; the other whose object is the ego-sense as qualified by reflection of consciousness. The first is by *lakṣaṇā* or indirect signification, the second is by direct signification.) *Nine Commentaries*, p. 293.

51. *kartṛtvaṃ śārīrasya pradarśitam, tatpunaḥ svābhāvikam vā syādupādhinimittaṃ veti cintayate . . . tat saṃpṛktasyaivaivātmanaḥ kartṛtvam darṣtavyam. . . . upalabdhyapekṣaṃtveṣām karaṇānāṃ karaṇatvam, sā cātmaṇah. na ca tasyāmapyasya kartṛtvamasti; nityopalabdhisvarūpatvāt. ahaṃkārapūrvakamapi kartṛtvaṃ nopalabdhurbhavitumarhati. ahaṃkārsyāpyupalabhyamānatvāt. . . . tasmāt kartṛtvamapyātmana upādhinimittameveti sthitam.* BSBh II.3.40.

52. Ibid., I.1.4.

53. *na vastuyāthātmyajñānaṃ puruṣabuddhyapekṣaṃ. kiṃ tarhi? vastutantrameva tat.* Ibid., 1.1.2.

54. *jñānaṃ tu pramāṇajanyam. pramāṇaṃ ca yathābhūtavastuviṣayam. ato jñānaṃ kartumakartumanyathā vā kartumaśakyam. kevalaṃ vastutantrameva tat. na codanātantraṃ. nāpi puruṣatantraṃ.* Ibid., 1.1.4.

55. José Pereira translates *vivarta* as *transmogrification*, contrasting it with *pariṇāma* (transfiguration); *Hindu Theology: A Reader* (New York: Doubleday, 1976), pp. 201–6. I prefer the term "transformation" for *pariṇāma* because the word "transformation" suggests a conjunction of an unchanging form with changing modes, the presence of "form" in the mode of the expression pointing to it. This is precisely the sense in which *pariṇāma* is understood in Indian

philosophy. *Pariṇāma* is always *ekadeśa pariṇāma*, partial modification, and not a total one.

56. *Upadeśa*, XVIII. 96, 180, 182, 191.

57. BSBh, II.3.20.

58. PUBh, VI.2.

59. For Vijñānavādins, in the final analysis, ideas alone are real. For this school of Buddhism, the object of perception and perception itself are simultaneous, which results in their fusing the content and the act of cognition. All our experiences can be articulated and understood in terms of ideas alone. "As to ontology," notes Junjiro Takakusu, "this school adheres neither to the doctrine that all things exist, because it takes the view that nothing outside the mind (mental activity) exists, nor to the doctrine that nothing exists, because it asserts that ideations do exist." Takakusu, *The Essentials of Buddhist Philosophy* (Delhi: Motilal Banarsidass, 1978), p. 81.

60. Śaṃkara reiterates some of these points in BUBh, IV. 3.7.

61. *aṅgīkṛte ca tasminviṣayākārasya jñānenaivāvaruddhatvādanarthikā bāhyārtha sadbhāvakalpanā.* BSBh, II.2.28.

62. Daniel H. H. Ingalls maintains that Śaṃkara derives this argument from the following verse by Dharmakīrti:

Sahopalambha-niyamād abhedo nīla-tad-dhiyaḥ
bhedaś ca bhrānti-vijñānair dṛśyeterdāv ivādvaye.

(Blue and the cognition of blue are not different entities, for the one invariably occurs with the other. One should recognize their difference as due to false cognition, like [the double moon seen by an astigmatic] in the moon, which is single.) Ingalls, "Śaṅkara's Arguments against the Buddhists," *Philosophy East and West* 3, no. 4 (January 1954): 300.

63. *nābhāva upalabdheḥ. na khalvabhāvo bāhyasyārthasyādhyavasātum śakyate. kasmāt? upalabdheḥ. upalabhyate hi pratipratyayaṃ bahyo'rtaḥ—stambhaḥ kuḍyaṃ ghataḥ pata iti. na copalabhyamānasyaivābhāvo bhavitumarhati.* BSBh, II.2.28.

64. A *viśeṣaṇa* (attribute) is an invariable distinguishing feature, as redness in a rose. It is generally distinguished from *upādhi* (limiting adjunct), which is an imposed limitation, e.g., a crystal vase appears to be red because of the presence of the red flower near it. The distinction between *viśeṣaṇa* and *upādhi* plays a very important role in Advaita epistemology. See Chapter 5, note 24.

65. *vijñānaṃ vijñānamityabhyupagacchatā bahyo'rtha stambhaḥ kuḍyamityevaṃjātiyakaḥ kasmānnābhyupagamyata iti vaktavyaṃ. vijñānamanubhūyata iti cet, bāhyo'pyartho'nubhūyata eveti yuktamabhyupagantum. atha vijñānaṃ prakāśātmakatvātpradīpavatsvayamevānubhūyate na tathā bāhyo'pyartha iti cet, atyantaviruddhāṃ svātmani kriyāmabhyupagacchasyagnirātmānaṃ dahatītivat. . . . na cārthāvyatiriktamapi vijñānam svayamevānubhūyate, svātmani kriyāvirodhādeva.* BSBh, II.2.28.

66. *nanu vijñānasya svarūpavyatiriktagrāhyatve, tadapyanyena grāhyaṃ tadapyanyenetyanavasthā prāpnoti. api ca pradīpavadavabhāsātmakatvājjñānasya jñānāntaraṃ kalpayataḥ samatvādavabhāsyāvabhāsakabhāvānupapatteḥ kalpanānarthakyamiti. tadubhayamapyasat.* Ibid.

67. Andrew Fort, in his article "Sākṣin in Advaita Vedānta," maintains that "the sākṣin is an aspect of the the eternal, unchanging self" (*The Journal of Indian Philosophy* 12 [1984]: 281). I do not concur with this assessment. *Sākṣin*, in Śaṃkara, is self insofar as it fulfills a specific role; it is not an aspect of the self.

68. KUBh, I. 2–4.

69. This is in keeping with the fundamental position of the Advaita system. The later Advaitins call the former *svarūpa jñāna* and the latter *vṛttijñāna*.

70. Śaṃkara articulates *vṛtti* variously, e.g., *buddhivṛtti* (BUBh, IV.3.7); *manasovṛtti* (*Upadeśa*, I.17.36); *mānasavṛttiḥ* (*Upadeśa*, I.13.6); *dhiyovṛttiḥ* (*Upadeśa*, I.17.35), etc.

71. *taccātmana upādhibhūtamantaḥkaraṇaṃ mano, buddhirvijñānaṃ cittamiti cānekadhā tatra tatrābhilapyate. kvacicca vṛttivibhāgena saṃśayādivṛttikaṃ mana ityucyate, niścayādivṛttikaṃ buddhiriti.* BSBh, II.3.32

Dharmarājādhvarindra in his *Vedānta Paribhāṣā* states: "*sā ca vṛttiś caturvidhā—saṁśayaḥ, niścayaḥ, garvaḥ, smaraṇaṃ iti. evaṃ sati vṛttibhedena ekam api antaḥkaraṇaṃ mana iti buddhir iti ahaṁkāra iti cittam iti cākhyāyate.*

taduktam—
mano buddhir ahaṁkāraś cittaṃ karaṇam āntaram.
saṁśayo niścayo garvaḥ smaraṇaṃ viṣayā ime.

(Mental modes are of four kinds: doubt, certitude, egoism, and retro-cognition. Considering this division of the mental mode, the internal organ, although one, receives different appellations, namely, mind [*manas*], intellect [*buddhi*], ego-sense [*ahaṁkāra*], and retro-cognition [*citta*].

[Accordingly], it has been said:

the internal instruments are *manas, buddhi, ahaṁkāra*, and *citta*, and the [their] contents [functions] respectively are: doubt, certitude, egoism, and retro-cognition.) *Perceiving in Advaita Vedānta*, p. 225.

72. *mūṣāsiktaṃ yathā tāmraṃ tannibhaṃ jāyate tathā*
rūpādīn vyāpnuvac cittaṃ tannibhaṃ dṛśyate dhruvam. Upadeśa, II.14.3

73. *vyañjako vā yathāloko vyangyasyākāratāmiyāt*
sarvārthavyañjakatvād dhīrarthākārā pradṛśyate. Ibid., II.14.4

74. N. K. Devaraja, *Śaṅkara's Theory of Knowledge* (Delhi: Motilal Banarsidass, 1972), p. 96.

75. Mayeda, *A Thousand Teachings*, pp. 35–36.

76. BSBh, II.2.28.

77. BUBh, III.9.20

78. *anyathā hyanabhyupagamyamāne tasminnityopalabdhyanupalabdhiprasaṅgaḥ syāt. ātmendriya viṣayāṇāmupalabdhisādhanānāṃ sannidhāne sati nityamevopalabdhi prasajyeta.* BSBh, II. 3. 32.

79. *ābhāsa eva caiṣa jīvaḥ parasyātmano jalasūryakādivatpratipattavyaḥ.* Ibid., II.3.50.

80. *Upadeśa*, 18.70.

81. *Upadeśa*, 18:32, 33.

82. Rāhu is the cause of the eclipses, and the term is also used to designate

the eclipse itself. Mythologically, Rāhu is a *daitya* or demon who is supposed to seize the sun and the moon and swallow them, thus obscuring their rays and causing eclipses. In Indian mythology, a lunar eclipse is caused by the dragon Rāhu's attempt to swallow the moon.

83. BUBh, III.8.20.

84. *tarhi dṛṣterdṛṣtā, śṛteḥ śrota, matermantā, vijñātervijñātā, sa ātmā iti.* Ibid., I.4.10.

85. *tarhi dṛṣṭyādisākṣitvena ātmā uktā.* Ānandagiri, ibid.

86. *yadi dṛṣterdṛṣtā, yadi vā ghatasya dṛṣtā, sarvathāpi dṛṣtā eva.* Ibid., I.4.10.

87. *yo dṛṣterdṛṣṭā, sa dṛṣṭiścedbhavati, nityameva paśyati dṛṣṭiṃ, na kadācidapi dṛṣti na dṛśyate dṛṣṭā; tatra dṛṣṭudṛṣṭyā nityayā bhavitavyaṃ.*" Ānandagiri on BUBh, ibid.

88. Ibid., IV.3.23.

89. *vṛttimadantaḥkaraṇāvacchinnaṃ savikāro ghatadṛṣṭā kutaṣthacinmātrasvabhāvaḥ sannidhimātreṇa buddhitadvṛttināṃ dṛṣṭā iti.* Ānandagiri takes it to be the *sākṣin* of seeing, etc. BUBh, I.4.10.

90. *dṛṣṭiriti dvividhā bhavati laukikī pāramārthikı cetī. tatra laukikī cakṣuḥsaṃyūktāntaḥkaraṇavṛttiḥ. sā kriyata iti jāyate vinaśyati ca. yā tvātmano dṛṣṭiragnyuṣṇaprakāśādivat sā ca draṣṭuḥ svarūpatvānna jāyate na vinaśyati ca.* BUBh, III.4.2.

91. Gupta, *Perceiving in Advaita Vedānta*, p. 221.

92. See the fourth characterization of *sākṣin* in Section III.

93. "If the *brahman*, which is other than worldly things which are denied, exists, then why is it not known? [The reply is] because it is unmanifested and not accessible to the senses, [and] it is the witness of all that is seen [known]." *yat pratiṣiddhāt prapañcajātādanyatparaṃ brahma, tadasti cetkasmānna gṛhyata iti? ucyate-tadavyaktamanindriyagrāhyam; sarvadṛśyasākṣitvāt.* BSBh III.2.23. The opponents contend that if the phenomenal world is negated and only the transcendental *brahman* exists, why then is it not perceived? Śaṃkara in response says that it exists as the witness in all that is apprehended. It is a permanent witness. It is unevolved and therefore unperceivable by the sense organs.

94. "The *jiva*-hood which is falsely superimposed upon the intelligence which is one's own, the seer, beyond all qualities and actions and of the nature of direct awareness and bliss, is not real, and ceases to be with the removal of ignorance, for it is by nature a nonentity."

svasya draṣṭurnirguṇasyākriyasya
pratyagbodhānandarūpasya buddheḥ
bhrāntyā prāpto jīvabhāvo na satyo
mohāpāye nāstyavastusvabhāvāt. VC, 196.

95. See the eighth characterization of *sākṣin* in Section III.

96. "*dṛṣṭā* is the seer of all intellects." *sarvabuddheḥ dṛṣṭā.* AV, II.1.

97. See the first characterization of *sākṣin* in Section III.

98. See the fifth characterization of *sākṣin* in Section III.

99. See the second characterization of *sākṣin* in Section III.

100. *The Journal of Indian Philosophy* 10 (1982): 341.

101. D. P. Dryer, *Kant's Solution for Verification in Metaphysics* (London: Allen and Unwin, 1966), p. 2.

102. Ibid., p. 18.

103. Ibid.

Chapter 4. *Sākṣin* and Advaita Epistemology

1. In the Advaitin tradition, immediately following Śaṃkara, we find three different schools of interpretation:

(a) The first line of interpretation originated with Sureśvara (800 C.E.) and his pupil Sarvajñātman Muni (900 C.E.). Sureśvara was one of the direct disciples of Śaṃkara and his chief works are *Naiṣkarmyasiddhi* (NS), *Tattirīyopaniṣad Bhāṣya-Vārtika* (TUBV), and *Bṛhadāraṇyakopaniṣad Bhāṣya-Vārtika* (BUBV). Sarvajñātman was the author of *Saṃkṣepaśārīraka* (SS).

(b) The second line of interpretation originated in the writings of Padmapāda (820 C.E.), Śaṃkara's closest disciple. He wrote *Pañcapādikā* (PP), an exposition of Śaṃkara's commentary on the first four aphorisms of *Brahmasūtras.* Prakāśātman (1200 C.E.) wrote a commentary on PP entitled *Pañcapādikāvivarṇa* (PPV). It is the pillar of the Vivaraṇa school and the school is named after it.

(c) *Bhāmatī,* the third line of interpretation, is associated with Maṇḍanamiśra (800 C.E.) and Vācaspatimiśra (840 C.E.). Vācaspati's commentary on Śaṃkara's *Brahmasūtras,* from which this school receives its name, is known as *Bhāmatī* (the lustrous).

2. BSB, I.4.3.

3. Vidyāraṇya in *Pañcadaśī* (PD) makes a distinction between *māyā* and *avidyā, māyā* being the adjunct of *jīva* and *avidyā* being the adjunct of *Īśvara.* PD, I.16. Vidyāraṇya of *Vivaraṇaprameyasaṃgraha,* however, does not make a distinction between the two. He gives the following common definition of *māyā* and *avidyā*: "While being indescribable, it is the cause of obstructing the presentation of the truth and of the manifestation of the erroneous." *anirvacanīyate sati tattvāvabhāsapratibandha viparyayāvabhāsayor hetutvaṃ lakṣaṇam taccobhayoraviśiṣṭam. The Vivaranprameyasaṅgraha of Bhāratītīrtha,* trans. S. S. Suryanarayana Sastri and Saileswar Sen (Kumbakonam: Sri Vidya Press, 1941), Andhra University Series, No. 24, p. 44. Henceforth this edition will be referred to as VPS.

4. *evam avidyāsahitabrahmopādānaṃ jagat jāyate.* Bhāmatī, I.1.2.

5. Maṇḍana is regarded as a contemporary rival of Śaṃkara. He was the author of the work known as *Brahmasiddhi.*

6. *cinmātrameva avidyāviṣayaḥ . . . svaprakāśatvena prasaktaprakāśe tasmin āvaraṇakṛtyasaṃbhavācca, nānyat, tasyājñānakalpitatvāt, aprasaktaprakāśatvena āvaraṇakṛtyabhāvācca.* AS, p. 586.

7. Sureśvara, Sarvajñātman, and the Vivaraṇa School in this regard follow Śaṃkara, who regards *māyā* and *avidyā* as one and not many.

8. Sureśvara, *The Tattirīyopaniṣad Bhāṣya-Vārtika of Sureśvara,* ed. R. Balasubramanian (Madras: University of Madras, 1984), p. 140. Henceforth this edition will be referred to as TUBV.

9. *mūlājñānasyaiva avasthābhedāḥ, rajatādyupādānāni śuktikādijñānaiḥ sahādhyāsena nivartante.* PPV, p. 99.

10. *tadvṛttidvārā viṣayākārajanane'pi caitanasya na kūtasthatvavyāhatiriti. Vartikaṃ* on "Adhyāsabhāṣyaṃ," *Nine Commentaries,* p. 447.

11. *tasya ca abhivyaktasya caitanyasya ekatvepi abhivyanjakāntaḥkaraṇabhāgabhedāt tridhā vyapadeśo bhavati. kartṛbhāgāvacchinnaścidaṃsaḥ pramātā. kriyābhāgāva'chinnaścidamśaḥ pramāṇaṃ viṣayagata abhivyakti yogyatvabhāgāvacchhinnaścidamśaḥ pramitiḥ prameyaṃ tu viṣayagataṃ brahmacaitanyamevājñātaṃ tadevaṃ ca jñātaṃ satphalaṃ.* SB, pp. 78–79.

12. *trividhaṃ caitanyaṃ: viṣayacaitanyaṃ pramāṇacaitanyaṃ pramātṛcaitanyaṃ ceti. tatra ghaṭādyavacchinnacaitanyaṃ viṣayacaitanyaṃ. antaḥkaraṇavṛttyavacchinnaṃ caitanyaṃ pramāṇacaitanyaṃ. antaḥkaraṇāvacchinnaṃ pramātṛcaitanyaṃ.* VP in *Perceiving in Advaita Vedānta,* 3.17, p. 167.

13. "Perceptibility" and "perceptuality" are often used interchangeably. From a technical point of view, however, there is a distinction between the two: "Perceptibility" refers to the circumstance of the object being perceived; "perceptuality" is used when speaking with reference to the percipient or to the perceived knowledge.

14. *tatra yathā taḍāgodakaṃ chidrānnirgatya kulyātmanā kedārān praviśya tadvad eva catuṣkoṇādyākāraṃ bhavati tathā taijasaṃ antaḥkaraṇaṃ api cakṣurādidvārā nirgatya ghaṭādiviṣayadeśaṃ gatvā ghaṭādiviṣayākāreṇa pariṇamate. sa eva pariṇāmo vṛttir ity ucyate. anumityādisthale tu nāntaḥkaraṇasya vahnyādideśagamanaṃ, vahnyādeś cakṣurādyasannikarṣāt. Perceiving in Advaita Vedānta,* pp. 167–68.

15. See P. K. Sundaram, *Advaita Epistemology* (Madras: University of Madras: 1984), p. 4.

16. S. S. Suryanarayana Śāstrī, *Siddhāntaleśasaṃgraha of Appaya Dīkṣita,* Madras Government Oriental Series, vol. 155 (Madras: Governmental Oriental Manuscript Library, 1958), I. 51.587. Hereafter this edition will be cited as SLS.

17. Dharmarāja, the author of *Vedānta Paribhāṣā* (VP) was a seventeenth-century Advaitin. VP for the first time provides a systematic exposition of the Advaita theory of knowledge. It is because of his efforts that epistemology began to be treated as an independent discipline.

18. *tathā ca "ayaṃ ghaṭaḥ" ityādipratyakṣasthale ghaṭādes tadākāravṛtteś ca bahir ekatra deśe samavadhānāt, tadubhayāvacchinnaṃ caitanyam ekam eva; vibhājakayor apy antaḥkaraṇavṛttighaṭādiviṣayayor ekadeśasthatvena bhedājanakatvāt. ata eva maṭhāntaravartighaṭāvacchinnākāśo na maṭhāvacchinnākāśād bhidyate. Perceiving in Advaita Vedānta,* pp. 167–68.

19. Nondifference in this context must not be construed to mean total identity; it is rather "unity" or "coincidence" because the limiting adjunct of each consciousness endures.

20. *antaḥkaraṇapariṇāmāḥ sarve'pi sākṣivedyatvādaparokṣāḥ.* VPS, p. 223.

21. *"ayaṃ ghaṭaḥ" iti pratyakṣasthale ghaṭākāravṛtter ghaṭasaṁyogitayā,*

ghaṭāvacchinnacaitanyasya tadvṛittyavacchinnacaitanyasya cābhinnatayā, tatra ghaṭajñānasya ghaṭākārāṁśe pratyakṣatvam.

sukhaduḥkhādyavacchinnacaitanyasya, tadvṛittyavacchinnacaitanyasya ca, niyamenaikadeśasthitopādhidvayāvacchinnatvān niyamena "ahaṃ sukhī, dukhī" ityādijñānasya pratyakṣatvam. Perceiving in Advaita Vedānta, p. 171.

22. *vṛtter bahirnirgamanena idamaṁśāvacchinnacaitanyaṃ vṛttyavacchinnacaitanyam pramātṛcaitanyaṃ cābhinnaṃ bhavati. tataś ca pramātṛcaitanyābhinnaviṣayacaitanyaniṣṭhā śuktitvaprakārikāvidyā cākacikyādisādṛśyasandarśanasamudbodhitarajatasaṁskārasadhrīcīnā kācādidoṣasamavahitā rajatarūpārthākāreṇa rajatajñānābhāsākāreṇa ca pariṇamate. Perceiving in Advaita Vedānta,* p. 258.

23. *na hi niradhiṣṭhānaḥ adhyāso dṛṣṭapūrvaḥ sambhavī va.* Padmapāda on "Adhyāsabhāṣyaṃ."

24. *atyantagrahe atyantāgrahe na cādhyāsaḥ.* Bhāmatī on "*Adhyāsabhāṣyaṃ.*"

25. *nanu—evaṃ vṛttibhede jñānaikyānubhavavirodhaḥ. . . .*" AS, p. 653.

26. *viṣayorabhedhādhyāse jñānayorapyabhedādhyāsa iti asya upacāraśabdārthatvena anubhavavirodhābhāvat.* Ibid.

27. *tasya ca viṣayacaitanyasya tadantaḥkaraṇopahitacaitanyābhinnatayā viṣayacaitanyādhyastam api rajataṃ sākṣiṇy adhyastaṃ kevalasākṣivedyam. . . . Perceiving in Advaita Vedānta,* p. 263.

28. *ātmāśrayāvidyātmakatve'pi sarvaireva gṛhyateti, na iti āha— . . . idamākārāvacchinnasākṣicaitanyasamāśritya rajatasya śuktikāsambhedo'pyavidyātmaka iti, sukhādivadananyavedyatvam.* (To the objection that if the [illusory] silver were a product of ignorance whose locus is *ātmā,* then the silver ought to be perceived by everyone, the answer is that this is not so, because the silver is of the nature of ignorance whose locus is the witness-consciousness as limited by the "this"; like pleasure, etc., it cannot be apprehended by the other.) *Pañcapādikāvivaranaṃ* on "Adhyāsabhāṣyaṃ," *Nine Commentaries,* p. 211.

29. PD, "*Kūtasthadīpaḥ,*" verse 16.

30. N. Veezhinathan, ed., *The Saṃkṣepaśarīraka of Sarvajñātman* (Madras: University of Madras, 1972), 1.31, p. 165. Also see 1.36, p. 167. Hereafter this edition will be cited as SS.

31. *nanu sākṣiṇi adhyastatve "ahaṃ rajatam" iti pratyayaḥ syāt, "ahaṃ sukhī" itivat. . . . yasya yadākārānubhavāhitasaṁskārasahakṛtāvidyākāryatvaṃ tasya tadākārānubhavaviṣayatvam ity evānugataṃ niyāmakam. Perceiving in Advaita Vedānta,* p. 265.

32. *Tattvaśuddhi* by Jñānaghanapāda, edited by S. S. Suryanarayana Śāstrī and E. P. Radhakrishnan (Madras: University of Madras: 1941), section 35.

33. *iti ced ucyate; svagocaravṛttyupahitacaitanyabhinnasattākatvābhāvasya viṣayāparokṣatvarūpatayā rajatasya aparokṣatvasiddhaye tadabhyupagamāt. Perceiving in Advaita Vedānta,* p. 269.

34. Ibid.

35. *kintu avidyaiva bāhyadoṣanimittakāraṇāpekṣayā rajatākāreṇa sākṣicaitanyasya rajatāvacchedajñānābhāsākāreṇa ca pariṇamamāṇā svakāryeṇa saha sākṣicaitanyasya viṣayabhāvaṃ pratipadyate iti te matam.* PPV, pp. 153–54.

36. AS, p. 544.

37. "If anything is *a priori* in the sense of being the non-empirical condition

of the possibility of experience—in a large segment of Indian thought—*avidyā* or ignorance may be said to be that. It is non-empirical, for ignorance has—in Buddhism as well as Vedānta—no origin: it is beginningless (*anādi*)." J. N. Mohanty, *Reason and Tradition in Indian Thought* (Oxford: Clarendon Press, 1992), p. 270.

38. AS, p. 544.

39. Citsukha, *Tattvapradīpikā* with *Nayanaprasādinī* of Pratyaksvarūpa and editor's Hindi commentary, ed. Yogīndrananda (Bombay: Nirṇayasagar Press, 1915), p. 374. Hereafter this book will be cited as TP.

40. *bhāvābhāva vilakṣaṇasya ajñānasya abhāva vilakṣaṇatva mātreṇa bhāvatvopacārāt.* Ibid.

41. The Advaitins argue: *pramāṇavṛttyupārūḍhaprakāśatvena nivartakatvaṃ brūmaḥ, na tu jātiviśeṣeṇa, prakāśatva mātreṇa vā.* (We say the property of removing ignorance is only qua manifesting as depending on a mode of *prāmaṇa,* but not qua the universal feature of mere manifestation.) AS, p. 590.

42. *sākṣīṇi yadajñānavirodhitvamanubhūyate tannājñānanivartakatvanibandhanaṃ kintu svaviṣaya icchādau yāvatsattvaṃ prakāśādajñānāprasaktinibandham.* Ibid.

43. TUBV, 176, p. 365.

44. "*Pramā* is a cognition which has for its content an entity that is not already known." *Perceiving in Advaita Vedānta,* p. 112.

45. *āśrayaviṣayajñānāni trīṇi api ekenaiva sākṣiṇāvabhāsyante. tathā ca āśrayaviṣayoḥ sādhayannayaṃ sākṣī tadvadeva ajñānamapi sādhayati eva, na tu nivartayati. tannivartakaṃ tu antaḥkaraṇavṛttijñānameva.* (All three—the locus, the object and the ignorance—are manifested by the same witness-consciousness. This witness-consciousness, after establishing the locus and the object, likewise establishes the ignorance, but does not destroy it [ignorance]. What destroys ignorance is the cognition that is a modification of the inner sense.) VPS, p. 20.

avidyāsvarūpam tu sākṣicaitanyādeva sidhyati. (The ignorance in itself is established by the witness-consciousness.) Ibid., p. 55.

ajñānasādhakasākṣicaitanye "ahamajñaḥ" iti ajñānāśrayatāyā eva anubhavāt. (In "I am ignorant," that ignorance is located in the witness-consciousness, which establishes the ignorance, is directly experienced.) Ibid., p. 56. Also see TUBV, 176.

46. *ajñānasya svarūpeṇaiva sākṣivedyatvāt.* (Ignorance, in its own nature, is cognized by witness.) AS, p. 557.

A little later, Madhusūdana adds: "*sā ca āvidyā sākṣī-vedyā, na tu śuddhacitprakāśyā. . . . rāhuvat svāvṛtacaitanyaprakāśyā'vidyeti.*" (That *avidyā* is known by *sākṣī,* it is not manifested by pure consciousness. . . . Like Rāhu, ignorance is manifested by the consciousness which it conceals.) Ibid., p. 575

sākṣiṇaścāvidyānivartakatvābhāvo 'vidyāsādhakatvenaiva dharmigrāhakamānasiddha. (Witness does not remove ignorance, but rather establishes it.) Madhusūdanasarasvati, *Siddhāntabindu,* ed. M. V. S. Abhyankar, Government Oriental Series—Class A, No. 2 (Poona: Bhandarkar Oriental Research Institute, 1962), p. 115. Hereafter this edition will be cited as SB.

47. *sākṣiṇi avidyo'pahitaciti. Laghucandrikā*, p. 545; *sākṣī ca avidyāvṛtti pratibimbita caitanyaṃ.* AS, p. 575.

48. PPV, p. 262.

49. Also see Sureśvara's *Sambandha Vārtika*, 178a–180.

50. *ātmāgrahātirekeṇa tasyā rūpaṃ na vidyate*
amitravadavidyeti satyevaṃ ghatate sadā. TUBV, II. 179, p. 366.

51. Ibid., II. 180, p. 367.

52. *ātmano'grahonāma āvaraṇaṃ ācchādanaṃ.*

53. *ahaṃ ajñaḥ iti jñānasya . . . abhāvavilakṣaṇaviṣayatvaṃ.* AS, p. 555.

54. *tatra ca ajñāne "ahamajño māmanyaṃ ca na jānāmī" ti pratyakṣaṃ, "tvaduktamarthaṃ na jānāmī" ti viśeṣataḥ pratyakṣaṃ, "etāvantaṃ kālaṃ sukhamahamasvāpsaṃ na kincidavediṣamiti" parāmarśasiddhaṃ śauṣuptapratyakṣaṃ ca pramāṇam.* Ibid., pp. 548–51.

55. *ajñānāśrayībhūtacaitanye antaḥkaraṇatādātmyādhyāsena ekāśrayatvasambandhena upapatteḥ.* Ibid., p. 548.

56. The Advaitins make a distinction between two functions of ignorance (*ajñāna*): that which envelops the existence of an object, thereby creating the notion that the object does not exist (*asattvāpādaka*), and that which prevents the revelation of the object, thereby creating the notion that the object is not manifest (*abhānāpādaka*). In the case of the erroneous perception of shell-silver, the nescience is present in the first of its functions. In an illusory cognition, before its occurrence, nescience exists, which causes the notion that the object does not exist.

Madhusūdana clarifies the distinction further: *dvibidhamāvaraṇaṃ. ekamasattvāpādakamantaḥkaraṇāvacchinnasākṣicaitanyaniṣthaṃ. anyadabhānāpādakaṃ viṣayāvacchinnabrahmacaitanyaniṣthaṃ.* (There are two kinds of covering. One presents nonexistence, and belongs to the witness-consciousness as limited by the inner sense. The other presents nonperception, and belongs to *brahma*-consciousness as limited by the object. The former is removed by *pramā* knowledge in general, both immediate and mediate. The latter is removed by immediate knowledge alone.) SB, p. 65.

57. *kevalacinmātraṃ na sākṣī, kintu avidyāvṛttyupahitaṃ, tathācāsthirāvidyāvṛttyupahitasya sākṣiṇo'pyasthiratvena tatsattvaparyantamavasthāne'pyavidyādernivṛttirupapadyata.* AS, p. 545.

58. *viśeṣaṇajñānasya viśiṣtajñānajanakatve mānābhāvat.* Ibid., pp. 550–51.

59. In this work I have translated "*pakṣa*" as "the minor term," "*sādhya*" as "the major term," and "*hetu*" as "the middle term." This, however, should not be taken to mean that there is a one-to-one correspondence between the terms that occur in the Indian syllogism and their Western counterparts. In other words, the Indian *sādhya, pakṣa,* and *hetu* (reason, or *liṅga*) are not equivalents of the Aristotelian major, minor, and middle terms respectively. Indian logic deals with entities rather than terms. In Indian logic, *sādhya* or *dharma* is a property, which the *pakṣa*, the *dharmin*, possesses, and the *hetu* or *liṅga* is the mark, by means of which the *sādhya* is inferred in the *pakṣa*. For Indian logicians to say "Socrates is mortal" amounts to saying that "Socrates" (*pakṣa*) has the property of mortality

(*sādhya*). Aristotelian logic, unlike Indian logic, deals with terms rather than entities. The validity of a syllogism in Aristotelian logic depends on the extension of the minor term. The extension of the minor term "Socrates" (in the example "all human beings are mortal, Socrates is a man, therefore, Socrates is mortal") is subsumed under the middle term "human being" and the extension of the middle term under that of the major term "mortal." As long as one keeps this in mind, there is no harm in using "the minor term," "the major term," and "the middle term" in an Indian context.

60. *ajñānasya ajñānavṛtti pratibimbita sākṣibhāsyatvena vṛtti nāsad eva saṃskāropapatteḥ.* AS, p. 557.

61. *tataśca suṣuptau anubhūta ānandaḥ ātmā bhāvasvarūpājñānaṃ ca trayaṃ apyutthitena parāmaṛśyate "sukhaṃ ahaṃ asvāpsaṃ," "na kiñcid avediṣam" iti. nanu etat trayaṃ suṣuptau nāntaḥkaraṇavṛttibhir anubhūyate, tāsāṃ tatrābhāvāt . . . avidyaivoktatrayagrāhakavṛttitrayākāreṇa suṣuptau vivartate.* VPS, p. 73.

62. Sureśvara, *Naiśkarmyasiddhī*, II. 55–56. Hereafter this book will be cited as NS.

63. *na suṣuptagavijñānaṃ nājñāsiṣamiti smṛtiḥ, kālādyavyavadhānatvānna hy ātmasthaṃ atītabhāk. na bhūtakālaspṛk pratyak na cāgāmispṛgīkṣyate, svārthadeśaḥ parārtho 'rtho vikalpastena sa smṛtaḥ.* BUBV, I. 4. 300–301.

64. AS, p. 606.

65. *nanu, parāmarśaḥ kimanumānaṃ, kimvā smaraṇaṃ. ādya jñānābhāva eva anumīyatām kiṃ bhāvarūpa ajñānena? . . . dvitīye nāsti upapattiḥ, saṃskārāsambhavāt.* Ibid., p. 556.

66. According to *Advaitasiddhi*, an indeterminate mode of nescience can also cause memory (*nirvikalpakasyāpi smaraṇajanakatvāt*), p. 559.

67. See *Siddhāntabindu*, verse 8.

68. *ekasya eva vṛtteḥ ahaṃarthāṃśe pratyakṣatvaṃ, sākṣyaṃśe smṛtitvamiti bhāvaḥ.* AS, p. 595.

69. Ibid.

70. The mode of nescience in deep sleep is the same as the *nidrāvṛtti*, i.e., the mode of sleep of Patānjali yoga. Only for Advaita Vedānta, the mode of sleep is not a mode of the inner sense, for the inner sense is dissolved in sleep. During the waking state, this mode of sleep does not exist, but its residual impressions do—hence memory.

71. *vikalpaḥ na tu smṛtirūpanirvikalpaḥ. . . . na avediṣam iti pratyaḥ vikalpatām ghatayati.* AS, p. 558.

72. *evam etāvantaṃ kālaṃ na kiñcidavediṣamiti parāmarśasiddhaṃ suṣuptaṃ pratyakṣamapi bhāvarūpājñānaviṣayameva.* Ibid., p. 556.

73. Ibid., p. 559.

74. The concepts of *vṛtti-vyāpya* and *phala-vyāpya*, as they relate to the manifestation of an object, play a very important role in Advaita epistemology. As pointed out earlier, in every case of perception the mind goes out through the senses, pervades the object, and assumes the form of the object. Such a modification of the mind when it is pervaded by the object is known as *vṛtti-vyāpya*. However, in the system of Advaita, the contact of the mode, though

necessary, is not sufficient to manifest an object. What is needed is the reflection of the consciousness conditioned by the object in that particular mental mode. This is known as *phala* or the result of the functioning of the mental mode.

To appreciate this distinction one must recall the dynamics and the mechanics involved in the perception of an object. Let me explain these notions further with the help of the example of the perception of a particular object, say, a pitcher. When the sense of sight comes in contact with a pitcher, mind also "comes out" and reaches the place of the object and comes into contact with the pitcher. This is *vṛtti-vyāpya*. The mental mode, inspired by the reflection of consciousness in it, destroys the ignorance, resulting in a contact between the object and the consciousness reflected in the mental mode. In this process the manifestation of the pitcher is the "fruit" (*phala*), while the pitcher itself is the content of this "fruit."

75. *vivādagocarāpannaṃ pramāṇajñānaṃ svaprāgabhāvavyatirikta svaviṣayāvaraṇa svanivartya svadeśagata vastvantara pūrvakaṃ bhavitumarhati aprakāśita arthaprakāśakatvāt andhakāre prathamotpanna pradīpa prabhāvat iti.* PPV, p. 85.

76. Dharmarāja, *Vedānta Paribhāṣā*, trans. Swami Mādhavānanda (Calcutta: Advaita Ashrama, 1983), p. 117.

77. The unlimited bliss and manifestation of *brahman* is not possible of the *jīva*. This is a proof of that. (*jīvasya anavacchinnabrahmānandaprakāśānyārthānupapattiśca tatra mānam.*) AS, p. 576.

78. Ibid., p. 544.

79. Without knowing the earlier noncognition, it is not possible to apprehend an object as being known now. (*pūrvānavagatim avijñāya idānimeva avagataṃ ityavadhāraṇāyogyāt.*) PPV, p. 95.

80. Ibid., p. 110.

81. Ibid., p. 262.

82. PD, 8.10.

83. G. R. Malkani, R. Das, and T. R. V. Murti, *Ajñāna* (London: Luzac and Co., 1933), p. 152. Hereafter this book will be cited as *Ajñāna*.

84. K. C. Bhattacharyya, *Studies in Vedāntism* (Calcutta: Calcutta University, 1909), p. 8.

85. *māto' nadhigatatvasya siddhiḥ syāt athavā anyataḥ*
svato vā jñātāyāśca kutaḥ siddhiritīryatāṃ. See SV, 685.

86. *jñātatvasya māvyāpteḥ pūrvameva prasiddhitaḥ.*
tataśca mānataḥ siddhirnājñātatvasya kutracit. Ibid., 686.

87. *avidyāyā avidyātve idaṃ eva tu lakṣaṇaṃ. mānāghātāsahiṣṇutvaṃ asādhāraṇaṃ iṣyate.* Ibid., 181.

88. *avijñātārtha gantṛṇi pramāṇānīti vādināṃ; sarveṣāṃ abhyupeto'arthaḥ kuto'sāviti cintyate.* BUBV I.4.221.

89. "It does not exist, it is not manifested." This usage establishes ignorance. (*āvaraṇakṛtya. nasti na prakāśate. itivyavahārāpādanaṃ.*) AS, p. 587.

90. *Ajñāna*, p. 152–53. Professor Murti is following K. C. Bhattacharyya in this regard.

91. Ibid., p. 177.

92. *ata eva sākṣijñānasya satyāsatyaviṣayatayā prāmāṇyāniyamād aprāmāṇyoktiḥ sāmpradāyikānāṃ. Perceiving in Advaita Vedānta,* p. 270.

93. *ajñānādisatyamithyāvastusādhāraṇena sākṣimātreṇa vedyatvāt.* (The witness-consciousness alone apprehends all objects, ignorance, true and false entities in common.) *Pañcapādikāvivaraṇaṃ. Nine Commentaries,* p. 497.

sāksiṇaḥ pramāṇatvābhāvāt. na ca mithyāvabhāsena virodhaḥ, satyasya eva niṣedhapratiyogitvāt. mithyābhūtasya sākṣivedyatvena pratīti—niṣedhayorbhinnaviṣayatvāt iti bhāvaḥ. (The witness-consciousness does not possess the property of being a means of true cognition. There is nothing contradictory about manifestation of a false entity; what is real alone is the counterpositive of negation, if the false is manifested by witness-consciousness, then apprehension and negation have different objects.) *Ṛjuvivaraṇaṃ,* ibid.

sākṣisiddhaṃ paramārthasat iti niyantuṃ na śakyaṃ, mithyāvastuno'pi paramārthasat iti niyantuṃ na śakyaṃ, mithyāvastuno'pi sāksyadhīnasiddhitvāt. (It is not possible to say that what is established by the witness-consciousness is real, for the false object also is established by the witness-consciousness.) *Tattvadīpana,* ibid.

94. Given below are some of the objections that Madusūdana anticipates in his *Advaitasiddhi* on behalf of the opponents.

95. *pratyakṣasya vartamānamātragrāhitve śuktirūpyādeḥ pratipannopādhu traikālikaniṣedhapratiyogitvarūpaṃ mithyātvaṃ kathaṃ pratyakṣaṃ syāt?* AS, p. 351.

96. *atha tatra rajatatvavirodhiśuktitve sākṣātkṛte tadanyathānupapattyā ca rajatatvābhāve niścite mithyā eva rajatamabhāt iti tādṛg niṣedhapratyayaḥ svasambandhasarvābhāsakena sākṣiṇaivopapannaḥ.* Ibid.

97. *tarhi sākṣāt svaviṣayasya gaganāderbhāvikālaniṣedhāpratiyogitvaṃ sakalakālagrāhiṇā sākṣiṇā gṛhyatāmiti.* Ibid.

98. *na, sākṣiṇo vidyamāna sarvāvabhāsakatvena avidyamānabhāvibādhābhāvābhāsakatvānupapatteḥ, sākṣijñānasya bhramapramāsādhāraṇatvena pramāṇabādhakatvācca.* Ibid.

99. *nanu—jñānaprāmāṇyaṃ gṛhṇan sākṣi ghatādigatamabādhyatvaṃ gṛhṇātveva, na hi viṣayābādhamanantarbhāvya prāmāṇyagrahaṇam nāma iti cet.* Ibid.

100. *na, vyavahārakālābādhyatvamātreṇa pravṛttāvapi sambādopapatteḥ tadrūpagataprāmāṇyasya sākṣiṇā grahaṇe'pi virodhābhāvāt.* Ibid.

101. The most detailed and systematic treatment of this issue is found in Jñānaghanapāda's *Tattvaśuddhi.*

102. Ibid., p. 219.

103. Ibid.

104. The commentator once again is refuting the Nyāya theory that a cognition does not manifest itself; that it does not manifest either the subject or itself. The Advaitins affirm that the Nyāya position that a cognition, while itself unperceived—like the eyes, etc.—establishes its own objects—such as desire, etc.—leads to infinite regress.

105. It is worth noting that some schools of Advaita accept a mode of nescience in this case, not a mode of the inner sense.

106. P. K. Sundaram, *Advaita Epistemology,* pp. 30–31.

107. *Vṛtti* at times has been translated as "psychosis" (see S. S. Suryanarayana

Sastri's translation of VP). Such a translation, however, having pejorative psychological connotations, is misleading. *Vṛtti* refers to an epistemic process or act. Therefore, it is more appropriate to translate it as "a mental mode."

108. T. M. P. Mahadevan, *The Philosophy of Advaita*, pp. 33–34.

109. Plato states: "And of the organs they first contrived the eyes to give light, and the principle according to which they were inserted was as follows. So much of fire as would not burn, but gave a gentle light, they formed into a substance akin to the light of everyday life, and the pure fire which is within us and related thereto they made to flow through the eyes in a stream, smooth and dense, compressing the whole eye and especially the center part, so that it kept out everything of a coarser nature and allowed to pass only this pure element. When the light of day surrounds the stream of vision, then like falls upon like, and they coalesce and one body is formed by natural affinity in the line of vision, wherever the light that falls from within meets with an external object. And the whole stream of vision, being similarly affected in virtue of similarity, diffuses the motions of what it touches or what touches it over the whole body, until they reach the soul, causing that perception which we call sight." Plato, *Timaeus*, trans. Benjamin Jowett (Princeton, N.J.: Princeton University Press, 1980), 45b–c.

110. *ghaṭāder viṣayasya pratyakṣatvaṃ tu pramātṛabhinnatvaṃ . . . pramātṛabhedo nāma na tāvad aikyaṃ, kintu pramātṛsattātiriktasattākatvābhāvaḥ. tathā ca ghaṭādeḥ svāvacchinna-caitanyādhyastatayā viṣayacaitanyasattaiva ghaṭādisattā; adhiṣṭhānasattātiriktāyā āropitasattāyā anaṅgīkārāt. viṣayacaitanyañ ca pūrvokta-prakāreṇa pramātṛcaitanyaṃ eveti pramātṛcaitanyasyaiva ghaṭādyadhiṣṭhānatayā pramātṛsattaiva ghaṭādisattā nānyeti siddhaṃ ghaṭāder aparokṣatvaṃ. Perceiving in Advaita Vedānta*, pp. 201–3.

111. Jadunath Sinha, *Indian Psychology*, vol. 1 (Calcutta: Sinha Publishing House, 1958), 137.

112. Aristotle, *De Anima*, 424a18.

113. Aristotle, *Posterior Analytics*, 99b33–100b5.

114. Thomas Aquinas, *Summa Theologica*, Ia. lxxviii. 3. *Saint Thomas Aquinas: Philosophical Texts*, trans. Thomas Gilby (New York: Oxford University Press, 1960), p. 227.

115. Ibid.

116. Ibid., p. 237.

117. Brentano echoes the same point in his theory of intentionality when he articulates the object as "inexistent" in the mind. "Inexistent" here should be taken to mean not that the object is only in the mind, but rather that only the form of the object exists in an intentional act that apprehends that object.

118. *astītyādi tadviṣayaka vyavahārapratibandhakājñānanivartana yogyat-vasya . . . tadākaratvarūpatvāt.* AS, p. 483.

119. *na ca āśrayapratiyogijñānabhūtamapi sākṣicaitanyaṃ bhāvāntarasya ajñānasya nivartakaṃ tasya ajñānaviṣayapratibhāsatvāt.* PPV, p. 82.

120. Ibid., p. 247.

121. Ibid., p. 259.

122. *āvaraṇāvidyā tu brahmatattvākāramācchādayantyapi svāvabhāsakaṃ sākṣicaitanyākāraṃ na āvṛṇoti. na cet avidyā eva niḥsākṣikā sati na sidhyet.* VPS, p. 73.

123. T. M. P. Mahadevan, *The Philosophy of Advaita*, p. 12.

Chapter 5. *Sākṣin* and Advaita Metaphysics

1. BSBh, II.3.50.
2. Ibid., I.5.7; I.2.6; II.1.20 & 22; II.3.17 & 49.
3. Ibid., I.1.17; III.2.21.
4. SS, III. 277–79.
5. Ibid., III.132.
6. Ibid., III.67.
7. Ibid., II.29.
8. Ibid., II.30.
9. *vārtikakāramate tu Īśvara eva sākṣin iti.* SB, p. 90.
10. Abhyankar in his commentary on *Siddhāntabindu* points out that for Sureśvara, the words "*sākṣin*" and "*Īśvara*" refer to the same entity. The Vivaraṇa view is that *sākṣin* is common to *jīva* and *Īśvara*. The distinction between *jīva* and *Īśvara* does not correspond to the *bimba* and *pratibimba* distinction. *Sākṣin* is common to *śuddhacinmātra, jīva*, and *Īśvara*, with one important difference: *Īśvara* is *pratibimba* in primal nescience, but the *jīva* is *pratibimba* in derivative nesciences. Ibid., p. 90.
11. *atastadavadhiḥ sarvasya bādhastena tanmātrasya bādhābhāvāt svataśca viśeṣānupalabdhaḥ kūtastha aprokṣaikarasacaitanyāvadhiḥ sarvasya bādhaḥ.* Padmapāda on "Adhyāsabhāṣyaṃ." *Pañcapādikā*, Vizianagaram Sanskrit Series, No. 3 (Benaras: E.J. Lazrus and Co., 1891), p. 12. Hereafter this edition will be cited as PP.
12. Ibid., pp. 35–36.
13. Ibid., p. 94.
14. Bhāmatī on BSBh, I.1.1: "*evamahaṃpratyayinaṃ . . . adhyasyati.*" Vācaśpati explains "*ahaṃpratyayinaṃ*" = "*ahaṃpratyayo vṛttiryasminnantaḥkaraṇādau so'haṃpratyayī taṃ.*"
15. In his commentary on I.1.4, "*nanu ātmā . . . tatsākṣī,*" Vācaśpati explains "*tat sākṣītvena.*" *ahaṃpratyayaviṣayo yaḥ kartā kāryakāraṇasaṃghātopahito jīvātmā tat sākṣītvena paramātmano'haṃpratyayaviṣayatvasya pratyuktatvāt.*
16. In his commentary on II.1.9, "*evamavasthātraya sākṣī eko.*" The term "*avasthātraya*" occurs in Śaṃkara's commentary on the *Brahmasūtra*. Vācaspati explains "*avasthātraya*" as *utpattisthitipralayāḥ*, i.e., "origin, existence, and dissolution."
17. *tasmādyathā cchettā chidayā chedyaṃ vṛkṣādi vyāpnoti, na tu chidāṃ chidāntareṇa, nāpi chidā eva cheṭṭi, kintu svataḥ eva Devadattādi . . . , evaṃ pramātā, prameyaṃ nīlādi pramayā vyāpnoti, na tu pramāṃ pramānāntareṇa, nāpi pramā eva pramātrī, kintu svata eva pramāyāḥ pramātā vyāpakaḥ.*
18. The commentary *Kalpataru* on the above passage clarifies the meaning further: *vijñānagrahamātra eva asmābhiḥ svīkṛiyate vijñānasākṣiṇaḥ vijñānaviṣayagrahaṇāntarākāṅkṣānutpādāditi.* (We admit only apprehension by

knowledge. With regard to the witness of the knowledge, there is no desire for another knowledge which would have that knowledge for its object.)

Also, "*sākṣīviṣayagrahaṇākāṅkṣānutpādāt*" means that "there does not arise a desire to have an apprehension whose object is the witness-consciousness."

Kalpataruparimalaḥ, a commentary on *Kalpataru*, further adds: *avidyāvacchinno jīva eva sākṣī, sa ca viṣayapradeśe'pi asti iti viṣayasyāpi tatsambandhaḥ tulya. . . . vyāpako'pi sākṣī, svacchāntaḥkaraṇāvacchinno'nāvṛto viṣayāvacchinnaḥ tu āvṛta iti āvaraṇabhangārthaṃ vṛttyapekṣā ityarthaḥ.* (The witness is the *jīva* limited by ignorance. It exists also at the location of the object, and the object's relation to it is equal. Although the witness is all-pervading, the witness as limited by the clear inner sense is not covered up. The witness as limited by the object is covered up; a mental modification is needed to destroy this cover.)

19. *Tattvaśuddhi*, pp. 217–24.

20. This text investigates the issues discussed in the first four aphorisms of the *Brahmasūtra*. The tone of the book is polemical in nature. The manuscript is yet to be published. My account of this text is based on Appaya Dikṣita's *Siddhāntaleśasaṃgraha*, ed. S. S. Suryanarayan Śāstrī (Madras: University of Madras, 1935), pp. 206–67. Henceforth *Siddhāntaleśasaṃgraha* will be cited as SLS. Also see S. N. Dasgupta's *History of Philosophy*, vol. 2, pp. 204–14.

21. SLS, p. 207.

22. A. G. Warrier, *The Concept of Mukti in Advaita Vedānta* (Madras: University of Madras, 1961), p. 339.

23. Madhusūdana explains *upalakṣaṇa* as follows: "That which, while making its coloring (effect) neutral, generates a cognition of differentiation through presenting a differentiating property in the substantive, that is '*upalakṣaṇa*,' as in the case of crow, etc." AS, chap. 1, sec. 27, p. 449.

The point that is being made is as follows: *Upalakṣaṇa* is an ascribed or an indicative characteristic. The crow on the roof of Devadatta's house distinguishes his house from the remaining houses on the block. In singling out Devadatta's house from other houses, the crow functions as an indicative characteristic. Although the crow is only an accidental attribute of the house, it nevertheless identifies the house; the function of identification is the significance here, it is never lost, although the crow may fly away. The point that must not be lost sight of is that for the Advaitins, it is not necessary that an essential property must serve as the mark to distinguish one object from the other. An accidental property could do the job as well.

24. Madhusūdana Sarasvatī explains the distinction as follows: "That which, by its own coloring, generates the cognition of differentiation in the substantive object is *viśeṣaṇa*; it colors the substantive at the time of the cognition of differentiation, as in the case of cowness. . . . that which neither colors, nor presents a separate property, and yet differentiates, is *upādhi*, as in the application of the word '*paṇkaja*,' the property of 'being the lotus.' " Ibid.

In other words, a *viśeṣaṇa* or *lakṣaṇa* is an invariable distinguishing feature. It enters into the very being of an object and distinguishes that object from other objects, e.g., blueness in a lotus. An *upādhi* (limiting adjunct), on the other hand, is a limitation, a separable, distinguishable feature, e.g., a red flower in the proximity of a crystal that appears to be red on account of the presence of the red flower near it. The distinction between *viśeṣaṇa* and *upādhi* is of utmost importance in Vedāntic thinking, thereby distinguishing its perspective from the Nyāya and other schools of Indian philosophy. Ibid.

25. TP, p. 374.

26. *sarvapratyagbhūtaṃ viśuddhaṃ brahma atra jīvabhedena sākṣin iti pratipādyate.* Ibid., p. 375.

27. SLS, p. 207.

28. PD, VIII.25.

29. *adhiṣṭānatayā dehadvayāvacchinnacetaṇaḥ, kūtavannirvikāreṇa sthitaḥ kūṭastha ucyate.* PD, VI.22.

30. PD, VI.18.

31. PD, X–10.

32. PD, X–12.

33. PD, VIII. 1–3.

34. PD, VIII.59.

35. *asminmate padārtho dvividhaḥ, dṛk dṛśyaṃ ca. . . . tatra dṛkpadārthaḥ ātmā pāramārthika ekaḥ, sarvadā ekarupo'pyupādhibhedena trividhaḥ, Īśvaro, jīvaḥ, sākṣin ceti. tatra kāraṇībhūtājñānopādhirīśvaraḥ. antaḥkaraṇatatsaṃskārāvacchinnājñānopahiko jīvaḥ . . . avidyāpratibimbeśvarapakṣe bimbacaitanyaṃ sākṣin, bimbeśvarapakṣe tu bimbapratibimbamukhānugatamukhasvarūpavajjīveśvarānugatasarvānusandhātṛcaitanyaṃ sākṣin iti ucyate. Vārtikakāramate tu Īśvara eva sākṣin iti. dvaibidhyameva jīveśvarabhedena dṛśaḥ. Madhusūdanasarasvati, Siddhāntabindu* with *Nyāyaratnāvalī*, ed. S. Subrahmanyasastri, Grantha Ratna Manjusha—No. 16, (Mount Abu: Mahesh Research Institute, 1978), p. 139. Hereafter this edition will be cited as SBMA.

36. *avidyātatkāryānyatarapratiphalitacaitanyasya eva sākṣītvāt.* AS, p. 754

37. *sākṣī jīvakotirvā, brahmakotirvā, ubhayānugataṃ cinmātram vā.* Ibid.

38. *sākṣī jīvakotirvā, brahmakotirvā, ubhayānugataṃ cinmātram vā. nādyaḥ, jivo buddhyupādhiko'ṇuriti pakṣe idaṃamśāvacchinnacidvedyasya śuktirūpyasya sākṣīvedyatvāyogāt cakrakādyāpātāt, ajñānopādhikaḥ sarvagata iti pakṣe'pi ajñānasyāpi sākṣyadhīnasiddhikatvenānyonyāśrayatā.* Ibid.

39. *na dvitīyaḥ, brahmaṇa eva sākṣīvedyaduhkhādidhī na jīvasya iti vaiparītyāpātāt. anyathā anavacchinnānandadhīrapi jīvasya iti syāt, brahmacaitanyaṃ ghatādiprakāśakamiti mate ajñānābhibhavadvārā tasya jīvacaitanyābhedābhivyanjakāntaḥkaraṇavṛttitvāttādṛśavṛttyabhāvācca.* Ibid.

40. *Īśvareṇa eva cinmātreṇāpi saṃsāriduḥkhasya tadgatatvena grahaṇe'pi yadbhāgo muktaḥ tasya cinmātrasya duḥkhādullekharūpopaplavāpātāt.* Ibid.

41. *suptamaitraṃ prati maitryājñānādermaitrīyatayā eva jāgratcaitrīyatayā duḥkhāderapi caitrīyatyā suptamaitraṃ prati pratītiprasangeṇa maitreṇa etāvantakālaṃ duḥkhaṃ na avediṣamiti parāmarśa ayogāt.* Ibid.

42. *śuddhabrahmātiriktasya buddhyupādhikajīvātiriktasya sākṣiṇo'ngīkṛtatvena, tatpakṣoktadoṣābhāvāt.* Ibid.

43. *tathāca avidyāvṛttipratiphalitaṃ caitanyaṃ sākṣī, suptau eva avidyāvṛttisvīkārasya prāgukteḥ.* Ibid.

44. *sākṣiṇaḥ sarvajıvasādhāraṇye'pi tattajjīvacaitanyābhedenābhivyaktasya tattaddukhādibhāsakatayā atiprasaṇgābhāvāt.* Ibid., p. 754–55.

45. *atha sukhādāvaraṇābhāvānna tadbhāne manovṛttyapekṣā, tarhi jīvasyaiva ghatādau vṛttidvārā sukhādau svataḥ sambandhāt sākṣītvasambhavena brahmaṇah sākṣitva ukti ayukta.* Ibid., p. 754.

46. *upaplavo hi na duḥkhaviṣayakatvamātraṃ, Īśvarasya api tatsattvāt, kintu yaṃ prati duḥkhādau mithyātvamāvṛtaṃ, tattve sati duḥkhādisambandhitvaṃ. tacca na muktabhāgasya iti dhyeyaṃ.* Ibid.

47. *Catrīyaduḥkhādeḥ Caitriyatayā bhāsakatvamistameva; Caitraṃ prati tatsattvāt, suptamaitraṃ prati Caitriyatayā bhāsakatvaṃ tu na sambhavati; puruṣāntarīyaduḥkhādeḥ puruṣāntaraṃ prati āvṛtatvena pramāṇavṛttiṃ vinā taṃ prati sākṣimātrasyābhāsakatvāt.* Ibid., pp. 754–55.

48. *jñānānandaikarūpamadvitīyaṃ nityaṃ sākṣī ca brahme iti siddhaṃ.* Ibid., p. 755.

49. *vyabhicāro mitho yadvatpramātrādeḥ sasākṣikaḥ.*
sākṣiṇo'vyabhicārastu tathā kiṃ sākṣiko bhavet.

Vidyāraṇyasvāmī, *Bṛhadāraṇyakopaniṣadbhāṣyavārtikasāra* (Kasi: Acyuta Grantha Mala, 1942), 22, p. 1705. Hereafter this book will be referred to as BUBVS.

50. *dṛṣṭṛdarśanadṛśyāṇāṃ sākṣiṇaḥ svaprabhasya tat*
pramāṇāgocaratvaṃ tu vastusvābhāvyato bhavet. Ibid., 54, p. 1722.

51. *cakṣurjanyamanovṛttiścidyuktā rūpabhāsikā.*
dṛṣtirityucyate dṛṣṭā dṛṣteḥ karteti laukikaiḥ. Ibid., 56, p. 1723.

52. *ātmeti ca pramātrādeḥ svarūpamabhidhīyate*
pramātrādyāgamāpāya sākṣītvāt tatsvarūpatā. Ibid., 20, p. 1704.

53. *yadyasmin vyabhicāryeta tatsvarūpaṃ na kutracit.*
kundalitvaṃ yathā puṃsaḥ sākṣī tvavyabhicāravān. Ibid., 212, p. 1705.

54. *naustho nāvo gatiṃ kā'pi vīkṣate na tatasthavat.*
tathaivaṃ buddhyabhinnasya na syāddhīvṛtti sākṣīta. Ibid., 115, p. 2078.

55. *dhīvikārastataḥ kalpyo buddhi sākṣiṇyāśaṅkite.*
sākṣisākṣyatvamithyādhīstattvajñānānnivartate. Ibid., 117, p. 2079.

56. *ato dṛṣtidvayaṃ vācyaṃ nityānityavibhedi tat*
manovṛttiranityā'nyā sākṣīcaitanyarupiṇī. Ibid., 60, p. 1724.

57. *buddhirjaḍā'pi cicchāyāvaśato dṛṣṭṛtvaṃ vrajet.*
paśyatītyeṣa śabdo'tastasminneva prayujyate. Ibid., 325, p. 2197.

58. *yo budhyupādhiko dṛṣta suptatvātsa na paśyati.*
cidātmā'pi dvitīyasyā'bhāvādatra na paśyati. Ibid., 330, p. 2198.

59. *cillopābhāvataḥ sākṣī paśyannevetyudīryate.*
akartaryapi kartṛtvāropeṇaitadudīraṇaṃ. Ibid., 331, p. 2199.

60. *pratyakṣākṣyatirekeṇa nā'bhāvo'pi prasiddhyati.*
kimu bhāvo jagatyasmin sākṣī ca'nanyasiddhikaḥ. Ibid., 72, p. 1729.

61. *dṛṣṭṛdarśanadṛśyānı yaḥ svapne prasamīkṣata.*
tadabhāvaṃ suṣupte ca sa ātmetyabhyupeyatāṃ. Ibid., 65, p. 2039.

62. Also see Sureśvara, *Sambandha Vārtika*, verses 793–96. Hereafter this text will be cited as SV.

63. Sureśvara, NS II. 70–77.

64. *sākṣisākṣyābhisaṃbandaḥ pramātrādau yathā tathā sākṣivastuni naiva syātkevalānubhavātmati.* SV, 151.

65. NS, II. 106.

66. *kiñca jīvaviṣayā vṛttirvidyāvṛttiḥ, na tu pramāṇavṛttiḥ; tasyā evajñāvirodhitvāt.* AS, 591.

67. *ahaṃkārastāvad icchādiviśiṣṭa eva gṛhyata ityāvayoḥ samānam. suṣuptau ca na icchādayaḥ iti kathaṃ tadā'hamarthānubhavaḥ?* Ibid., p. 595.

68. Abhyankar, one of the commentators on SB, refers to two views in this regard: *saṃskārāṇāṃ sākṣisvarūpāntargatatve sākṣibhedaprasaṇgah. saṃskārāṇāṃ nānātvāt. sākṣibhedastu na iṣyate. . . . saṃskārādisannihito'pi cinmātrarūpa eva sākṣī na tu upādhiviśiṣṭaḥ.* SB, p. 135.

69. *tatra jīvo nāma antaḥkaraṇāvacchinnacaitanyam; tatsākṣin tv antaḥkaraṇopahitacaitanyam. antaḥkaraṇasya viśeṣaṇatvopādhitvābhyām anayor bhedaḥ. Perceiving in Advaita Vedānta,* p. 238.

70. Karl Potter, "*Vedāntaparibhāṣā* as Systematic Reconstruction," *Perspectives on Vedānta,* ed. S. S. Rama Rao Pappu (Leiden: E. J. Brill, 1988), p. 111.

71. M. Hiriyanna, *Outlines of Indian Philosophy* (London: Allen and Unwin, 1973), p. 344.

72. *ayañ ca jīvasākṣin pratyātmaṃ nānā; ekatve caitrāvagate maitrasyāpy anusandhānaprasaṅgaḥ. Perceiving in Advaita Vedānta,* p. 240.

73. *tatsaṃskārasya ca nimittakāraṇatvena, sākṣyāśritakāryopādānakatvapraveśānna tadbhedena sākṣibhedaḥ.* SB, p. 135.

74. *jāgaraṇe tu antaḥkaraṇasya pramātrāśritakāryopādānakotau praveśāttadbhedena pramātṛbheda eva.* Ibid., p. 136.

75. *ajñānasya tu sarvatrābhinnatvāt . . . sākṣīcaitanyasya na kadācidapi bhedabhānam.* Ibid., p. 43.

76. SBMA, p. 88.

77. SB, p. 137.

78. *sa ca draṣṭā ekaḥ; tat nānātve mānābhāvāt. nanu–kathameka eva jīvaḥ; pratiśarīram "ahaṃ sukhī, ahaṃ duḥkhī, ahaṃ saṃsārī, ahaṃ asvāpsam" ityādhyanubhavavirodhāditi—cenna; avidyāvaśāt brahmaivaikaṃ saṃsarati. sa eva jīvaḥ. tasya eva pratiśarīramahamityādibuddhiḥ. Svāpnaśarīre "ahaṃ sukhī, ahaṃ duḥkhī," ityeva yatra buddhina tvahaṃ sukhītyādi, tattu nirjīvaṃ. yatra tu ahaṃityādi tat sajīvam . . . bandhamokṣādivyavasthānupapattistatra mānamiti cet na; bandhamokṣaguruśiṣyādivyavasthāyāḥ svapnavad yāvadavidyāmupapatteḥ. . . .*

na ca evaṃ tasminnekasminneva jīve supte samastajagadapratītyāpatteḥ, samaṣṭyabhimānino mukhyajīvasyāsuptatvāt. tasmin layakāle prasupte jagadapratīteḥ. . . .

antaḥkaraṇāvacchinne jīvābhāse tu, supte tameva prati jagadapratītiḥ, na tvanyānapi prati, tadupādhīnāmapralīnatvāt. . . .

Caitramaitrādisarvābhimanino jīvasya kalpakatvena tava mama ityādivikalpānupapatteh.

nanu—sarvābhimānino Hiraṇyagarbhasya jīvasya svīkāre tasya kalpānte muktyā sarvamuktyāpattiriti. . . . saguṇabrahmānamityupāsakānāmapunarāvṛttya brahmalokasithatānām kaivalyaprāpti bodhyate, na tu kalpānte avaśyam seti bodhyate. (Gauḍabrahmānandī)

anekaśarire ekajīvavādasyāngīkārāt. . . . bhinnabhinnāntaḥkaraṇābhedādhyāsena tattadantaḥkaraṇamādāya pratyaktvaparāktvāhamityādibuddhiviṣayatvavyavasthā upapatteḥ. na ca Caitrasukhaduḥkhādīnām Maitreṇa anusandhānāpattiḥ, antaḥkaraṇāvacchinnenāvidyāvacchinnena vā. nādyaḥ, tatra parasparam bhedāt. na dvitīyaḥ, iṣṭāpatteḥ. ata eva—Caitrasya śuktisākṣātkāreṇa rajatabhramanivṛttāvanyeṣāmapi tannivṛttiḥ syāditi—nirastam; antaḥkaraṇabhedena vyavasthā upapatteḥ. . . .

anādimāyayā supto yadā jīvaḥ prabudhyate ityādiśrutiṣu ekavacanaprāptaikatvavirodhena udāhṛtaśrutīnāmanekatvaparatvābhāvāt. . . .

samaṣṭyabhimānino jīvasya sarvajñatvasarvakartṛtvādisvīkārāt. AS, pp. 539–41. The rest of the section cites scriptural texts in support of his thesis. *Gauḍabrahmānandī explains "*nirjīvam*" as "*nirjīvam jīvāvacchedakamanaḥsukhādyanavacchedakam.*"

79. It is obvious to the reader that the *jīva* occupies a prominent place in the writings of Madhusūdana. It is indeed true that *brahman* is the highest reality, better yet, the only reality in the system of Advaita. However, from an empirical perspective, the importance of the *jīva* cannot be underestimated—insofar as the teachings of Vedānta are meant for the *jīva,* because in the final analysis, it is the *jīva* who realizes *mokṣa.*

80. *sākṣinānātvam sasākṣikam cet anavasthā. asākṣikam cet na eva sidhyati.* SB, p. 137.

81. *sākṣin tu sarvānusandhātā sarvānugataḥ turīyākhya ekavidha eva.* Ibid., p. 93.

82. *kevalaḥ sākṣin turīyākhyohamasmītyarthaḥ.* SB, p. 141.

83. Ibid., p. 142.

84. *mātṛmānaprabhede'pi pratideham na bhidyate*
sākṣī bāhyyārthavadyasmātsa ātmetyucyate tataḥ
vyābhicāro mitho yadvatpramātrādeḥ svasākṣikaḥ
sarvamātrādyabhāvārthasākṣitvānna tathātmanaḥ.

According to Sureśvara, there is only one *sākṣin* during the waking stage. BUBV, III. 4. 54–55. Also see SB, p. 137.

85. SB, p. 143.

86. Ibid., p. 89.

87. *ātmanaḥ suṣuptisākṣitvāt.* (The self is the witness of deep sleep.) Ibid., p. 19.

88. *ātmanaḥ suṣuptisākṣitvānna tatra tadabhāvaḥ. anyathā mūdho' hamāsamiti parāmarśānupapatteḥ. mātṛmānamitimeyānām vyabhicāritve'pi tadbhāvābhāvasākṣiṇaḥ kālatraye'pyavyabhicārāt.* SBMA, pp. 58–59.

89. *ātmanaḥ suṣuptisākṣitvāt.* SB, p. 19.

90. VPS, p. 79.

91. *Dṛgdṛśyaviveka,* 1.

92. *sākṣiṇa eva cādhikopādhiviśiṣṭasya pramātṛtvātnna anusandhānānupapattiriti.* SB, p. 136.

93. The commentary *Nyāyaratnāvali* attempts to clarify the intent of what is said in the original text. It is noted there:

mūle sākṣimātrāśritatvarūpaṃ sākṣyāśritatvaṃ smaraṇādeḥ yaduktaṃ tadavidyāgatacidābhāsaḥ sākṣīti vārttikmatamabalamvyaiva. ata eva manogatacidābhāsasya jīvatvena tanmate avidyāyāḥ jīvānupādhitvena bhedāsvīkārāt sākṣiṇaḥ sarvajīveṣu aikyameva. bimbapratibimbānugataśuddhacit sākṣī iti mate tu smṛtyādikāryaṃ na sākṣimātrāśritaṃ, kintu avidyāviśiṣṭacidābhāsāśritamapi.

In the original text (i.e., *Siddhāntabindu*), when it is said that memory, etc., are located in the mere *sākṣin,* that is said following the view of Sureśvara that *sākṣin* is the reflection of consciousness in ignorance. If the *jīva* is taken to be the reflection of consciousness in the inner sense, then, since on that view ignorance is not different according to difference of the *jīva*-s, the *sākṣin* will be the same in all *jīva*-s. On the theory that *sākṣin* is the pure consciousness common to the reflected and the reflection, memory, etc., are not located in mere *sākṣin,* but rather in the reflection of consciousness as qualified by ignorance. SBMA, p. 169.

It further adds that on some views *sākṣiñ* is the consciousness as limited either by the mind or by its residual impressions On such a view, *sākṣin* is different in each body. Ibid., p. 170.

94. *nanu ajñāna sukhānubhavayoḥ sākṣicaitanyasya cāvināśinaḥ saṃskārābhāve kathamutthiṣṭasya trayāṇāmanusmaraṇam syāt? ucyate—ajñānagatacaitanyābhāsajanmopādhitvādajñāna sukhasākṣivikalpānubhavākṣya . . . sambhāvyate. Nine Commentaries,* p. 325.

95. *ajñānaṃ svasukhasākṣyākāreṇa pariṇamate, tatra ca pariṇatājñāne caitanyābhāsa upajāyate.* Ibid.

96. *sākṣicaitanyaṃ hi suṣuptāvanubhūtānsukhādīnahaṃkārāśrayatvena smaratīti bhāvaḥ.* SB, p. 124.

97. *ahaṃkārasya ca pramāṇajanyajñānāśrayatvaniyamāt.* Ibid.

98. *smṛtisaṃśayaviparyayāṇāṃ sākṣicaitanyāśrayatvaniyamāt.* Ibid., p. 124.

99. *apramājñānam na manovṛttirūpaṃ, kintu avidyāvṛttirūpaṃ sākṣyāśrayam.* Ibid.

100. *sākṣin tu satyaḥ. sa ca na dṛṣtā. kintu dṛgrūpaḥ.* SB, p. 131.

101. *nanu mahadetadindrajālaṃ, pramāśrayānakūtasthān vihāya, kūtasthamapramāśrayameva pramāṇarājaḥ sarvasākṣiṇaṃ karotīti.* SBMA, p. 62.

102. *bāḍhaṃ. Indrajālamevetatsvapnavat avidyāvilasitatvāt.* Ibid.

103. Ibid., p. 60.

104. *pramātuśca pariṇāmitvena dṛśyatvāt ekasya kūtasthasya eva sarvasākṣitvāt.* Ibid.

105. T. M. P. Mahadevan, *The Philosophy of Advaita,* p. 190.

106. If the *brahman*-consciousness is the *sākṣin,* then taking into account Caitra's mental modifications, Maitra should say "I perceive the pitcher." (*caitrīyamanovṛttimādāya maitrasyāpi "ghataṃ sākṣātkaromi" iti vyavahārāpatteḥ.*) SBMA, p. 109.

107. *atra ca yasminpakṣe antaḥkaraṇāvacchinno jīvaḥ, yasminśca pakṣe*

sarvagato'sango'vidyāpratibimbo jīvaḥ, tatrobhayatrāpi pramātṛcaitanyoparāgārthā viṣayagatacaitanyāvaraṇabhangārtha ca antaḥkaraṇavṛttiḥ. Ibid., pp. 105–6.

Chapter 6. *Sākṣin* and Western Phenomenology

1. Immanuel Kant, *Critique of Pure Reason,* trans. Norman Kemp Smith (London: Macmillan, 1973), B-1. Henceforth, this edition will be cited as *Critique of Pure Reason.*

2. *Critique of Pure Reason,* B2.

3. *Ajñāna,* p. 173.

4. In the Advaita view *all* objects are superimposed upon consciousness. The function of the witness-consciousness is simply to manifest. However, the pure consciousness and the witness-consciousness are the same consciousness wearing different hats. So, one could say that objects are superimposed on the witness-consciousness; although, technically speaking, all objects are superimposed on *brahman.*

5. *Critique of Pure Reason,* A104.

6. *Critique of Pure Reason,* B132.

7. *Critique of Pure Reason,* B414–15. Also see footnote B415.

8. *Critique of Pure Reason,* B131–32.

9. Henry E. Allison, *Kant's Transcendental Idealism: An Interpretation and Defense* (New Haven, Conn.: Yale University Press, 1983), p. 155.

10. *asmatpratyaye yo'nidam aṃśas cidekarasaḥ tasminstadbalanirbhāsitatayā lakṣaṇato yuṣmadarthasya manuṣyābhimānasya sambhedaivāvabhāsaḥ sa eva adhyāṣaḥ.* PP, p. 3.

11. For a discussion of this issue, see Chapter 4.

12. Edmund Husserl, *Cartesian Meditations,* trans. Doris Cairns (The Hague: Martinus Nihjoff, 1973), p. 26.

13. J. N. Mohanty, *The Concept of Intentionality* (St. Louis: Warren H. Green, 1972), p. 56.

14. Eugen Fink, "Husserl's Philosophy and Contemporary Criticism," in *The Phenomenology of Husserl,* ed. R. O. Elveton (Chicago: Quadrangle Press, 1970), p. 115.

15. Ibid.

16. Ibid., pp. 115–16.

17. Joseph J. Kockelmans, "What Is Phenomenology?" in *Phenomenology: The Philosophy of Edmund Husserl* (New York: Doubleday Anchor, 1967), pp. 34–35.

18. "Husserl's Phenomenology and Existentialism," in ibid., p. 229. See Ludwig Landgrebe, *Phänomenologie und Metaphysik* (Hamburg: Schröder, 1949), pp. 87–94.

19. Preface to Fink's "Husserl's Philosophy and Contemporary Criticism," in *The Phenomenology of Husserl,* ed. R. O. Elveton (Chicago: Quadrangle Press, 1970), p. 74.

20. Sartre, *The Transcendence of the Ego,* trans. Forrest Williams and Robert Kirkpatrick (New York: Noonday Press, 1957), pp. 40–42.

21. Ibid., pp. 44–45.

22. "Neuroses aren't simple diseased abnormalities—but rather another sort of mental functioning. However, neuroses allow glimpses into the hidden depths of the mind which aren't 'normally' open to inspection." Richard Appignanes, *Freud for Beginners* (New York: Pantheon Books, 1979), p. 67.

23. Sigmund Freud, *The Essentials of Psychoanalysis*, with an introduction and commentary by Anna Freud (Harmondsworth: Penguin, 1986), p. 147.

24. C. G. Jung, *The Archetypes and the Collective Unconscious*, trans. R. F. C. Hull (Princeton, N.J.: Princeton University Press, 1959), p. 283.

25. Ibid., p. 287.

26. Sartre, *The Emotions: Outlines of a Theory*, trans. Bernard Fechtman (New York: Philosophical Library, 1948), p. 91.

27. Sartre, *Being and Nothingness*, trans. with an introduction by Hazel Barnes (New York: Philosophical Library, 1956), p. 48. Henceforth this edition will be cited as *Being and Nothingness.*

28. Ibid., pp. 55–56.

29. Ibid., p. 49.

30. Ibid.

31. *Freud for Beginners*, pp. 60–65.

32. *Being and Nothingness*, p. lv.

33. *Transcendence of the Ego*, p. 45.

34. *Being and Nothingness*, p. liii.

35. *Transcendence of the Ego*, p. 42.

36. David Smith, *The Circle of Acquaintance* (Dordrecht: Kluwer Academic Publishers, 1944), pp. 91–92.

37. Noam Chomsky, *Knowledge of Language* (New York: Praeger, 1986), p. 3.

38. The Yogacāra Buddhists seem to allow for unconscious cognitions in their theory of *ālayavijñāna.*

Glossary

abādhita	noncontradicted
ābhāsa	appearance, semblance
abhāva	absence
ādhāra	container, support, receptacle
adhiṣṭāna	substratum, locus
adhyāsa	superimposition
aham	I
ahaṃkāra	ego-sense
ahaṃpratyaya	the I-consciousness
aja	unborn
ajñāna	ignorance
ajñāta	unknown
ajñātāartha viṣayakatva	the property of having an object which was previously unknown
ākāśa	space
akṣara	unchanging
antaḥkaraṇa	inner sense
antaḥkaraṇavṛtti	modification of the inner sense
antaryāmin	the ruler inside
anupalabdhi	non-perception
anuvyavasāya	cognition of (primary) cognition
anuyogin	the locus of a relation or of an absence

anyonyābhāva	mutual absence
apariṇāmin	that which does not change or transform
apramā	false cognition
arthāpatti	postulation
ātmajyoti	self-shining
ātman	self
avabhāsaka	that which manifests
avabhāsya	that which is manifested
āvaraṇa	concealment
avidyā	nescience, ignorance
avidyāvṛtti	modification of nescience
avyakta	unmanifested
bhāvajñāna	knowledge of something positive
bhāvarūpa	positive
bījanidrā	the seed sleep, dormant darkness
bimba	that which is reflected
buddhi	intellect
cidābhāsa	manifestation of consciousness
cit	consciousness
citta	retro-cognition, memory
dharma	property
dharmin	substantive
dhīuāsanā	the trace of cognition
doṣa	defect
dṛṣṭā	seer
dṛśya	object of seeing
dṛśyam	perceivable
dṛṣterdṛṣṭā	the seer of seeing

duḥkha	pain
guṇas	qualities
hetu	middle term, reason, cause
Ī śvara	God
Īśvarasākṣin	God's witness-consciousness
Īśvaratva	the property of being God
jaḍa	unconscious
jīvasākṣin	individual's witness-consciousness
jñānābhāva	absence of knowledge
jñāpana	disclosure in knowledge
jñātārtha	known object
jñātṛ	knower
jñeya	knowable, object of knowledge
kevalasākṣībhāsya	manifested by the witness alone
kartā	agent
kośas	sheaths
kūṭastha	transcendent, immutable
kūṭasthacinmātra	that whose only nature is the transcendent consciousness
lakṣaṇa	definition
manaḥ	mind
māyā	illusion
mohaśakti	the power to produce confusion
mūlāvidyā	root nescience, primal nescience
nirguṇa	propertyless
nirmāṇaśakti	power of creating
nirvikalpaka	non-conceptual cognition
nirviśeṣa	without distinguishing features

nityasākṣin	eternal witness
pāda	foot
pakṣa	the minor term (of a syllogism)
parāmārśa	consideration, recollection, reflexion
paramparayā	through a series or chain of conditions
pariṇāmin	that which undergoes change or transformation
pāramārthika	pertaining to the highest being
phala-vyāpya	pervaded by the resulting cognition
pracāra	manifestation
prājña	the wise
prakṛti	nature
pramā	true cognition
pramāṇa	cognition, means of true cognition
pramāṇacaitanya	consciousness as limited by a means of true cognition
pramāṇajanyāntaḥkaraṇavṛtti	mode of the inner sense brought about by a means of right cognition
pramāṇasiddha	established by a means of true cognition
pramāṇavṛtti	modification caused by a means of right cognition
pramātā	cognizer
pramātṛcaitanya	consciousness as limited by the inner sense
pramātṛgata ajñāna	ignorance belonging to the cognizer
pramātva	the truth or validity
pramāviṣaya	object of true cognition
prameya	the object of cognition
pramiṇomi	I know
pramiti	true cognition

prāṇa	life-energy
prāpyakāri	that which reaches what is to be reached
prasiddha	well established
prātibhāsika	the illusory
pratibimba	the reflected image
pratiyogin	counter-positive
pratyagātman	the inner or the innermost self
pratyayin	the subject of cognition
pravṛtti	practical response
sādhya	major term (of a syllogism)
saguṇa	with properties
sajātīya	belonging to the same class
sākṣijñāna	witness-cognition (awareness)
sākṣitva	the property of being a witness, witnesshood
samprasanna	extremely delighted, gracious, propitious
saṃskāra	trace
sārūpya	similarity of form
sarvadṛk	the perceiver of all
sarvasākṣin	the witness of all
satkāryavāda	theory that the effect was existent prior to production
savikalpaka	conceptual cognition
saviṣayakatva	the property of having an object
smṛti	memory, retro-cognition
śuddhacaitanya	pure consciousness
sukha	happiness
suṣupti	deep or dreamless sleep
svagata	internal to oneself

svarūpajñāna	the knowledge which is the nature of one's being
svataḥ pramāṇya	intrinsic validity
svayṃjyoti	self-shining
svayaṃprakāśa	self-manifestation
svena bhāsā	by one's own light
tūlāvidyā	derivative nescience
turīya	the transcendent, or the 'fourth' experience
upādhi	limiting adjunct
upalakṣaṇa	accidental qualification
vastu	thing (actual object)
vidyā	knowledge
vijātīya	belonging to a different class
vijñāna	cognition
vijñātā	knower
vikalpa	alternative, false notion, merely conceptual entity
vikṣepa	projection
viṣaya	object (the intentional object)
viṣayacaitanya	consciousness as limited by the object
viṣayagata ajñāna	ignorance pertaining to the object
viṣayo nasti	the object does not exist
viśeṣaṇa	adjective
viśiṣtajñāna	determinate cognition
viśiṣṭavṛtti	determinate mode
viśva	the universe
vivartavāda	theory of apparent transformation
vṛtti	mental modification

vṛtti-vyāpya	pervaded by the cognitive mode
vṛttijñāna	cognition which is a mental mode
vyāpya	pervaded
vyāvahārika	empirical

Bibliography

Recommended General Works on Indian Philosophy

Chatterjee, Satischandra, and Dhirendramohan Datta. *An Introduction to Indian Philosophy.* Calcutta: University of Calcutta, 1960.

Dasgupta, Surendranath. *A History of Indian Philosophy.* 5 vols. New Delhi: Motilal Banarsidass, 1975.

Edgerton, Franklin. *The Beginnings of Indian Philosophy.* London: Allen and Unwin, 1965.

Hiriyanna, Mysore. *The Essentials of Indian Philosophy.* London: Allen and Unwin, 1932.

———. *Outlines of Indian Philosophy.* Bombay: Allen and Unwin, 1973.

Potter, Karl. *Presuppositions of India's Philosophies.* Englewood Cliffs, N.J.: Prentice-Hall, Inc., 1963.

Prasad, Jwala. *History of Indian Epistemology.* Delhi: Munshi Ram Manoharlal, 1958.

Puligandala, R. *Fundamentals of Indian Philosophy.* New York: Abingdon Press, 1975.

Radhakrishnan, Sarvepalli. *Indian Philosophy.* 2 vols. London: Allen and Unwin, 1923–27.

Radhakrishnan, Sarvepalli, and Charles A. Moore, eds. *A Sourcebook in Indian Philosophy.* Princeton, N.J.: Princeton University Press, 1957.

Sharma, Chandradhar. *Indian Philosophy: A Critical Survey.* New York: Barnes and Noble, 1962.

Smart, Ninian. *Doctrine and Argument in Indian Philosophy.* London: Allen and Unwin, 1964.

Zimmer, Heinrich. *Philosophies of India.* Ed. Joseph Campbell. London: Routledge and Kegan Paul, 1952.

Primary Sources

Abhyankar, M. V. S., ed. and trans. Madhusūdanasarasvati's *Siddhāntabindu.* Government Oriental Series—Class A, No. 2. Poona: Bhandarkar Oriental Research Institute, 1962.

Aiyer, S. Venkataramana. The *Sambandha Vārtika of Sureśvarāchārya.* Varanasi: Chaukhamba Amarabharati Prakashan, 1981.

Alston, A. J., trans. *The Naiṣkarmya Siddhi of Śrī Sureśvara.* London: Shanti Sadan, 1959.

Alston, William P., and George Nakhnikian, eds. *The Idea of Phenomenology* by Edmund Husserl. The Hague: Martinus Nijhoff, 1966.

Apte, V. M., trans. *Brahma-Sūtra-Shānkara-Bhāshya.* Bombay: Popular Book Depot, 1960.

Baillie, J. B., trans. and ed. Hegel's *The Phenomenology of Mind.* New York: Harper Torchbook, 1967.

Balasubramanian, R., trans. *The Taittirīyopaniṣad Bhāṣya-Vartika of Sureśvara.* Madras: University of Madras, 1984.

Barnes, Hazel, trans. Sartre's *Being and Nothingness.* New York: Philosophical Library, 1956.

Cairns, Doris, trans. Edmund Husserl's *Cartesian Meditations: An Introduction to Phenomenology.* The Hague: Martinus Nijhoff, 1973.

Devanji, Prahlad Chandrashekhar, trans. *Siddhāntabindu of Madhusūdana with the Commentary of Purushottama.* Gaekwad Oriental Series, vol. 64. Baroda: Oriental Institute, 1933.

Fechtman, Bernard, trans. Sartre's *The Emotions: Outlines of a Theory.* New York: Philosophical Library, 1948.

Gambhirānanda, Swāmī, trans. *Brahma-Sūtra-Bhāṣya of Śrī Śaṅkarācārya.* Calcutta: Advaita Ashrama, 1983.

———. *Eight Upaniṣads with the commentary of Śaṅkarācārya.* 2 vols. Calcutta: Advaita Ashrama, 1965.

Gilby, Thomas, trans. *Saint Thomas Aquinas: Philosophical Texts.* New York: Oxford University Press, 1960.

Hiriyanna, Mysore, ed. *The Naiṣkarmya-Siddhi of Sureśvarācārya with the Candrikā of Jñānottama.* Bombay Sanskrit and Prakrit Series no. 38. Poona: Bhandarkar Oriental Research Institute, 1980.

Hull, R. F. C., trans. Jung's *The Archetypes and the Collective Unconscious.* Princeton, N.J.: Princeton University Press, 1959.

Hume, Robert Ernest, trans. *The Thirteen Principal Upanishads.* Oxford: Oxford University Press, 1967.

Jagadānanda, Swāmī, trans. *Upadeśa Sāhasrī of Śrī Śankarāchārya* ("A Thousand Teachings"). Mylapore, Madras: Sri Ramakrishna Math, 1961.

Jha, Ganganath, trans. *Advaitasiddhi of Madhusūdana Sarasvatī. Indian Thought,* vol. 6, 1914; vol. 7, 1915; vol. 8, 1916; vol. 9, 1917.

Jowett, Benjamin, trans. Plato's *Timaeus.* Princeton, N.J.: Princeton University Press, 1980.

Lauer, Quentin, trans. *Edmund Husserl's Phenomenology and the Crisis of Science.* New York: Harper Torchbook, 1965.

Mādhavānanda, Swāmī, trans. *The Bṛhadāraṇyaka Upaniṣad with the Commentary of Śaṅkarācārya.* Mayavati, Almora, Himalayas: Advaita Ashrama, 1941.

———. *Vedānta Paribhāṣā* by Dharmarāja Adhvarīndra. Mayavati: Advaita Ashrama, 1983.

Mahadevan, T. M. P., ed. and trans. *The Saṃbandha-Vārtika of Sureśvarācārya.* Madras: University of Madras, 1958.

Madhusūdanasarasvati. *Advaitasiddhi*. Delhi: Parimal Publications, 1988.

Mayeda, S. trans. *A Thousand Teachings: The Upadeśasāhasrī of Śaṅkara*. Tokyo: University of Tokyo Press, 1979.

Mohanty, J. N. *Gaṅgeśa's Theory of Truth*. Shantiniketan: Centre of Advanced Study in Philosophy, 1966.

Nikhilānanda, Swami, trans. *Dṛgdṛśyaviveka*. Mysore: Sri Ramakrishna Ashrama, 1976.

———. *The Māṇḍūkhyopaniṣad with Gauḍapāda's Kārikā and Śaṅkara's Commentary*. Mysore: Sri Ramakrishna Ashrama, 1974.

———. *Self-Knowledge: An English Translation of Śaṅkarāchārya's Ātmabodha*. Mylapore, Madras: Sri Ramakrishna Math, 1947.

———. *Vedāntasāra: or the Essence of Vedānta of Sadānanda Yogīndra*. Mayavati, Almora, Himalayas: Advaita Ashrama, 1949.

Padmapāda, *Pañcapādikā*. Vizianagaram Sanskrit Series, No. 3. Benaras: E. J. Lazrus and Co., 1891.

Radhakrishnan, Sarvepalli, trans. *The Brahma Sūtra: The Philosophy of Spiritual Life*. New York: Greenwood Press, 1968.

———, trans. *The Principal Upaniṣads*. New York: Harper and Bros., 1953.

Śaṃkara, *Brahmasūtra Saṃkara Bhāṣya with the Commentaries of Bhāmatī, Kalpataru, and Parimala*. Delhi: Parimal Publications, 1988.

Śāstrī, Anantakṛṣṇa, ed. *Brahmasūtra-Śaṅkara-Bhāṣyam*. Calcutta Sanskrit Series, 3 parts. Calcutta: Metropolitan Printing and Publishing House, 1941. Cited as *Nine Commentaries*.

———. *Paribhāṣā Prakāśikā*, a commentary on *Vedānta Paribhāṣā*. Calcutta: University of Calcutta, 1927.

Śāstrī, Kuppuswami, ed. *Brahmasiddhi*. Madras: Madras Government Press, 1937.

Śāstrī, Srirama, trans. *The Pañcapādikā of Padmapāda*. Madras Government Oriental Series, vol. 155. Madras: Government Oriental Manuscript Library, 1958.

Sastri, S. Srirama, and S. R. Krishnamurthi Sastri, eds. Prakāśātman's *Pañcapādikāvivaraṇa*. Madras: Madras Goverment Manuscripts Library, 1958.

Śāstrī, S. S. Suryanarayana, trans. *Siddhāntaleśasaṅgraha of Appayya Dīkṣita*. Madras Goverment Oriental Series, vol. 155. Madras: University of Madras, 1935.

———. *Vedānta Paribhāṣā* of Dharmarāja Adhvarīndra. Adyar: Adyar Library, 1942.

Śāstrī, S. S. Suryanarayana, and Raja C. Kunhan, eds. and trans. *The Bhāmatī of Vācaspati: on Śaṅkara's Brahmasūtrabhāṣya* (*Catussūtrī*). Madras: Theosophical Publishing House, 1933.

Śāstrī, S. S. Suryanarayana, and E. P. Radhakrishnan, eds. and trans. Jñānaghanapāda's *Tattvaśuddhi*. Madras: University of Madras, 1941.

Śāstrī, S. S. Suryanarayana, and Saileswar Sen, eds. *Vivaraṇaprameyasaṅgraha*. Madras: Sri Vidya Press, 1941.

Shastri, Hari Prasad, trans. *Pañcadaśī. A Treatise on Advaita Metaphysics by SwāmīVidyāraṇya*. London: Shanti Sadan, 1956.

Subrahmanyasastri, S. *Madhusūdanasarasvati's Siddhāntabindu* with *Nyāyaratnāvalī*.

Grantha Ratna Manjusha—No. 16. Mount Abu: Mahesh Research Institute, 1978.

Smith, Colin M., trans. Merleau-Ponty's *Phenomenology of Perception.* London: Routledge and Kegan Paul, 1962.

Smith, Norman Kemp, trans. Kant's *Critique of Pure Reason.* London: Macmillan, 1973.

Thibaut, George, trans. *The Vedānta-Sūtras with the Commentary of Śaṅkarācārya.* Vols. 34 and 38 of *Sacred Books of the East,* ed. Max Muller. Oxford: Clarendon Press, 1890, 1896. (First Dover edition was published in 1962, the second in 1970.)

Veezhinathan, N., ed. *The Saṃkṣepaśārīraka of Sarvajñātman.* Madras: University of Madras, 1985.

Venkataramiah, D., trans. *The Pañcapādikā of Padmapāda.* Gaekwad Oriental Series, vol. 107. Baroda: Oriental Institute, 1948.

Vidyāraṇyasvāmī, *Bṛhadāraṇyakavārtikasāra.* Kasi: Acyuta Grantha Mala, 1942.

Williams, Forrest, and Robert Kirkpatrick, trans. Sartre's *The Transcendence of the Ego.* New York: Noonday Press, 1957.

Yogīndrānanda, ed. and trans. Citsukha's *Tattvapradīpikā Nayanaprasādinī* of Pratyaksvarūpa and editor's Hindi commentary. Bombay: Nirṇayasagar Press, 1915.

Secondary Sources

Allison, Henry E. *Kant's Transcendental Idealism: An Interpretation and Defense.* New Haven, Conn.: Yale University Press, 1983.

Alston, William P., and George Nakhnikian, eds. *Readings in Twentieth-Century Philosophy.* London: Free Press of Glencoe, 1963.

Appignanes, Richard. *Freud for Beginners.* New York: Pantheon Books, 1979.

Arapura, J. G. "*Māyā* and the Discourse about Brahman." In *The Problem of Two Truths in Advaita Vedānta and Buddhism,* ed. Marvin Sprung. Dordrecht, Holland: D. Reidel Publishing Company, 1973.

Belvalkar, S. K. *Vedānta Philosophy.* Poona: Bilrakunja Publishing House, 1929.

Bhattacharya, Asutosh Sastri. *Studies in Post-Śaṅkara Dialectics.* Calcutta: University of Calcutta, 1936.

Bhattacharyya, Kalidas. *A Modern Understanding of Advaita.* Ahmedabad: L. D. Institute of Technology, 1975.

Bhattacharyya, Kokileswar. *An Introduction to Advaita Philosophy.* Calcutta: University of Calcutta, 1924.

Bhattacharyya, K. C. *Studies in Vedāntism.* Calcutta: University of Calcutta, 1909.

Chakraborty, Nirod Baran. *The Advaita Concept of Falsity—A Critical Study.* Calcutta College Sanskrit Series no. 57. Calcutta: Sanskrit College, 1967.

Chatterjee, A. K., and R. R. Dravid, *The Concept of Sākṣin in Advaita Vedānta.* Banaras: Banaras Hindu University, 1979.

Chatterjee, Tara. "The Concept of Sākṣin." *The Journal of Indian Philosophy* 10 (1988).

Chaudhuri, Anil Kumar Ray. "The Concept of Sākṣin." *Our Heritage*, Vol. 1, 1953.

———. *The Doctrine of Māyā*. Calcutta: Dasgupta and Co., 1950.

———. *Self and Falsity in Advaita Vedānta*. Calcutta: Progressive Publishers, 1955.

Chisholm, Roderick M. *Realism and the Background of Phenomenology*. New York: Free Press, 1964.

Chomsky, Noam. *Knowledge of Language*. New York: Praeger, 1986.

Coward, Harold G., ed. *Studies in Indian Thought*. Delhi: Motilal Banarsidass, 1983.

Datta, Dhirendra Mohan. "Inward and Outward in Advaita Vedānta." *Philosophical Quarterly* 30 (October 1957): 165–72.

———. *The Six Ways of Knowing: A Critical Study of the Vedānta Theory of Knowledge*. 2d rev. ed. Calcutta: University of Calcutta, 1960.

de Bary, William Theodore, ed. *The Buddhist Tradition in India, China, and Japan*. New York: Modern Library, 1969.

Deussen, P. *The System of the Vedānta*. New York: Dover Publications, 1973.

Deutsch, Eliot, and J. A. B. van Buitenen, eds. *A Sourcebook of Advaita Vedānta*. Honolulu: University Press of Hawaii, 1971.

Devaraja, N. K. *An Introduction to Śaṅkara's Theory of Knowledge*. Delhi: Motilal Banarsidass, 1962.

Dravid, Raja Ram. *The Problem of Universals in Indian Philosophy*. Delhi: Motilal Banarsidass, 1972.

Dryer, D. P. *Kant's Solution for Verification in Metaphysics*. London: Allen and Unwin, 1966.

Farber, Marvin. *Foundations of Phenomenology*. Cambridge, Mass.: Harvard University Press, 1943.

Fink, Eugen. "Husserl's Philosophy and Contemporary Criticism." In *The Phenomenology of Husserl*, ed. R. O. Elveton. Chicago: Quadrangle Press, 1970.

Fort, Andrew. "Sākṣin in Advaita Vedānta," *The Journal of Indian Philosophy* 12 (1984).

Freud, Sigmund. *The Essentials of Psychoanalysis*, with an introduction and commentary by Anna Freud. Harmondsworth: Penguin, 1986.

Guenther, Herbert V. *Buddhist Philosophy in Theory and Practice*. Baltimore: Penguin Books, 1972.

Gupta, Bina. *Perceiving in Advaita Vedānta: Epistemological Analysis and Interpretation*. Lewisburg, Pa.: Bucknell University Press, 1991.

Gupta, Bina, and William C. Wilcox. "'*Tat tvam asi*': An Important Identity Statement or a Mere Tautology." *Philosophy East and West* 34, no. 1 (1984).

Hacker, Paul. "Śaṃkara's Conception of Man." In *Kleine Schriften*. Wiesbaden: F. Steiner, 1978.

Ingalls, Daniel H. H. "Śaṅkara's Arguments against the Buddhists," *Philosophy East and West* 3, no. 4 (January 1954).

Kar, Bijayananda. *The Theories of Error in Indian Philosophy*. India: Ajanta Publications, 1978.

Kockelmans, J., ed. "What Is Phenomenology?" In *Phenomenology: The Philosophy of Edmund Husserl.* New York: Doubleday Anchor, 1967. Cited as *Phenomenology.*

Landgrebe, Ludgwig. *Phänomenologie und Metaphysik.* Hamburg: Schröder, 1949.

Larson, Gerald, M. *Classical Sāṃkhya.* Delhi: Motilal Banarsidass, 1969.

Mahadevan, T. M. P. *The Philosophy of Advaita.* New Delhi: Arnold-Heinemann Publishers, 1976.

———. *Superimposition in Advaita Vedānta.* New Delhi: Sterling Publishers Private, 1985.

Maitra, Sushil Kumar. *Fundamental Questions of Indian Logic and Metaphysics.* Calcutta: University of Calcutta, 1974.

Malkani, G. R. *Vedāntic Epistemology.* Amalner: Indian Institute of Philosophy, 1953.

Malkani, G. R., R. Das, and T. R. V. Murti. *Ajñāna.* London: Luzac and Co., 1933.

Matilal, Bimal K. *Nyāya-Vaiśeṣika.* A History of Indian Literature Series, vol. 6, ed. Jan Gonda. Wiesbaden: Otto Harrassowitz, 1977.

———. *Perception.* Oxford: Claredon Press, 1986.

Mohanty, J. N. *The Concept of Intentionality.* St. Louis: Warren H. Green, 1972.

———. *Reason and Tradition in Indian Thought.* Oxford: Clarendon Press, 1992.

Mukherjee, A. C. *The Nature of Self.* Allahabad: Indian Press, 1938.

Murti, T. R. V. *The Central Philosophy of Buddhism.* London: Allen and Unwin, 1960.

Pereira, José, ed. *Hindu Theology: A Reader.* New York: Doubleday, 1976.

Potter, Karl, ed. *Advaita Vedānta up to Śaṃkara and His Pupils.* Princeton, N.J.: Princeton University Press, 1981.

———. "*Vedāntaparibhāṣā* as Systematic Reconstruction." In *Perspectives on Vedānta,* ed. S. Rama Rao Pappu. Leiden: E. J. Brill, 1988.

Radhakrishnan, S. *An Idealist View of Life.* Bombay: Allen and Unwin, 1971.

Raju, P. T. *Idealistic Thought of India.* Cambridge, Mass.: Harvard University Press, 1953.

Sarma, V. A. *Citsukha's Contribution to Advaita.* Mysore: Kavyalaya Publishers, 1976.

Satprakāshānanda, Swāmī. *Methods of Knowledge.* Calcutta: Advaita Ashrama, 1975.

Sengupta, Bratindra Kumar. *A Critique of the Vivaraṇa School.* Calcutta: Dr. Bratindra Kumar Sengupta, 1959.

Singh, Ram Pratap. *The Vedānta of Śaṃkara—A Metaphysic of Value,* vol. 1. Jaipur: Bharat Publishing House, 1949.

Sinha, Debabrata. *The Idealist Standpoint: A Study in the Vedāntic Metaphysic of Experience.* Santiniketan: Visva Bharati, Centre of Advanced Study in Philosophy, 1965.

Sinha, J. N. *Indian Epistemology of Perception.* Calcutta: Sinha Publishing House, 1969.

———. *Indian Psychology.* 2 vols. Calcutta: Sinha Publishing House, 1958.

Sircar, Mahendranath. *Comparative Studies in Vedāntism.* Bombay: Humphrey Milford, 1927.

Smith, David. *The Circle of Acquaintance.* Dordrecht: Kluwer Academic Publishers, 1944.

Sundaram, P. K. *Advaita Epistemology.* Madras: University of Madras, 1968.

Takakusu, Junjiro. *The Essentials of Buddhist Philosophy.* Delhi: Motilal Banarsidass, 1978.

Thèvenaz, Pierre. *What Is Phenomenology?* Chicago: Quadrangle Books, 1962.

Upadhyaya, Veeramani Prasad. *Lights on Vedānta.* Varanasi: Chowkhamba, 1959.

Warrier, A. G. *The Concept of Mukti in Advaita Vedānta.* Madras: University of Madras, 1961.

Index